Spaghetti In My Hair

by

Clare Stimpson

Bloomington, IN Milton Keynes, UK

authorHOUSE

AuthorHouse™
1663 Liberty Drive, Suite 200
Bloomington, IN 47403
www.authorhouse.com
Phone: 1-800-839-8640

AuthorHouse™ UK Ltd.
500 Avebury Boulevard
Central Milton Keynes, MK9 2BE
www.authorhouse.co.uk
Phone: 08001974150

This book is a work of non-fiction. Unless otherwise noted, the author and the publisher make no explicit guarantees as to the accuracy of the information contained in this book and in some cases, names of people and places have been altered to protect their privacy.

First published by AuthorHouse 10/10/2006

ISBN: 1-4259-0732-6 (sc)

Printed in the United States of America
Bloomington, Indiana

This book is printed on acid-free paper.

DEDICATION

I dedicate this book to the Bortolani family who befriended me in Italy and to Steph, who is greatly missed by all.

ACKNOWLEDGEMENTS

I should like to thank my parents who gave me encouragement and support whilst writing this book and my immediate family who assisted me with technical computer problems – and there were many along the way. Thanks also to those friends featured in the book, both English and Italian, particularly to Jemp, Teresa and the three Dorises. Some names have been changed for various reasons

Contents

PART ONE   THE EARLY DAYS

CHAPTER 1   CIAO ITALIA...1

CHAPTER 2   FOOD GLORIOUS FOOD 14

CHAPTER 3   BOLOGNA AND SIROLO 24

CHAPTER 4   FABULOUS FIRENZE 36

CHAPTER 5   SAN GEMIGNANO'S DAY AND MAGICAL
MODENA 48

CHAPTER 6   VILLA VITTORIA 59

CHAPTER 7   CASA DELLA FONTANA 68

CHAPTER 8   SPAGHETTI IN MY HAIR...................................83

CHAPTER 9   SUMMERS AT THE SEASIDE 92

CHAPTER 10   EARTHQUAKES AND FLYING PLATES 101

CHAPTER 11   SIENA AND THE PALLIO..............................114

CHAPTER 12   SEE NAPLES AND DIE 126

CHAPTER 13   PENNY AND HER PUPS 140

CHAPTER 14   LEAVING LA DOLCE VITA............................154

PART TWO   ITALY REVISITED

CHAPTER 15   SAN REMO..173

CHAPTER 16   MODENA REVISITED 193

CHAPTER 17   FROM ONE COAST TO ANOTHER................206

CHAPTER 18   THE GRAND TOUR.......................................225

PART THREE ENIGMATIC ITALY

CHAPTER 19 ALLA SICILIANA!..271

CHAPTER 20 BELLA ROMA...281

CHAPTER 21 VENEZIA - LA SERENISSIMA.........................290

CHAPTER 22 BOLOGNA AND MODENA AGAIN!.............322

PART ONE

THE EARLY DAYS

CHAPTER 1 CIAO ITALIA

My love affair with Italy began many years ago. My mother regaled me with stories of intrepid hitchhiking holidays spent in that fascinating country. She told me that she first saw Venice by moonlight, and that this romantic, artistic notion lit a fire deep within my soul and ignited my imagination.

Mother had travelled with one of her university friends as far down the Italian peninsula as Sicily - a tourist's no-man's land in the late 1940s. As their money had been stolen, they had to resort to sleeping on the beach - and were subsequently arrested by the local police or Caribinieri, who thought they were vagabonds and associates of Salvatore Giuliano, the infamous Sicilian folk-hero and bandit. My poor grandmother, who lived in respectable Guildford, nearly had a fit when she read in an eminent English newspaper that her own daughter had been slung into a foul, mephitic, Italian jail.

The story turned into a family myth. It made Italy seem even more exciting to me - a convent girl from the Wirral, who craved an adventurous lifestyle. From an early age, I knew that I had to live there in that land of dreams.

By the time I had left college and taught for a year in London, a burning desire compelled me to escape the drudgery of the three day week that epitomised the early 70s in England.

A college friend and I had managed to get ourselves jobs teaching English as a Foreign Language, in a small provincial Italian city called Modena, situated in the flat Po valley, in the province of Emilia-Romagna. One early sun-dappled September morning, when swinging London had ground to a halt we boarded a dusty train at Victoria Station and thus began our adventure.

That morning, we were wide-eyed with excitement. My huge blue trunk, containing enough belongings for a year, accompanied me into the unknown. As a natural hoarder and perhaps not quite as adventurous as I tried to appear, I needed to surround myself with familiar junk from home. Balanced on top of my trunk was a basket stuffed with precious things. Precariously perched on top of this, was my faithful radio. Radio Luxemburg was a constant companion in those days and I was not prepared to give this up.

My friend Jemp and I laughed, as we struggled to board the train.

"We look like a couple of bag ladies," I giggled.

"I wish I had sent my trunk on, like you did," I remarked to Jemp.

Sensibly, my friend had thought of this solution and was hoping to find her trunk waiting for her on arrival in Modena. Jemp and I had studied art together at teacher training college and we both dressed in a fairly bohemian style, with the long flowing skirts of the day. My friend had a particularly individual look as she had bleached two stripes in her long dark hair, one on either side of her face.

An uneventful journey lay ahead. Next morning, the train shuddered to a halt in Milan station. Bleary eyed through lack of sleep, we unloaded ourselves and our luggage into Milano Centrale.

There was great hustle and bustle in this huge railway terminus which was built in the days of Mussolini. It is a masterpiece of Fascist architecture, boasting great high ceilings and lots of creamy marble.

Elegant, animated Italians gesticulated and shouted at each other. People were shoving suitcases through the open windows in the impossibly crowded trains. This was a short cut that we would often see in the future. There were no orderly queues. As soon as a train arrived, the waiting public all scrambled at once to gain access to its dim interior, pushing and elbowing each other, some even following their luggage through the window.

Jemp and I were agog. We stood dazed, drinking in the atmosphere, savouring the foreign element and theatricality of the scene before us.

Well-dressed businessmen with a purpose and small brief cases passed by. Women, expensively dressed, dripping with jewels and tottering about in beautifully crafted shoes, looked up and down at Jemp and me as if to say 'How scruffy!' We were both kitted out in our best frayed hippy jeans and sleeveless vests. Hair was long and straight in those days and our feet were clad in clumpy flat sandals. Indeed, we felt a crumpled mess having slept on the train in our

3

clothes, and we were unprepared for the sophisticated demeanour of the Northern Italian.

In our imaginations, most Italians were a small, lively, ice cream eating nation and we were surprised to find that our preconceptions were entirely wrong. Elegance and style, charm and quick-wit are the words I would now use to describe this varied nation. According to the writer Ennio Flanio, being an Italian is a profession - flexibility and adaptability are in the genes.

The train to Modena was late. It was two or three hours '*in ritardo*' (late). This was not unusual in those days. Trains could sometimes be days '*in ritardo,*' as the main railway line cuts through the length of the country, from Milano in the north to Reggio di Calabria in the Sicilian south. Milano to Reggio in those days, was roughly a twenty four hour journey, and all sorts of problems could be amassed on its way from the north to the '*Mezzogiorno*' - another name for the south.

Eventually '*il treno per Modena*' arrived, puffing and snorting. The waiting crowds all rushed to greet it. It was pleasantly empty, so we did not have to frantically shove our luggage through the grimy windows. The grey and rather utilitarian train sped on its way, slicing across the flat lowlands of the Po valley. Unending plains, cultivated with corn and vines, stretched as far as the eye could see. The landscape was repetitive and I was beginning to wish that I had taken another job that had been offered to me, further south, in coastal Brindisi.

Emilia-Romagna is a vast agricultural plain. Everywhere, tractors plough the Po's deposits of fertile silt, and the area is reminiscent of

East Anglia. Modena is on the main north to south railway line, and we passed through the pretty and historic towns of Piacenza and Parma, before arriving at our destination two and a half hours later.

The city of Modena seemed to have ground to a halt. It was about 2.30p.m, but the town was definitely asleep. Jemp and I decided to take a taxi to the language school, where hopefully we would be pointed in the direction of our accommodation for the next year.

"Do you speak English?" Jemp asked the taxi driver, expecting "no" as a reply.

"A little." He grinned. "Where do you wanna go?"

We gave him the address of the City Language School in the centre of Modena, and soon we were whizzing through colonnaded cobbled streets, horn beeping every few seconds, even though there was no-one in sight.

"Where is everyone and why is it so quiet?" I asked the driver.

"Siesta," he replied laughing. "Everyone's asleep!"

The City Language School had employed us, solely because we could not speak Italian. They stated in their glossy brochure that all their teachers spoke only mother tongue English. We were not supposed to learn Italian, which was rather a tall order considering we had to live in the country. The powers who thought up these rules, decided that if we could not speak Italian, our students would learn English quicker. In future lessons this proved to be chaotic on occasions, although surprisingly, sometimes it worked.

The cab stopped abruptly.

"Here you are ladies," exclaimed the driver.

He sped off at a dusty roar, once we had paid our fare.

We stood in the scorching, early afternoon heat. The cobbles were shimmering, and the shutters in the nearby buildings were closed tight against the sultry sun.

In front of us, was the City Language School. It did not look very prepossessing. The door was a shabby flaky green colour and a few straggly plants careered down well-worn steps.

Jemp pressed the bell.

"Chi è?" (Who is it?) asked a woman through the intercom, with a high-pitched voice.

"It's Jemp and Clare," we answered confidently.

"Chi?" asked the puzzled voice on the other end.

"The new English teachers," Jemp explained more diffidently.

"Ah, bene, bene. Come up, come up!" the voice announced.

We trundled up the old stone stairway. The interior was a cool relief to the fiery heat of outside. Thankfully I left my luggage downstairs. It felt good to be free of it. Maria, the portly wife of the school proprietor, met us with out-stretched arms.

"Come state?" (How are you?) she shrieked, grabbing us both in a big bear hug.

We were glad to have arrived. After various introductions had been performed, Jemp asked about her luggage which had been addressed to the school. Sadly it had not arrived.

"Never mind," I said. "You can always borrow some of my stuff."

We expected a taxi to take us to our new abode, but instead, a sort of three wheeled affair called an *Ape* was summoned.

Jemp and I giggled. Was this contraption that went about two miles an hour really going to take us to our apartment? My luggage was hauled on board and we set off at a very slow, noisy pace.

Our destination was Via Ferrari, a dilapidated, grey, forlorn and dusty looking street. The three wheeled truck left our baggage and us outside and scuttled off. We looked around disappointedly. It was not what we had expected.

We moved into the shade, as the sun was glaring like a glazed ball of yellow sulphur.

"It might be better inside," I said hopefully.

Jemp looked around doubtfully.

The crumbling old building was entered via a huge arched wooden doorway. Inside, the floor was cobbled. Rickety stairs led up on to various floors - about four in all. Of course, ours had to be at the very top! We grabbed my trunk and hauled it up, bumping it and making quite commotion.

An ancient, wizened woman peered out from behind one of the front doors.

"*Buon giorno,*" we chorused, gasping for breath.

She retreated inside without as much as a gesture. She had obviously seen too many English girls go up and down that staircase.

At the top, we were met by flaky brown painted double doors. Jemp produced the key and threw the entrance open.

The flat was surprisingly airy. Old terracotta flagstones worn by generations, were laid on the floor. A small corridor led to two largish bedrooms, a very basic but functional kitchen and a narrow bathroom.

The windows were painted a vibrant red. Quaint shutters, also coloured in a radiant crimson, were there to shut out the intense Modenese heat.

"Wow!" enthused Jemp. "This flat has character."

"Yes, it's great - I love it!" I shouted back, running through the rooms.

"Jemp!" I shrieked. "Look at this bathroom! The shower goes straight onto the floor!"

Jemp turned around to look.

The bathroom was very rustic and basic. An old chrome showerhead protruded from the whitewashed wall. There was no bath or curtain around it - just the floor underneath and a waste outlet set into the red quarry tiles. I think it was the forerunner of what we now call a wet room.

"This will be fun," I muttered sarcastically.

Then I laughed. "At least the toilet and sink will get a clean every time we take a shower - one advantage, I suppose."

The shower turned out to be very efficient, even if it did leave the rest of the room dripping wet for a few hours. In the heat of summer it soon dried out, but in winter it was a different icier story.

I moved over to the window. The view was panoramic. Pantiled roofs stretched into infinity. Different sized chimney pots and a vast number of T.V. aerials, standing like sentinels, jostled for space in that rooftop scene.

Disappointingly, we did not have a balcony but directly opposite us was an old house, which we later found out to be a post office sorting depot. Its veranda was bursting with a riot of gorgeous geraniums.

Reluctantly, we tore our eyes away from the enticing view of jumbled terracotta roofs and thrusting chimney pots, and decided between ourselves which rooms to have.

My room seemed bare, as was the rest of the apartment. The furniture was funny old 1950's stuff with no apparent character, although the flat with its red paint work and stone floor had bags of potential. I opened my trunk and pondered. Inside, was a lovely Indian table-cloth that I thought I might use as a bedcover. It was red and green paisley patterned and matched the crimson window frames. I decided to hang the Indian cloth on the bare white walls, which produced instant colour and cosiness! Over the next few weeks, I promised myself that I would try to find or make some pictures to fill the other blank areas.

I later discovered that our apartment contained a secret room. It smelt of lingering heat and pungent mothballs, and was filled with lovely old country furniture and sepia portraits of long gone Italians. There was an early 1900's iron bedstead with a painted medallion containing a river scene, inlaid with opalescent mother of pearl. The mattress was hard and lumpy and stuffed with what appeared to be horsehair.

Next to the bed were matching walnut bedside cabinets, topped with marble. Intricately woven cane rug beaters hung from the peeling crumbling whitewashed walls, and an ancient faded Persian mat gave warmth underfoot. An air of musty nostalgia filled the chamber and cobwebs hung like decorations. Miss Haversham would have been proud!

The door to this room was always locked. We were never told about it, and thought it was just a broom cupboard. Months after moving into the flat, we found the key and were amazed that such a room should exist.

We finished unpacking our few belongings. Jemp had almost nothing and wanted to investigate the possibility of her luggage having arrived at Modena Station.

Outside, the atmosphere was humid. A searing heat rose from the baked ground. In summer and early autumn, Modena has the climate of a tropical jungle. Rivulets of warm sweat ran down our limbs.

There was no news of Jemp's luggage at the station, so we decided to go and explore the city centre - *'il centro città.'* It was five o'clock, and in marked contrast to earlier, the place was buzzing. Snippets of Italian laughter and the whirr of mopeds and bicycles mingled in the late balmy afternoon air.

A very beautiful cathedral dominates Modena. Romanesque in style, it sits along one edge of a huge, cobbled square. The other three sides are surrounded by colonnades and little old fashioned individual shops. The bell-tower or 'Ghirlandina' rises loftily over the city roofs and when the damp foggy November weather sets in, it is shrouded and sometimes obscured by mist. Inside on display is a bucket, which was stolen from Bologna in 1325, and this theft resulted in a war between the two cities. The incident was immortalised by the celebrated poet Tassoni in his poem *'La Secchia Rapita'* (The Stolen Bucket).

Two dignified, but madly grinning pale stone lions, guard the entrance to the cathedral. They sit on either side of well-worn steps leading to the impressive doors.

Sitting on the steps next to the grinning creatures, we surveyed the scene before us. We felt as if we were part of a screen set. A fascinating drama was unfolding - beauty, wealth, colour and confidence paraded before our eyes.

The crumbling *palazzi* were painted in muted tones of yellow ochre and pale terracotta. Faded green shutters revealed windows and balconies, brimful with cascading crimson geraniums and all shades of pink begonias. Vaulted colonnades overflowed with people of all ages, elegantly dressed - beautiful from top to toe. No scruffy hippies here!

We watched for hours. Bicycles and mopeds, carrying three or more persons - some of whom were perched dangerously on handlebars, whizzed in and out of the traffic. Trolley buses zigzagged across the road in front of us, spewing out more perfectly dressed humans and carrying others to various destinations all over the city.

Modena is a small place by English standards. It is a micro city. The historic centre is tiny - more like a large town, but the *'periferia'* or the outskirts, are enormous and ever expanding. For such a small city, great amenities such as the theatre and symphony orchestra are enjoyed by the inhabitants. Pavarotti originates from Modena and often, open-air concerts featuring the great artist are arranged.

Via Emilia, an ancient Roman road cuts through the heart of the city. To the north on this same road is Parma - famous for its ham, violets, and more recently, its football team. To the south is Bologna, seat of the first European university and the gastronomic centre of northern Italy.

Modena is an extremely prosperous provincial city, with a great historical past. In 1288, the famous Este family gained control and the Duchy of Modena was created for Borso d' Este in 1452. This lasted until 1796 and was reconstituted in 1814-59, through an alliance that the Este family had with the House of Austria. Alfonso IV d' Este had a daughter, Mary of Modena, 1658-1718, who subsequently married James II. He eventually became king of England.

Before the Second World War, the area around Modena was largely agricultural. Its present day wealth harks back to post-war times, when industries such as ceramics and knitwear sprang up around the region.

Modena is also famous for the Maserati family and that great status symbol of a car - the Ferrari, founded by Enzo Ferrari in Marenello just outside the city.

After sitting on the sun drenched steps and drinking in the atmosphere, Jemp and I voted to look around the *Duomo* or cathedral.

The beautiful interior was cool and dim after the glittering heat of outside. A red marble floor and pale reddish arcades, cast a rosy comforting glow. A myriad of candles blazed at the back of the huge church, and a wonderful stained glass rose window threw intense dappled colours onto the floor and walls, giving an atmosphere of peace and security. Some of the walls are painted with frescoes and there are coloured sculptures representing the Evangelists and scenes of the Passion.

I felt calm and peaceful in this great house of God. It was a refuge from the oppressive swelter and clatter of the streets outside.

"I think I'll say a prayer for my luggage," whispered Jemp. "I've got a funny feeling about it."

She was right. Her trunk did not arrive for another three weeks.

We blinked as we returned to the outside world. The incandescence of the day had softened and a warm breeze blew about our faces. It was getting late and we thought about going home to Via Paolo Ferrari.

Walking around the exterior of the Duomo, we returned to the west portal. Across the front of the facade were four bas-reliefs with stories from Genesis, which we later found out to be by Wiligelmus in 1100.

The north side of the cathedral is connected to the Ghirlandina tower by two Gothic arches, and as we walked under them, we marvelled at the fairy tale quality and Gothic beauty of the whole building.

By now, the light was fading - mellow and much cooler. Our train journey across Europe was catching up with us. Any unsolved problems and questions would have to be answered tomorrow. Right now, we needed our beds.

CHAPTER 2 FOOD GLORIOUS FOOD

Before we could be let loose teaching English to the Italian public, Jemp, I and four other English girls who had been employed by the School, had to undertake a special course in E.F.L. (English as a Foreign Language). It would last for one week and was called the 'Direct Method.' This endowed us with the knowledge of how to teach English to non English speaking people, by literally acting out most words and speaking very directly and slowly to the pupil. It was exhausting to say the least!

We attended classes every morning. Our teacher's name was Lindsay and she had lived in Italy for four years and had married into the culture.

"Now!" she said "You must say the words by doing the actions, for example, I am sitting on a chair."

She demonstrated this piece of information to us by getting up, moving her chair and then pointing to it. Next, she lowered herself onto the chair, saying the words very clearly and slowly, as if speaking to a very small child.

I suppressed a torrent of giggles and dared not look Jemp in the eye. If I did, I knew we would both explode with mirth. The other girls were looking quite serious.

We had to practise the 'Direct Method' technique on each other.

"Of course," said Lindsay, "some Italians cannot pronounce 'sitting' easily. They either say 'seating' or even 'shitting' - I am shitting on a chair."

We all laughed at this and the ice was broken.

The training course was very intensive. We felt a little less nervous towards the end, being better equipped to face our students, knowing that they knew that we would be teaching using the 'Direct Method.' It was written so, in black and white in the glossy prospectus - never mind if it was boring!

The 'Direct Method' was really for the beginners in English.

Complicated grammar would have to be revised independently for intermediate classes. The advanced groups proved to be the easiest, as all they required was stimulating conversation and debate, with occasional grammar corrections. I prayed that I would get my fair share of the more articulate and fluent speakers as these lessons appeared to be by far the most interesting.

At the end of the course we went out to celebrate. Lindsay took us to her favourite pizzeria.

"Buona sera, signora, signorine," beamed the rotund waiter.

"Venite, venite con me." (Come with me).

He led us to a huge circular table in the centre of the room.

"*Quante bellisime Inglese,*" he chuckled and bowed.

The pizzeria was wonderful. Bottles of Chianti in raffia caskets and an assortment of other wines, hung from the beamed ceiling. The large tables were covered with cheerful white and blue cloths and serviettes.

There were softly glowing candles and striking landscape paintings hung on the walls.

An overwhelming aroma of garlic and other appetising cooking smells wafted over, adding to the cosy comforting atmosphere.

"We must drink Lambrusco," declared Lindsay. "It's the wine made in Modena and around these parts."

I had never heard of this wine before. The year was 1974 and most English people rarely drank wine in those days, except on special occasions. Nowadays, we have very European habits - sometimes it is hard to tell different nations apart. Now we have Benetton, Gucci and Prada in our big shopping malls. We can find Chianti, San Giovese and Lambrusco on our supermarket shelves, along with Panettone at Christmas, Amaretti di Saronna and Balsamic Vinegar, which originates from Modena.

A couple of litres of Lambrusco were ordered and the wine tasted a little like sour raspberryade. The Lambrusco in Modena is different from the sweet, frothy stuff that we find in our English supermarkets. The Modenese wine is much stronger and stiffer, with more of a kick.

However, to us it tasted like pop and its alcoholic content only became apparent after downing several glasses. We were all, including Lindsay, very merry by the time our pizzas arrived.

The type of pizzas that we now have available to us in England did not exist in 1974. Pizzaland was one of the few places that sold pizza on a grand scale and there were no takeaways or pizzarias as we know and love them today.

So back then, a visit to an Italian pizzeria was really something - an unforgettable experience. The waiters were jolly and jokey, topping up empty glasses with the foamy, purple coloured Lambrusco. One of the chefs who was in view, was hurling freshly made pizza bases into the air, whilst another was adding different, delicious toppings to them as they landed. Yet another tall dark extrovert Italian was thrusting the finished pizzas into a great fiery oven with a long spade.

"They're oven baked," said Lindsay, noting our interest. "They have a lovely charcoaly taste, which really you only get with stone baked pizza."

She forgot to add that in Modena, the chefs often used old orange boxes to fuel the ovens, and sometimes an astonished client would find nails in their pizza bases!

Inebriated and full to the brim with pizza, we ended our evening on a happy note.

~

Italian cooking really took me by surprise. Previously, I had not had much interest in food. During my three years at college, where

17

I trained to be a teacher, I ate very little. This was possibly due to the fact that the food was practically inedible, or maybe because I just could not be bothered to go down to the dining area which was nicknamed the 'Crash-Hall.' In those days I lived on chocolate.

Before I set sail, or rather rail, for the Italian shores, I was employed by the City Language School, to teach a group of Italian students for three weeks, during the summer holidays at Reading University. Most of these students hailed from Modena. They amazed me, because the majority of them had lugged great suitcases over Europe, filled not with clothes, as you would imagine, but with spaghetti, Italian coffee and perculators, salami and even tins of tomatoes. I was amused at such behaviour. At this point I did not understand the enormous part food has to play in Italian society.

Meal times are probably the most important feature in the structure of the Italian day. Breakfast is a rather 'hit and miss' affair, but lunch has to be eaten at 1.00 p.m. on the dot. At that time of day, every Italian worth his salt is sitting at a carefully set table, complete with wine. The whole nation is at home, or at the restaurant, *a l'una* - at one o'clock!

After this, they have a nap or a siesta. They need to, as they have consumed so much they can barely move. Pasta is eaten as a *'primo piatto,'* and meat with salad as a *'secondo,'* followed by lots of wine - Lambrusco for the Modenese - of course! Then comes cheese and fruit and finally, a tiny cup of coffee in the form of an *espresso.* Sometimes, there will be a *'digestivo'* such as *'Nocino'* or brandy, to wash it all down and of course, settle the overflowing stomach.

This culinary experience will be repeated at eight o'clock sharp.

Dinner is probably a little more elaborate - maybe more cheese and wine, or a bigger plate of pasta. I could not understand why the women were so slim. I now realise - we all do - that the Mediterranean diet is one of the best in the world. Lots of olive oil, protein, complex carbohydrates and fruit form the basis of their daily food. Not many cakes, puddings or chocolates cross their lips! They also have pots of nervous energy to work off all those calories.

Cakes are reserved for Sundays. *'Pasticcerie'* are the only shops open on the day of rest. Delicate little pastries, often with an almond base, are packed into a pretty box which is tied with an exquisite cascade of shiny ribbons. It looks like an extravagant and beautiful gift. Almost too special to open and eat!

One bar that I particularly liked in Modena, was called 'Molinari.' Situated right in the heart of the city on the Via Emilia, it was a typical stand up bar where coffee, cakes, ice cream or spirits could be served at any time of the day. Its speciality was an invigorating, delicious drink called *'Frullato di frutta.'* This is a wonderful whizzed-up mixture of different fruits - very healthy and energising. Molinari bar was elegant and stylish, and also served the most delicious *gelati* or ice cream.

I once ate a very decadent ice cream there. It was piled high with wonderful fruity flavours and topped with an enormous dollop of whipped cream, and drizzled with liquid chocolate.

In the evenings, Via Emilia would be heaving with humans of all shapes and sizes. Families with small children, groups of chatting teenagers, chic young couples and old people in their best attire, paraded up and down the busy street. Ubiquitous mopeds zipped in and out, and precariously balanced bicycles wobbled through the crowds. In the evening, Italians come out en masse to *'fare la passeggiata.'* This means walking up and down the main thoroughfare, ice cream in hand, people watching. I can thoroughly recommend it!

During the summer months, the balmy evening air is slightly fresher than the muggy lifeless heat of the day. This entices people out.

To the south of the city there was, and to my knowledge probably still is, a 'Luna Park,' a sort of ribbon development of outdoor cafés and bars, which came alive in the warm summer evenings. Tables and chairs were placed along the pavements and people could drink beer or sip wine or order great chunks of juicy red water melon, which were sold by the barrelful.

At the 'Luna Park', a favourite spot for the younger generation, the air would be lively with endless chatter as the Modenese folk thronged in and out of the brightly lit area. Laughter, music, and the drone of televisions from nearby open apartment windows rose up to meet the velvety star-studded sky.

~

During our early days in Modena and before we could speak any Italian, Jemp and I decided to visit a little food shop situated at one end of Via Paolo Ferrari, We entered the tiny store and looked around. We wanted some yoghurt.

Consulting my dictionary, I said in halting Italian: *"Vorrei un uomo, per favore."*

The old woman behind the counter glared at us and issued a tirade of what sounded like scolding Italian.

"Non vendiamo gli uomini qui!" (We do not sell men here!) She shouted at us. *"Andate via!"* (Be off with you!)

The brand name of the yoghurt I wanted was '*Yomo*' and the Italian word for man is *uomo*. I had unknowingly mispronounced the word.

Needless to say, we did not return to that particular shop again.

The Italian nation has a liking for certain English words which are inappropriate and funny to us Brits. I once saw a portable toilet, which was called a 'Jolly Box' and many times I have been given 'Bum' bubble gum, usually instead of small change in shops. Small change in lira was often in short supply and sweets or chewing gum were given instead!

After our Direct Method course, we were issued with our teaching placements and classes. We had been told before the course began, that many of us would not be teaching in Modena but in other schools some kilometres away.

I was disappointed to be one of the teachers selected for two small language schools in Sassuolo and Carpi, tiny provincial towns in the province of Modena. I had hoped to stay in the city I was growing to know and love.

My way of life was to be turned upside down. Instead of teaching during daylight hours, I would have to begin at five o'clock and work through until ten p.m. I was not madly happy about this and wondered how I would keep my energy levels up during the long exhausting evenings.

Monique, a French girl to whom I was introduced, was also placed in the Sassuolo and Carpi language centres teaching French. She possessed a Citroen *'Deux Chevaux'* and offered to drive me home each evening. Feeling somewhat placated, Monique and I became great friends, sharing many secrets during our fog bound late evening journeys along the Via Emilia.

Originally, Monique hailed from Paris and had previously worked with a wealthy Modenese family, teaching their children French. In fact, it was this eminent family who had presented her with the *'Deux Chevaux.'*

Monique had amused us all by recalling that before arriving in Italy, her parents had instructed her to buy new clothes, especially a coat.

"You never know - the Italian shops may not be any good." they said.

We chuckled at this. The Italian shops were full of beautiful, fashionable coats, probably even better than those in Paris.

This young French girl who was of a similar age to us, seemed very independent, sophisticated and Italianised. She did not speak English, so in her company I learnt many new Italian words. Over the years most of the English girls left Modena, but Monique remained until she married a Greek boy and departed to live in Athens, sometime in the late 1970s.

CHAPTER 3 BOLOGNA AND SIROLO

Before settling down to the serious job of teaching, which was to begin in October, we were given the rest of September as an interim holiday.

Jemp was very into the rock music of the day and strains of 'Led Zeppelin' nearly always filled our flat. Even now, when I hear 'Stairway To Heaven,' a mental picture of the apartment in Via Paolo Ferrari vividly floods my consciousness.

One warm September day as I was inside pottering about, Jemp burst headlong through the front door in great excitement.

"Guess what!" she exclaimed. "I've got two tickets to see Frank Zappa! He's playing in Bologna!"

She held them up gleefully, as she danced around the room.

"Wow, great!" I responded, not too enthusiastically. I was not sure if I liked Frank Zappa, but I decided that an evening out in Bologna would be fun anyway. It was time we explored somewhere other than the provincial, arcaded streets of Modena.

We put on our best hippy gear - long, flowing, flower printed skirts with plaits in our hair. In high spirits we set off by train to the capital of Emilia-Romagna.

Arriving early, we decided to explore the great city before the concert began. We tumbled out of the train and on to one of the biggest stations. I had ever seen. The main north to south line has numerous junctions here. On the 2nd August in 1980, it was to be the scene of one of Italy's most terrible terrorist attacks ever probably perpetrated, by an extreme right wing organisation known as the outlawed P2 (Propaganda Two), who were engaged in acts of political espionage and terrorism.

They planted a massive bomb on Platform 1, and about eighty-six people were killed and two hundred injured on that fateful day. The country was devastated and in mourning. In recent years, a poignant memorial was built into the glass of either the waiting-room or the restaurant, honouring and remembering the dead.

The late 1970s was to witness some of the bloodiest outbursts of terrorism ever seen in a modern industrialised society. Important factory bosses were in danger of being knee-caped, kidnapped, or worst still, murdered by subversive terrorist gangs. Potential victims did not often venture out of their homes without a tourniquet, in case they were shot in the legs. There were revolutionary parties galore.

These dramatic years of fear were called the *'Anni di Piombi'* (Years of lead), so called after the lead bullets favoured by the Red Brigades. In the winter of 1976, the industrial north was in turmoil terrorised by this gang. On March 16th 1978, Italy's Christian

Democrat leader, Aldo Moro, was kidnapped by the Red Brigades, and his five men escort, machine-gunned to death.

Moro lay in his 'people's prison' for forty-five days, blindfolded somewhere near Rome. During this period, Italy seethed with anxiety and growing horror. Almost two months after his disappearance, Moro's body was found in the boot of a car in Rome, ridden with bullets.

After the bombing atrocity in Bologna in 1980, it seemed as if Italy was on the brink of entering a Neofascist period of terrorism. The extreme right wing MSI party had been founded immediately after World War II and the Fascism of the Mussolini era would always simmer beneath the surface of what seemed to be a respectable Italy.

~

As we entered the sun lit world of Bologna, full of deep sharp late afternoon shadows, we gradually threaded our way down narrow streets towards the centre. There was much more traffic here than in Modena.

Cars, buses and mopeds crowded, jammed and jostled together as people wove their way in and out.

Pedestrian crossings were a joke. Nobody stopped when the lights went red. Finally, we took our lives in our hands trying to get across the main road. With determination, we strode across, holding our arms up as if to halt the traffic. Miraculously, it squealed to a halt, the drivers grinning and waving as we traversed from one side to the other.

Bologna is a very beautiful city. It is one of the oldest in Italy and seat of a famous university. The old town is permeated with a rosy glow, as it is built almost exclusively of reddish brick. The bustling streets are bordered by arched porticoes, which cast a welcome shade and give some respite from the scorching summer sun. In winter, the endless arcades lend protection from the bitterly cold winds. In fact, one can roam around Bologna without ever having to come into contact with any adverse weather conditions at all - apart from having to cross the death-trap roads.

In the early 1970s, Bologna was one of the centres of Communist Italy. Many old apartments displayed ubiquitous red awnings over their windows, to provide shade. I do not think that I saw any other hue or colour - only red, on these material canopies. I remember reading somewhere that 'even the dogs in Bologna carry little red flags in their mouths.' One of Bologna's nicknames is *La Rossa* (the red).

During the few occasions that I visited Bologna in the 70s, there was always student unrest, political trouble and confusion. However on a recent trip to that venerable city, it seemed to be an oasis of calm and prosperity with few hints of its recent, turbulent past.

It seemed to me that young Italians were much more aware of politics than their English counterparts back home - that is, apart from my own family who always enjoyed a good political debate, and were never happier than when shouting back at the T.V. at some well meaning or conniving politician. In Italy, politics would creep into every conversation. Modena and Bologna were both represented by the Communist party. However it was a sort of Eurocommunism - very diluted.

Over the years, I became acquainted with the family of one of the left wing Communist mayors of Modena. He was well versed in the theory of Marx and Engles, but he lived in a big villa containing wonderful works of modern art. Another property belonging to this very charming and hospitable family was situated in a near-by fashionable seaside town. Not quite the Communism of the Eastern Block!

I was rather amused one day when visiting the family, to find that the loo was devoid of toilet paper. Instead, numerous pages of a right wing Italian newspaper, were carefully rolled onto the holder. I have never been sure if this was complete disdain for right wing political views, or just plain parsimony.

On another visit to Bologna, I was involved in a rather unpleasant political incident. I was on my own and had boarded a trolley bus which was headed for the city centre. Suddenly, the bus came to a shuddering standstill. People were talking excitedly to one another. Everyone stood up quickly and hurried off, beckoning to me, so of course I followed them.

Minutes later, the bus was overturned and set on fire. Absolutely horrified and frightened, I ran back towards the station. Masked students were rampaging up and down the narrow streets, pushing over cars and buses.

Riot police with shields and tear-gas bombs, were marching en mass towards these young activists. The miasmic smell of tear-gas reeked and hung heavily in the air. My shopping trip was ruined, and

I returned to Modena, feeling disheartened. It seems I had exchanged one country threatened by the terrorism of Northern Ireland, for another with a similar problem.

On the day of the Frank Zappa concert, Jemp and I wandered around Bologna. We marvelled at the beautiful medieval architecture and were especially smitten with the *Due Torre* or the two towers which stand tall, or rather lean slightly, at the end of the Via della Independenza.

We made our way to the university area, and were surprised to see the arcades there disfigured and painted with lurid red graffiti. It was much scruffier than the rest of the town. Bars blared out rock music in Italian and English and groups of students with books under their arms sat at pavement cafés, deep in intellectual discussion, smoking, drinking and laughing.

Winding our way down to Via Zamboni, we joined up with a surging throng of young people, all presumably heading for the Frank Zappa concert. We clutched our tickets and intermingled with the group.

Suddenly, the crowd started running. Arms flailed. Shrieks pierced the darkening evening air. Confusion broke out.

"*Porca miseria!*" the crowd shouted, screamed and scuffled.

"*Puttana Eva!*" they swore.

Stunned, we looked around.

Policemen with great clanking chains were starting to chase us all.

Jemp and I hitched up our skirts and ran for our lives. We had no idea why we were running, where we were running, or who we were running from. Some primal instinct told us that if we did not escape along with the rest of the hoard, we would probably be bashed to death.

At some point, I was actually lifted off the ground by the surging, pushing crowds. It seemed terrifying and unreal.

Looking back on this horrific incident, I do not recall where we went. All I remember is the chaos and the terror of the situation - the panic, the mayhem and the pain in my legs at having to run so fast.

Later, we discovered that this sort of scenario was fairly common at demonstrations and large potentially unruly gatherings. Apparently, a great number of concert goers did not have tickets, so the heavy-handed police came out in force, brandishing dangerous chains, indiscriminately.

The Italian police continued to scare me during my stay there. They were not like our friendly British Bobbies on the beat. Armed with great guns attached to their uniforms, they stood outside banks and other public places and appeared officious and unapproachable. There are many different types of Italian police, including the Carabinieri and the Polizia di Stato, which can get confusing

After our adventure in Bologna, we thought that we would travel down to the coast for a few days, to catch the last of the glorious September sunshine. The leaves on the trees were turning colour, just tinged with russet and gold, just starting to crinkle and crack and fall to the ground to be crunched on.

The east coast sounded promising. Jemp had a friend called Marco who lived in Cesenatico, a picturesque fishing village south of Venice.

We decided to call in on him and then head south to a small seaside town by the name of Sirolo.

~

Sirolo was a dream destination. A pretty seaside village where time had stood still. The silky beach was covered with pure white sand, and the sea was sparkly glittering cobalt turning translucent on the far away horizon line. Small fishing craft were dotted around on the water, and a few colourful beach umbrellas flapped gently in the light breeze.

Jemp and I dug our toes into the luxuriously soft sand.

"Io sono, tu sei, lei è," we chanted in unison and then fell about laughing, trying to get our brains around the Italian verbs.

If anyone could hear us, they would think that we were completely bonkers. We had agreed to do little other than walk down to the beach every day of our short holiday, and give ourselves an intensive course of Italian. We would sprawl out in the sand with our grammar books, getting a tan, and at the same time we would equip ourselves for life back in Modena. What could be better!

Our journey to Sirolo took us through some spectacular countryside.

It was a difficult journey by train, so we chose to travel by *corriera* (coach) down to Ancona, and then on to Sirolo by local transport.

Our first port of call was Cesenatico where Marco had an apartment.

We planned to stop there overnight on our way further south.

Marco, a big, tall guy with long dark flowing tresses, met us at the coach station.

"*Ciao bellisime!*" He greeted us with outstretched arms. "*Come state voi due*? (How are you both?) Come let's walk around Cesenatico and find a good bar and get something to eat and drink."

We were travelling light with small rucksacks, so our luggage presented no problem. Cesenatico was charming. Rather like Venice, it is built on a system of lagoons. Quaint little bridges crossed the canals at intervals, and small colourful fishing boats trawled the waters.

Altogether it had a very sleepy air. It was as if it had been forgotten by time and man.

After a refreshing drink, we dumped our bags at Marco's place, freshened up and set out for our evening's entertainment.

"I know a good night-club," announced Marco in faltering English.

"It's very good! Once you pay to enter you can drink what you want."

This sounded promising. We strolled through Cesenatico, admiring the bobbing colourful fishing boats. The day's catch had been hauled up on to the quay side and various different types of fish gleamed silvery in the dying rays of the evening sun. A pungent smell of brine and oil permeated the air. This was a working port.

Along the quayside were an assortment of bars and restaurants. We tumbled into '*Il Gatto Grigio*' - The Grey Cat Club. Inside it was like the 'The Black Hole of Calcutta.' Ancient gloomy mirrors hung on the dark walls and a spooky atmosphere pervaded the air. It was also empty.

The bar man greeted us with a *"Buona sera"* and we ordered whiskey chasers. The turntable was blaring out the latest hit single by 'Deep Purple.'

"Why is it so empty?" we asked Gigi the bar tender.

"I don't know," he shrugged his shoulders expressively. "Maybe It's because it's Monday night."

Jemp made a face at me and I grimaced back.

"Oh well," said Jemp cheerfully. "At least we'll have the whole dance floor to ourselves. We can really move about. Yeah!"

She spun around, pirouetting across the shiny, black dance floor, her long silky hair splaying around her face.

We followed suit. We danced and drank, danced and drank. At midnight we decided to call it a night and get some sleep, as the following morning, we had a long journey to Sirolo.

Marco pushed open the door of the *'Gatto Grigio'* and the cold night air hit us like a sharp slap.

Stumbling onto the pavement we fell into a heap, one on top of the other, giggling like a bunch of drunken sailors. The free drinks were working their lethal damage upon us. The three of us just about managed to tumble and lurch our way home.

My head was spinning. I needed the bathroom quickly. Once back at Marco's flat, I rushed up there and locked the door. I had an overwhelming urge to lie down. A small balcony led off from the bathroom and outside the air was fresh and fragrant. I thankfully eased my weary body down to the floor and slept until morning.

Unbeknown to me, Jemp and Marco had been calling and knocking on the bathroom door all night long. They were worried that something had happened, and also needed to use the facilities. Blissfully unaware, I slept through all the commotion.

Needless to say, next morning, I was not a popular person. All three of us had terrific hangovers. Even to this day I cannot drink whiskey without a nauseous feeling in the pit of my stomach.

Subdued is the word to describe us on our journey to Sirolo. I slept for the first part of the way. I awoke in a daze and watched the countryside flashing past my window. The terrain was beautiful. Small, pocket-sized fields and hilly outcrops were interspersed with blue-green cypress trees and umbrella pines, waving softly in the breeze. Olives, grapes, peaches, grain, beans and flowers were growing together in an intensive pattern of garden farming. The patchwork landscape seemed familiar and I recognised images that had been there for centuries, locked in the paintings of the Renaissance artists.

The coach climbed through a stretch of mountainous region. We traversed vertiginous, spiralling roads, until we finally arrived at the coast and glimpsed the azure bays of the Adriatic.

Peace and tranquillity reigned in Sirolo. Each morning after a good breakfast at our small *pensione*, we would follow a short path through gloriously fragrant pine trees to a tiny, practically deserted beach.

We lay on our towels, with books in front of us, testing each other on Italian verbs and phrases, interspersed with chat and laughter. One word I remember learning in Sirolo, was *stuzzicadenti* which means toothpicks - a totally useless word - but what a beautiful sound! With words such as these, it is no wonder that the Italian language has a reputation for being musical!

When we had had enough of Italian grammar, we would plunge into the shimmering opalescent sea, frolicking and diving in the clear crystal waters, waving at passing fishing boats and generally chilling out.

However, all too soon it was time to return to Modena and our new teaching careers. Life in the big city was calling us back.

CHAPTER 4 FABULOUS FIRENZE

My life settled down into a comfortable routine. At around ten o'clock in the morning, I would stumble out of bed, breakfast in a nearby bar, and mooch around the shops until lunch time, when the whole city closed down for its siesta.

Back at my flat, I would have a quick meal followed by preparation for the evening's lessons. Struggling with the perfect tense, the past perfect and the conditional, I was probably only a few steps ahead of my students! At least I could speak English brilliantly, even if I did not always know why I had used one particular tense and not another.

At four o'clock I would venture out, and take the little old-fashioned train with wooden seats to Sassuolo or Carpi, where smaller versions of the City Language School were based. Both these towns were thriving enclaves of Modena.

Carpi is particularly picturesque, with an enormous piazza surrounded by typically Italian architecture. It is one of the most interesting places in the province of Modena, and boasts some fine palaces or *palazzi,* although its extensive suburbs are fairly industrial. In the 1970s, the periphery of the town housed numerous factories which produced exquisite cardigans and pullovers. Factory outlets existed where cheap versions of these chic numbers could be bought.

From 1327 to 1525, Carpi was a lordship of the Pio family, who were famous patrons of the arts. The Pio Castle now houses the Museo Civico which contains works by Bernadino, Loschi and Mattia Preti, as well as some beautiful scagliola works. Scagliola is a material made from selenite, which is often used to imitate marble and pietradura - a type of marble. Many famous scagliola works were situated in Carpi in the seventeenth and eighteenth centuries.

Another place of interest in Carpi is a museum that commemorates Second World War victims, who were deported to German Nazi concentration camps. About five kilometres from Carpi is the small town of Fossoli, where the largest Nazi internment camp was built in 1944. The brilliant writer Primo Levi describes this camp in one of the great books of the twentieth century - *'Se Questo e Un Uomo.'*

Levi suffered greatly and was deported to Auschwitz from Fossoli. A huge war memorial exists in Carpi, and many people from these smaller outlying towns are still not too keen on the Germans, remembering the atrocities committed against them during the latter years of World War II. Later on in my first year in Italy, my parents and younger sisters came to visit me, and we took a trip to Carpi.

Our family was mistaken for Germans as we were blond, foreign and drove around in a V.W. We received disdainful looks until it was somehow discovered that we were English. It was interesting how people's attitudes then changed completely.

Lessons at Carpi were quite low key. I would work from about five o'clock to about ten o'clock p.m. with a small break of five minutes at the conclusion of each lesson. Each group contained between eight to fifteen students and lessons were often great fun, with some older students producing bottles of wine and cakes to eat, drink and be merry, as we talked and discussed current affairs in English.

Some students who worked in, or even owned the local *maglieria* or knitware factories, would often bring gifts of tee-shirts and pullovers, for me and the other teachers. It was really more like a social occasion than work. After the last lesson at 10 o'clock, many of us including myself and Monique would pile into the local pizzeria and finish the evening on a high note.

Sassuolo was much the same. Situated south of Modena, this pretty little town is renowned for its ceramic industry. In those days it produced stunning innovative tiles, beautifully painted with intricate designs. Sassuolo is on the road to Abetone, a skiing resort in the Apennines. It leads the way to beautiful Tuscany and the countryside is fairly unpopulated and rich in flora and fauna.

~

Slowly I was accumulating more and more friends. The crowd I had taught at Reading were quick to offer me Italian hospitality, and happy evenings were arranged in their company. The other four

English girls who also worked for the City Language School were good fun and very pleasant, and a Canadian girl called Lisa became a firm friend.

During that first term, my new buddies and I travelled at weekends to some wonderful places such as Perugia, Turin, Verona, Venice and Florence.

I will never forget my first view of Florence or Firenze - city of the Renaissance. We travelled there by train down the spinal rail cord of Italy - the line that runs from north to south, a mere two hours from Modena.

After leaving Bologna, the terrain became mountainous and picturesque - such a contrast from the flat plains of Emilia-Romagna. We sped past hilly outcrops, deeply carpeted with groves of umbrella pines. From the windows, we could see massive viaducts supporting the motorway or *Autostrada del Sole* (motorway of the sun), transporting a myriad of gleaming cars to the ancient city of Florence.

On our journey, a long lonely tunnel swallowed us up somewhere between Bologna and Florence - it seemed to go on for ever. In later years, this tunnel was to be the gruesome scene of many a terrorist bomb. As we emerged from the long monotonous tunnel, the city I had always wanted to visit was ever nearer.

Soon a panoramic view of Florence, in an overwhelming beautiful landscape was spread before our eyes. There it was in the distance, like a perfect toy city - the huge ribbed dome of the Duomo or cathedral, overshadowing all other architecture.

Florence is the city of Dante and Beatrice, Petrarch and Boccaccio. In Dante's day, it was the centre of tremendous mercantile wealth. Its noble families were the bankers of Europe. The Renaissance started there. The most powerful family to probably live in Florence was the Medici, reigning over that city state. Florence's role on the European political stage at that time was enhanced by the intensity of its artistic culture, which has been unsurpassed before or since.

I caught my first glimpse of this beautiful city, as the train threaded its way towards the centre. Brunelleschi's giant dome and Giotto's tower stood strong and rosy against the late morning sunshine. The hills around us were becoming more populated with farms and pastel and ochre coloured villas, and the Tuscan countryside revealed olive groves and fruit orchards, splashed with dappled sunlight. In between the hamlets, the landscape was blanketed with cypresses and ilexes. The brick-red view of the city against this background was a sight I shall never forget.

We stood in the Piazza del Duomo feeling dazed. Where should we begin? Florence is packed with so many treasures. The ghostly presence of its turbulent and artistic past is powerful, and the narrow medieval stone streets are evocative. It is a city virtually unchanged for four hundred years. People milled around us. Cameras clicked. Buses, mopeds, bicycles, noise. It was a dizzy, slightly surreal sensation - as so many Italian cities are.

The Duomo, huge in its proportions loomed above us, like a giant wedding cake, richly ornate with walls of creamy Carrara and green Prato marble. The dome created by Brunelleschi and completed in 1436 is truly awesome. At the time it was constructed, nobody believed that it was possible to build so large a half sphere. Someone actually proposed building it over an immense mound of soil piled high inside the cathedral. They planned to hide money inside the pile of dirt and eventually when the dome was completed, the peasants from the surrounding area would be allowed to dig for the loot and cart away the soil at the same time. Luckily, Brunelleschi worked out the technique and engineering principles in time.

We looked at the Baptistery doors cast in bronze by Ghiberti, and marvelled at the façade of the Duomo and the beauty of its sculptures. The magic of Florence had beguiled us.

"Shall we go up inside the Dome?" I asked the others.

Monique declined as she was afraid of heights. The rest of us trundled up the spiral stone staircase, which was so narrow there was only room enough for one person to pass at a time. It felt cold and dank and slightly claustrophobic. We were out of breath by the time we reached the top, but it was well worth it. Florence was spread below - a kaleidoscope of terracotta. The River Arno gleaming in the afternoon sun snaked its way through the centre.

Returning down the steps was even more difficult than going up, and we had to press ourselves against the cold stone walls whenever we met anyone coming in the opposite direction.

We left the area around the Duomo and found our way to Via Tornabuoni, one of the most fashionable shopping areas in Florence. Inviting shoe shops and wonderful window displays captivated and seduced us, but unfortunately we had no money.

At the end of this road, we veered towards the river Arno - that wonderful expanse of water, bridged by the famous and romantic

Ponte Vecchio. This was where Dante met his Beatrice. We strolled about the market place near to the Ponte Vecchio, where leather goods, embroidered tablecloths and Florentine paper crafts were on display.

Crossing the bridge, the river glinted below us. Many buildings still showed the water mark left by the great flood of 1966. On 4th November of that year, the Arno broke its banks, and angry breakers mingled with foam, sediment and oil. The huge waves swelled over the embankment which had been built to hold back the often raging torrents. By early afternoon on that day, the Arno had plunged deep into the heart of Florence, devastating the city and engulfing it in fetid, silt-laden water and fuel oil.

Many of its citizens were marooned, and within hours, seventeen people had perished, and eleven thousand had abandoned their homes. At precisely 7.26 a.m. all electric clocks had stopped in every corner of the city. At that moment, San Nicolo, the most easterly of the seven bridges in Florence was being swallowed up, and the full fury of the flood was vent upon the city.

A thick slime of liquid mud containing the carcasses of animals, mingled with debris, including the contents of the sewers. Huge tree stumps caused untold damage as they brushed against other objects in the putrid water. Many say it was like Dante's 'Inferno.' More than one and a half million volumes from the Nazionale - an important library, disappeared under the flood. Many treasures were lost.

There is a remarkable story about an academic woman, who made twenty eight precarious trips along a third-storey ledge between the Museum of History and Science and the Uffizi Art gallery. She managed to save numerous treasures, including Galileo's telescopes.

The devastation was such, that many Florentines claimed that it was even worse than the Second World War. After the waters which had reached ten feet tall had subsided, the narrow streets looked as if they had been bombed. The violence of the waters had stirred an explosive mixture of stored chemicals, which blasted warehouses and artisan workshops apart. Cars covered with the slime of oil and other detritus clogged the streets and rubble lay everywhere.

The restoration of the city took ages. It was an extraordinary salvage operation manned by hundreds of students, foreigners and volunteers. Paintings were removed from the Uffizi for drying, and a hospital for art was set up in the *Limonaia* - a winter shelter for lemon trees at the Pitti Palace. Bit by bit, the city of the Renaissance was cleansed and put back together again. By the first summer after the flood, almost all the hotels had reopened and museums and art galleries were displaying their many treasures once more.

Later, we strolled down via dei Servi to the quiet workaday quarter of the city, where small individual shops or *botteghe*, sell useful household items. We continued to saunter down narrow streets, cool in the mid day sun, until we arrived in the area where the artisans worked and sold their goods. This fascinating part of Florence is called Oltr'arno which means the 'other side' of the river Arno.

Quaint, brightly lit work shops hummed with activity. Furniture makers, upholsters, picture framers, mirror makers working with gesso, restorers of beautiful paintings, silversmiths, carpenters and ladies ironing the clothes of the gentry, work long hours in this tucked away part of the city. There are tiny workshops making the softest leather goods; beautiful bags, gloves and exquisite shoes for which the Italians are so renowned. We often stopped, mesmerised by the activity and goods being created within these musty little workshops.

"Jemp and Monique," I called. "Come and look at this!"

I was gazing into the window of a furniture shop, where marble boxes were displayed, inlaid with silvery hues of mother of pearl, malachite and lapis. All the designs were different and intricately presented. I just had to have one.

"I must go in!" I begged.

"I don't think you can buy from these workshops" replied Jemp. "I'm sure there'll be some for sale in one of the markets. We could go back to the 'Ponte Vecchio' - I'm sure I saw some there."

Reluctantly, I tore myself away from the enticing workshops and joined the others. We retraced our steps back to the market and I purchased a pretty inlaid trinket box. Our party was about six in all - Jemp, Monique, and three of the other English teachers, Lucy, Jess and Helen and I.

Eventually, after spending some time in the market, we arrived at a wide piazza in front of the church of Santa Maria Novella. The Gothic interior of the church was quite a surprise. Strange frescoes by Fillippino Lippi adorned the walls, and there were episodes from the life of the Virgin in the chapel, painted by Ghirlandaio. We stayed in there for quite a while as we were all tired, and the calm atmosphere and the chance to sit down and contemplate the silence was welcoming.

The Uffizi was next on our hit list. By now it was late afternoon and we were beginning to flag. The dying embers of the sun felt warm and reassuring. Luckily, many tourists had departed and we were able to gain entry to this famous art gallery without having to queue. 'The Battle of San Romano,' by Paolo Uccello was one of the first pictures that I saw there. Its immense size and strong vertical perspective had a huge impact on me and has stayed in my memory ever since.

Outside, the air was now quite cool and the shadows sharp edged. We made for the Piazza della Signoria. Tables and chairs with umbrellas were set out around the great piazza, and we sat down for a coffee. Soon winter would be approaching and café life would continue indoors. It was great to feel the last rays of the sun's warmth, and to drink *cappuccini* or *cappucci* in such marvellous surroundings.

The piazza seemed an extension of the art gallery, and gigantic marble statues, many sculptured by the great Michelangelo, offered perching places for inquisitive pigeons. A sprinkling of lights in the cyan blue sky and a growing chill in the air told us that dusk was about to fall, and after an exhausting but wonderful day, we made our way back to the station and home to Modena.

~

Autumn did not slip gracefully into winter as it sometimes does in England. Instead it was a short sharp shock. The lovely balmy days of summer metamorphosed into a few crisp crunchy golden-leaved ones. Then the grey damp nebulous smoggy fog appeared, interspersed with a few beautiful, limpid crystal clear periods.

The fogs around Modena are legendary. As the city is situated in a river basin and below sea level, mists would rise and cover the flat landscape with white, cotton wool-like ectoplasm. It was dense and dangerous to those who were road-bound, and Monique and I often drove back from Sassuolo and Carpi in the midst of a real pea-souper. Slowly, hardly daring to speak, we negotiated the hazardous way, our eyes straining to catch sight of any other vehicles on the road, in front or behind. We searched for stray lights and familiar landmarks. The relief was palpable when we eventually arrived back in Modena.

Monique was a typical young French woman. She had that *'je ne sais quoi'* sort of style that just seems effortless - an innate chic. It was different from the glossy Italian elegance; it was quieter and more refined. We became good friends and often invited each other over for lunch. Monique taught me how to make the delicious and cheap *spaghetti al tonno* which became part of my staple diet. Even now when I eat this economical and nutritious dish, memories of Monique and Modena flood my memory. The recipe is as follows;-

- Fill a pan 3/4 with water; place lid on pan;
- While water is boiling, prepare the sauce, by finely chopping an onion; and two cloves of garlic; place these in another pan;
- Gently cook for about 4 mins; add a tin of tuna; cook this for another 4 mins; add a tin of chopped tomatoes; leave this to simmer on a low heat; season with salt and pepper;

- Meanwhile, go back to the first pan and when the water has boiled, add 4oz of spaghetti per person (or more if you want!); cook on a medium to high heat for approx. 11 mins;
- Drain the pasta; mix in the juicy sauce, and top with Parmesan cheese or any other cheese of your liking.
- Che economico!
- Enjoy with a big glass of red Italian wine. Valpollicella is good!

~

Jemp and I returned to England for Christmas to be with our families. Jemp had been homesick during our last few weeks in Italy and decided not to return to '*la bel paese.*' In January I had to make the long, lonely train trip alone, and return to Via Paolo Ferrari, without a flatmate.

CHAPTER 5 SAN GEMIGNANO'S DAY AND MAGICAL MODENA

January 31st is the feast of San Gemignano, the patron saint of Modena. All Italian cities have their own patron saint, believed to look after the inhabitants, and he or she generally protects and bestows gifts upon them.

Gemignano had been Modena's first bishop and was canonised after his death because in the 4th century, he had miraculously covered Modena with a blanket of dense fog and saved the city from the marauding Huns, who were about to attack the city. When the Huns again threatened Modena in the early 10th century, prayers were offered up to the saint and it was thought that he saved Modena once more from invasion. The fact that the city is usually covered with a thick carpet of fog during the winter months was, however, not taken into consideration.

So every January 31st, Modena was and probably still is, transformed into a fairyland *festa* or feast day. The arcaded labyrinth of streets put on a shimmering face, and glittering fairy lights were strung all around Piazza Grande, lighting up the plethora of stalls selling candy floss and sugared almonds, nut chocolate, huge slabs of chewy nougat that made your teeth clamp together, and all manner of interesting things.

On that evening the atmosphere was electric and the piazza took on a dramatic appearance. Lively old fashioned dance music emanated from behind the stalls, which had been set up earlier in the day by itinerant traders. Children wore multicoloured jester hats and groups of people chatted, laughed and jostled with each other. The smell of roasting chestnuts wafted on the air. It was magical.

In other parts of Italy many *feste* or feast days are religious, especially in the south. On days like Good Friday or the feast of the Immaculate Conception, evening torch lit processions bearing statues of Jesus or the Madonna or some saint, spiral their way through the streets and countryside, chanting the Rosary and singing hymns. The girls are usually dressed in white, resplendent brides of Christ, complete with veils and halos of flowers around their heads. The boys would be smartly attired in their Sunday best, shoes shining and hair carefully combed. Following them would be the rest of the town or village, bearing enormous colourful banners and sweetly singing the 'Ave Maria.'

Being a Catholic, I remember such processions from my childhood in the northwest of England. They usually occurred in May and were great flowery occasions, with an excuse to have a new pair of gleaming white sandals and a pretty white frock. Sadly, they no longer seem to take place in England.

However in Modena, the feast of San Gemignano was not really a religious affair, as few Modenese felt strongly about their old faith. Many folk were Communists, and on Sundays, the great churches of the city were nearly empty, save for a few old signoras dressed in black, their days probably numbered, hoping and praying for a place in Heaven.

~

Piazza Grande is the hub of Modena. It is a huge cobbled square in the heart of the city, bounded on one side by the Duomo or cathedral and the Ghirlandina, and on the other three sides by colonnaded arcades. On Monday mornings it is brimful of elderly men, all nattily dressed in black, complete with trilby style hat and the ubiquitous black bicycle, discussing business, politics and football - no doubt!

The first time I chanced upon this sea of hats and gesticulating maleness, I was dumbstruck. I was on my way to visit the cathedral and I had never seen such a sight. It was obviously a 'no-go' territory for the female gender, and I decided not to invade but to seek entrance to the Duomo through another door. Fortunately, this spectacle of chattering men only appeared to happen on a Monday morning, and I was free to roam in the beautiful *piazza* any other time I liked.

Another interesting *piazza* in Modena, houses the Palazzo Ducale or Ducal Palace. In days gone by, this was the residence of the Duke of Modena, but now it houses a prestigious military academy. Near to this wonderful terracotta coloured building, is a park with winding pathways and shrubby bushes. Trees provide welcome shade in the hot summer months and I seem to remember a small zoo area with animals such as monkeys, and birds such as flamingos, living there. It was not far from Via P. Ferrari and was a pleasant spot to eat lunch or read a book

Modena is a self-contained sort of place. Many northern Italian cities are self-sufficient and Modena is no exception. The quality of life in these little Emilian enclaves is extremely high. Bologna, just south of Modena, has been voted as the place with the best quality of life in the whole of Italy, and Modena follows closely.

These are comfortable places to live in, and the inhabitants are complacent and happy with their lot, and see no reason to ever move away. The food is wonderful, the home-made wine endless, and the fashion and clothes second to none. There are good universities on the doorstep and healthy industry in the environs. The Adriatic Sea and the Apennine ski resorts for weekend entertainment are just a drive away, and the extended family still maintains importance. Why should anyone want to move elsewhere? The writer Jonathan Keates has said of the Modenese 'There is little anguish or doubt or stress because the *piccolo mondo moderno* (little modern world) they inhabit is so full of certainties, life runs fairly smoothly.'

In spite of there being a 'northern Italian' character, the different regions in the North and indeed in the South, do have their own cultural distinctiveness, and regional rivalries abound. Many regions have their own dialects and there may still be some old folk who cannot speak Italian but only dialect.

Italians love to stereotype their fellow men and claim that the Venetians are secretive, those from Verona have right wing tendencies, the Milanese display materialistic qualities, and those from Genoa are mean. The Emilians and thus the Modenese, are supposed to be greedy (although I never saw any evidence of this), pampered and sensuous and so it goes on.

Most Modenese citizens would prefer to live in the city centre, or the ever expanding *periferia,* than in the surrounding rural hinterland. The neighbouring countryside is flat and evokes bad memories of peasant days and great hardship scraping a living together. In those days before the industrial boom, there was rarely enough to eat and many prefer to forget, enjoying the luxury that city life can offer them.

I remember in the mid 1970s, seeing a few little old women working in the fields, dressed from top to toe in black, as if from another much poorer era. They tilled the fields by hand, raking the soil, pulling up radici and other salad leaves and stacking them in great sacks on their old gnarled backs. These ancient peasant folk were really destitute and the juxtaposition of them against the wealth of Modena, collecting cardboard boxes from the streets to sell for a pittance, is something that will always remain in my memory.

In midwinter, Modena is a bleak place to be. Cruel winds howl down the arcades, and *la nebbia* or fog wraps its icy fingers around the city. All the women wear fur coats with little hats to match, in an effort to stay warm and chic. The men don smart Loden coats, which are long mid-calf elegant affairs with a pleat down the back.

During this time of year, the network of narrow streets, have their own evocative atmosphere which is slightly eerie. The old shop windows are brightly lit and look inviting through the spiralling mists. Sometimes the Ghirlandina can be lost altogether, clothed in fine white *nebbia*. This is a surreal but compelling sight

~

The weekday morning fruit and vegetable market in Modena was a real treat. From Via Paolo Ferrari, I used to wind my way down the maze of narrow streets, to the purpose built indoor market just off Piazza Grande. The small narrow alley type streets in Modena are called *vicolo* or in the plural *vicoli* and in one particular *vicolo* near to the market, there was a wonderful strong coffee aroma that always emanated from one of the bars strung along the way. The smell was pure heaven.

The market was old fashioned and probably built in the late 19th century, with intricate ironwork around the entrances and high vaulted ceilings. Great piles of fruit and vegetables, some of which I had never seen before, were heaped on every stall. There were juicy purple aubergines and fat green courgettes with which the Modenese make the delicious *polpette* - a sort of stuffed courgette topped with a tasty tomato sauce and grated parmesan cheese. There was an orange, gooey fruit called *cacci,* and persimmons with enormous pips. The tomatoes were as big as tennis balls, shiny and red and meticulously piled high in triangular shapes.

Spinach is a great favourite with Italians, and in Modena market it was sold already cooked and rolled into neat little balls, which could be eaten cold with a drop of olive oil or reheated. Many Italian vegetables are consumed cold, having already been previously cooked. They are absolutely delectable when eaten with a dressing of olive oil and balsamic vinegar.

The market was certainly a busy place. Stout housewives shopped every morning for fresh produce - tomatoes and basil for their daily pasta dishes and vegetables to eat cold with a great beef steak, a real favourite with Italians.

Monique and I would often visit the market on our way to the city centre. We were a little naïve and unaware of pick-pockets, who roamed the place looking for likely victims. On one memorable occasion, I was carrying two £10 notes that my mother had sent me. They were safely embedded in my pocket. That day, I was planning to buy a second-hand Singer sewing machine that I had seen for sale with the money, and was looking forward to being able to make my own curtains and cushions and other creative pieces.

We stopped off at the market to buy some onions. When we went to pay, I found to my bitter disappointment that my money was no longer in my pocket but had been stolen. £20 was a lot of money in those days. Besides buying the sewing machine, I could have fed myself for a week and paid my rent. I was so distraught that I began to cry.

Later that week, a good friend bought me the sewing machine as a present. It was an old treadle machine, which in time became a trusty piece of furniture - a much loved ally. I was sad that I had to leave it behind when I eventually returned to England.

Besides the wonderful fruit and vegetable market, there was also a fabulous flea market every Friday morning that snaked around one of the large arterial roads surrounding the city. All manner of interesting objects were for sale, from ornate Venetian mirrors and bric-a-brac to busy Lizzie plants and even baby chicks. Off-cuts of unusual patterned materials that local factories had discarded, were casually thrown together in a jumbled heap, and sat happily next to exquisitely embroidered sheets and tableware. In time, I made a lovely patchwork quilt from some of these scraps. There were cheap leather goods and shoes, and the latest in knitwear fashions. It was a vibrant and colourful place, and a very pleasurable way to spend Friday morning before taking the train to Sassuolo or Carpi.

The winter months were freezing. Often it rained. My students amused me by declaring that 'In England it always rains!' I replied by saying that I thought it rained more in Italy - especially in the winter, when great sheets of the stuff would almost knock you out as you battled your way along the street. One quaint sight in the rain was that of people riding bicycles and balancing umbrellas simultaneously. In time, I too acquired this amazing skill and often rode my bike feeling like Mary Poppins.

Back at the flat in Via P. Ferrari, we were kept warm with archaic gas-fired stoves in each of our rooms, which had great flues reaching up to the ceiling. Our apartment was on the top floor of the building, and the heat from the other flats would rise and warm us.

There were no radiators and I cannot remember how we dried our clothes, especially during the winter months. If the weather was good and breezy, we would precariously hang the washing out of the window to dry, as did the apartment below us.

On one occasion, I had washed my sheets in the kitchen sink - we did not have the luxury of a washing machine - and then hung them from my bedroom window to dry in the wind. I thought I would do some shopping and when I returned, my sheets would be crisp and dry.

I returned some hours later to find no sign of the sheets. They had disappeared. I searched the street below - maybe they had fallen down in my absence and blown around the corner. They had to be somewhere. In desperation, I knocked on the door of the flat below and asked in faltering Italian, dictionary in hand, if someone had seen my sheets fall from my window.

"Mi scusi signori, avete visto i miei lenzuoli?" (Excuse me, have you seen my sheets) I asked of the small hostile looking couple who answered the door.

"No, non abbiamo visto niente!" (We haven't seen anything), they declared and shut the door in my face.

They were suspicious of us English girls or *'signorine'* as they called us. They thought that we were up to no good as we were foreigners, and often, we would be denied the *'buon giorno'* or *'buona sera'* that was afforded to most of the population, when meeting each other going up or down the stairs, or in and out of the building.

In Italy, everyone says *'buon giorno'* to everyone else - it is considered rude not to. Another verbal practice, which I found funny, is the use of the word *'prego'* meaning both 'thank you' and 'you're welcome.' Sometimes conversations take on a farcical element, with many 'pregos' flying between two people, each person not quite knowing where to stop.

Two other widely used words which seem to have no equivalent in English are *'Be,'* pronounced beh (this can mean anything from 'Who knows?' to 'What's the world coming to!') and *'Ma'* which can be translated as roughly the same!

I never did find my clean sheets. I suspect that the residents in the flat below reached up and grabbed them for themselves when no one was looking.

~

From January to about May, flatmates came and went. The City Language School was always anxious to make money, and when they eventually found a replacement for Jemp - a girl called Lizzy from Manchester, she was sent around to inhabit Jemp's empty room.

Lizzy was a talented artist and she and I clicked straight away. We both enjoyed painting in watercolours, and I remember that Lizzy made several beautiful studies of the cathedral whilst staying in Modena.

Over Easter, I received the news that my family, including two of my three sisters, would be visiting me that summer. I was very excited and looked forward to showing them the sights of Modena, Parma and other local cities and towns. I asked the language school if my family could sleep in the 'hidden room,' which had always remained empty - the one that Jemp and I had discovered with the wonderful mountain beds. Reluctantly they agreed, and I spent part of the Easter holidays sorting it out and tidying it up.

The flat in Via Paolo Ferrari was gradually becoming more homely. I was able to cover grotty settees and make cushions and quilts, using my beloved sewing machine. Many a happy austere winter's evening was spent whirring away, with Radio Luxembourg in the background.

We had no luxuries in the flat - no vacuum cleaner, washing machine or tumble dryer. We would sweep the quarry tiled floor and pick up the dust with a pan and brush. We did however, become the owners of an ancient T.V. In those days in Italy, transmissions were still black and white - colour arrived much later than in England, for some unknown reason. Italian T.V. was dire - and I believe it still is - but the adverts had catchy tunes and I learnt many Italian colloquial phrases from them.

CHAPTER 6   VILLA VITTORIA

Towards the end of May, disaster struck. I had not been feeling too well for a couple of weeks, with a sharp pain in the right hand side of my stomach and a recurrent feeling of nausea.

I duly visited the doctor, who in this case was a *dottoressa*. Dottoressa Magli was in her mid fifties - a strong independent woman, who viciously chain-smoked even during her consultations. On my first visit to her some months before, I was very surprised when she greeted me at her surgery, cigarette in hand.

The Italians are obsessed with their livers. Practically every stomach ache is put down to a *mal di fegato* or bad liver, which is usually due to drinking too much of the red and white stuff, or indulging in heavy creamy sauces. The remedy for this malady is *una dieta in bianco* - literally a white diet, which includes any white food e.g. fish, potatoes, rice, milk and pasta. This should be consumed for at least one week, or until the patient feels better.

However, on this particular occasion, Dottoressa Magli did not smilingly inform me that I had a *mal di fegato*, as she had done so on previous occasions. No, this time, she looked serious and while taking several puffs of her cigarette and making scissor actions with her fingers, informed me that I had appendicitis and would have to have the offending article cut out at once.

My heart sank, and my mind cast back to about twelve years before, when one of my sisters had been carted off to hospital in an emergency ambulance, sirens wailing, with the same complaint. Caroline had been seriously ill and peritonitis had set in as a complication. I did not want a recurrence of this scenario, so I willingly agreed like a lamb to the slaughter, to go into hospital that same week and part with my grumbling and totally useless appendix.

Dottoressa Magli booked me into Villa Vittoria, a sort of cottage cum convent of a hospital, right in the centre of Modena. There was also a very large *Policlinico* or general hospital on the periphery of the city, but places there were reserved for the seriously ill, or accident and emergency cases.

I have no idea what the Italian public health service is like nowadays, but in the early 1970s in Modena, it was excellent. No sooner had my grumbling appendix been diagnosed than I was whisked away - no long waiting lists - no 'let's see how you are next week' - no writhing on the floor in agony, waiting for the thing to burst - a straight diagnosis and attention is what I received.

I found myself in a small clean ward. My operation was scheduled for the following day, so meals were very slight and light. Nuns attended to my every need. They must have been nursing nuns, because they took my temperature and blood pressure etc.

The chaplain visited and I decided to make my confession - being a Catholic - in case I did not pull through. Since my sister Caroline had almost died of appendicitis as a small child, I had always carried a subconscious fear that I too, would die in the same way. At least now if I died, I might go to heaven, and if I pulled through, my dark, irrational, predatory fears could be put to rest, and my soul would be free from sin - an added bonus!

The day of the operation dawned. I remember a large window in the ward looking out to the city street below. The sounds of busy life were in progress, and trees were bursting into beautiful fresh spring leaf. The trees were like a garden full of bird song - alive and melodious. I hoped beyond hope that I would hear these sounds again tomorrow.

Later that morning, the nuns came for me and lifted me onto what I imagined to be my 'trolley of death.' Luckily, some friends had called in to visit and they accompanied me to the operating theatre, jesting and trying to lift my pessimism. Once inside, the surgeons were reassuring as they joked with me in English.

I awoke feeling woozy but alive. I was deliriously happy that I was now minus my dubious appendix and not in too much pain. I was told not to laugh, as this would cause my scar to stretch and thus hurt. There were many occasions when I felt like laughing and I had to restrain myself.

Villa Vittoria became my home for ten long days. Every morning I had to rise, shine and make my own bed. We were not given bed pans as we would have had in England, but had to shuffle slowly to the toilets. Presumably this was to aid our swift recovery.

Most of the day was taken up with cleaning ourselves and keeping our areas tidy. The other ladies on the ward could not speak English, so during my stay my Italian improved considerably, as I had no option but to try to speak the language or remain mute. The first choice was definitely preferable.

During the time I had been in hospital, my salary at the language school continued to be paid, so when I eventually emerged into the late May sunshine, like a butterfly crawling out of its chrysalis, I had some spare cash for the first time in my life. Things were looking up! I was entitled to at least two weeks recuperation, I had said 'goodbye' to a feared and hated part of my anatomy, and I had some ready money in my pocket!

~

Not long after my hospitalisation, I started teaching private students to supplement my jobs in Sassuolo and Carpi. This was actually against the school's rules, but as our salaries were a pittance and no one in Italy actually pays much attention to the law, most teachers had a few private clients on their books.

At the beginning of June, I was approached by an old established Modenese family - the Benvenuti, and was asked if I would teach English to their five year old daughter, Diana. Count Benvenuti had been educated in England just after the war years, and his father had known various members of the English Cabinet and had been a personal friend of one of the British prime ministers of this era.

I was excited at the prospect of working with Diana. I was to go to the house in the countryside near Modena, and teach her there.

For just an afternoon's work I would receive 10.000 lira - about £6 in those days. It was considerably more than the language school were paying me.

Straight after lunch on a Tuesday, I would set off on my newly acquired bicycle, through the city and out into the early summer countryside, freshly green and interspersed with glorious flowering cherry trees. The warm sun cast bright shadows and melodious birdsong cut through the sweet air.

The Benvenuti family lived in a huge villa - very Modenese in style - square and terracotta coloured, with green shuttered windows. It was set in acres of rich farmland bearing the soft white cherry trees of the region. A massive entrance door gave way to a cool interior. Inside, the house was breathtaking. Huge high rooms with frescoed walls and ceilings, complete with sparkling chandeliers and heavy oak furniture.

Outside, Diana played merrily. She did not particularly want to learn English. I tried my best to interest her. My brief was to just speak *Inglese* or English but she would laugh capriciously and answer back in Italian. She invited me to talk with her dolls and animals - to play hide and seek and have a fun time. This we did, but I felt guilty. This way of earning money was too easy.

Another private student was called Marco. He was about eight years old and very solemn. A grand palazzo in the centre of Modena was home for this little rich kid. The outside of the palazzo was shabby, but the inside of the apartment was splendid and totally belied its exterior. Sumptuous antique furnishings, Persian rugs, an abundance of oil paintings framed in old intricately carved gold frames and enormous art nouveau lamps set the scene.

One day, while I was waiting for him to collect his books from his room, I picked up an art manual which was lying casually on a small side table. It featured the Italian Impressionists and as I flicked through the pages, I came across a painting that I particularly liked. I cannot remember the artist now, but the subject of the pointillist painting was of waves. The picture seemed familiar, and it was only then that I realized that the original was actually hanging on the wall in front of my very eyes. Such was, and probably still is, the wealth of Modena.

The prosperity of the place had amazed me, when I first arrived in September. One evening, Jemp and I had gone out for a pizza with the group that I had taught at Reading, before travelling to Italy. Gian Paolo, a medical student who seemed very ordinary, invited all of us back to his house afterwards for drinks.

The house which belonged to his parents was fairly dull from outside. However inside, it was expensively and tastefully decorated. I can remember visiting the bathroom, and looking in wonder and admiration at the beautiful floor to ceiling tiles with picture insets, gleaming dark blue bath (coloured suites were all the rage in the 70s), shower, W.C. and bidet with gold taps. These accessories were all quite common in Modenese society but reserved only for the rich and famous back in the old U.K.

Nowadays, of course, we have bathrooms to match anyone's. In fact in Britain, we have all gone bathroom mad, but in 1975, we Brits were stuck with our old post-war suites, whilst the Italians were well ahead in the posh stylish bathroom stakes. Many new apartments being built around the outskirts of the city during this era were equipped with two bathrooms, sometimes side by side, which seemed to me to be the height of luxury.

~

As June turned into July, so spring metamorphosed into summer. Slowly at first, but then with the raging heat that characterises the clammy suffocating torpid summers of the Po valley. The Afa, which is the summer version of the winter fog, had arrived, and for days on end, an expressionless limp whitish sky would glare above the rising city temperatures. It was impossible to stay cool.

Most schools had closed by now, including the City Language School. Italian school children have four months summer vocation and the majority of families head out of the cities to the cooler coastal resorts, or the near-by mountains, where the air is fresh and sweet.

My contract at the language school had not been renewed. In fact, all six of us English girls had been unofficially sacked. Earlier on in the year, we had become very friendly with a left wing student by the name of Giuseppe or Bepe for short.

Bepe informed us that we were being unfairly treated and badly paid, and suggested that we complain to the local *sindicato* - a kind of council which was run by the Communists, and have the school investigated. He suggested that we start by asking the language school for an increase in wages. When they refused, we declared that we would be taking the matter further with strike action. This we did and eventually our pitiful wages were slightly raised, but not surprisingly, none of our contracts were renewed for the following year.

In the meantime, the other five English girls had decided to return to the motherland and I alone was left in Italy. I found myself a new post at the Modena Language Centre, with much better pay and conditions. It was efficiently run by an elderly eccentric Italian spinster, by the name of Margherita or Rita for short.

When my contract at the City Language School finished, so too did my residency at Via Paolo Ferrari. Monique came to my rescue. She had just rented an apartment near the centre of Modena, in Via Georgi, and needed a flat-mate.

My new home was situated in a large block of purpose-built flats. They were modern and airy and to my eyes luxurious, although looking back they were actually quite ordinary by Italian standards.

The floors were laid with black marble tiles, and the two large bedrooms had small balconies, which were big enough to house some pots of geraniums or busy Lizzie plants. There was a well-equipped kitchen and a lovely bathroom, complete with bidet and half bath - one with a sort of step in it that you sit on while you are bathing – of which the Italians are very fond! The kitchen was a novelty as it overlooked an open-air cinema, and many a summer's evening was spent, squinting in the cool of the night, trying to catch a glimpse of the 'film now showing.'

A few months before I moved into Via Georgi, I acquired my first bicycle which cost me £13 second-hand. I remember it to this day. It was a red and green affair with a sweet little pixie bell. I was very proud of it and knew it would be useful for the following year, when I would be teaching in Modena and could therefore cycle to work.

One evening, Tricia, another English friend, who worked in yet another English Language school in Modena (there were about six in all), and I, cycled over to the outskirts, to visit an Australian girl whom we had recently met. We left our bikes outside her apartment and I swear that I locked mine up. However, when we returned at about midnight, my bike was missing and another older more battered one was leaning against the tree in its place. I was nonplussed and annoyed. Who on earth would want my old bike and how strange that the thieving low life had left me another in return!

The hour was getting late and there was nothing to do but use the substitute bike. I was pretty cross, as I had grown fond of my little red and green pixie-belled mode of transport. As we gathered speed downhill, I suddenly realised that this rusty excuse of a bike had no brakes, and I had to trail my feet along the ground whenever I wanted to stop which was fairly often. I decided not to use this bike again.

About one week later, I revisited Shelly the Australian - this time by bus. To my embarrassment, I found that my precious bike had not been stolen at all, but had been moved behind a nearby shed by a kindly old lady, to prevent it being taken. Now I was the guilty party, as I had inadvertently stolen someone else's bike. I was mortified and furtively returned the old rusty no brakes bike to its tree, hoping that no one had seen me in this dastardly act!

CHAPTER 7 CASA DELLA FONTANA

Around early summertime, my close friend Antonella invited me to the mountains near Modena, to spend some weeks of the long holiday vacation with her extended family. Antonella also happened to be the sister of my boy friend Paolo. She and I had become good friends, when I found her sitting by my bedside like a guardian angel, after the removal of my appendix.

Until this point, Paolo's family had been firmly in the background, disapproving I think, of the fact that he was going out with an English girl. His other sister, Gabriella, had gone off to America with an Englishman and the Contarini family were worried that Paolo would commit the same sin. However, the appendix episode changed all that. From the moment that offending part of my anatomy was torn from my body, I felt accepted, at least by Antonella, and the rest of the Contarini clan soon followed.

The first time I saw the Contarini's summer house in the mountains -Casa della Fontana - I was smitten. It was a bright early June day with the sun high in a cobalt blue sky. Antonella and I found ourselves racing up the hair pin bends of the Apennines, in a small red rattling Fiat 500. Casa della Fontana which comprised a wonderful group of farmhouses and outbuildings was bathed in sunshine, giving it a rosy glow.

Generations ago, Antonella and Paolo's family had farmed the land on these Apennine slopes. There were acres of pear, plum and vine trees and Signor Contarini made his own type of dark purple and white Lambrusco, which tasted a million times better than the shop bought stuff. After the Second World War, the Contarini, like countless other agricultural Italians moved to the nearby cities and trained for other jobs.

Signora Contarini, a kind and very emotional lady, had become a teacher and Antonella likewise. Paolo, who was the quintessential Italian male – tall, dark and handsome, was also a university student studying to become a vet, and he carried tomes of anatomy books around with him, from which he would revise whenever the mood took, as there always seemed to be an exam on the horizon. Signor Contarini appeared to have at least three jobs, which is often common in Italy. One of these was as some sort of engineer and of course, another was up in the mountains tending the fruit trees and producing delicious Lambrusco.

My first view of Casa della Fontana took my breath away. It was perfect. Nestling in a deep secluded valley, it was surrounded on all sides by the mysterious tree-covered Apennines. The house exuded a warm glow and the apricot coloured façade shimmered in the early afternoon sunshine. Typical faded green shutters were closed to the outside world, and an ancient pantiled roof was covered with mossy lichen. Gently rolling hills and fields, home to the orchards of pear trees and vines, surrounded the house.

"Do you like it?" asked Antonella.

"I love it," I answered. This was an understatement - I was enthralled.

"Come and meet la zia Vita" (auntie Vita), said Antonella, leading the way to an adjacent house across a small courtyard.

I had heard much about zia Vita from Paolo. According to him, she was the best cook in Modena and her wonderful cuisine could not be rivalled. Auntie Vita has since become a legend in our family. During my sojourn in Italy, my sister Caroline stayed with her whilst teaching English to her daughter Portia. Caroline was very fond of La zia Vita and we all grew to love her. She became an icon of glorious domesticity within our family. A true domestic goddess!

I was slightly apprehensive at meeting such a paragon, but my fears were soon quashed. Auntie Vita met me with outstretched arms. She was a lovely, lively matronly Italian lady. A real matriarch - in fact as time went by I grew to realise that she was the boss of the whole Contarini family. Everyone respected her.

"Ciao, venite dentro," (Hello, come in) she welcomed us. *"Come state? Venite mangiare!"* (How are you? Come and eat!)

We stepped inside a large room. In the centre was a huge table, groaning under the weight of the mountain of food placed upon it. There was an enormous fruit bowl and baskets of freshly made bread.

The table was set with pasta bowls and tall sparkly wine glasses. Several dark red bottles of Lambrusco were grouped around the centre of the table, and a massive cheese board was just waiting to be brought out after the meal.

"Sit down, make yourselves comfortable," Vita ordered, smilingly. "Tell me all the news from Modena!"

Auntie Vita had been up in the mountains since the beginning of May, when the weather in Modena had started to turn clammy and the days sweaty and claustrophobic. Life was pleasant in the mountain house with her husband Berto and daughter Portia. During the long days, she worked around the large house and prepared jars of preserves, using plum tomatoes, red and yellow peppers, artichokes and mushrooms, ready for the winter months in the city. Her ample larder was bursting full of them

We sat down to eat. Antonella was talking excitedly in Italian to her aunt, who was replying just as enthusiastically. I tried to follow the conversation. My Italian was growing better day by day, but often auntie Vita and uncle Berto lapsed into Emilian dialect which sounded to me like French. When she realized that I was looking bewildered, Vita laughed and apologised - until she forgot and spoke in dialect again.

The meal was superb with *pasta in brodo* (tiny pieces of pasta floating in a rich home-made chicken stock), followed by *zucchine ripiene* (stuffed courgettes) with *peperonata* (peppers and tomatoes roasted in olive oil). This was followed by a hefty salad tossed in virgin olive oil, sea salt, pepper and balsamic vinegar. Then there were the cheeses - *Pecorino* or goat's cheese - great slabs of *Parmigiano* and so on. Next there was fruit, washed down by several glasses of very strong Lambrusco. We sat back contented, our stomachs full to bursting.

"And now for the *digestivo*," announced auntie Vita.

Uncle Berto got up from the table and went over to a big stout cupboard built into the wall. He struggled back to the dinner table with his arms full of bottles such as Fernet Branco, Brandy, Nocino and others, the names of which I cannot remember.

"What would you like?" Berto asked me. "We made the Nocino ourselves," he added proudly. "Would you like to try some?"

"*Si, certo*," (yes of course) I replied cautiously, not really wanting to overload my stomach any more. I remembered the first time I had tasted *Grappa* - the Italian 100% pure alchoholic drink. It nearly blew my head off!

The *Nocino* was delicious - made from nuts and alcohol, it had a distinctly warming feeling as it rolled down my oesophagus.

The Italians consider a *digestivo* to be an important part of the meal. As its name suggests, it helps to digest the food just eaten and funnily enough it does just that. There was a great unloosening of belts and waistbands, and lengthy conversation and discussion flowed. Many Italians have an endearing habit of actually unzipping their skirts and trousers after they have eaten a huge meal and are completely uninhibited by this act.

After lunch we said our good-byes, promising to return later that evening. Antonella and I strolled back to her family's house and she showed me to the room where I would be staying.

It is customary in Italy, especially in the mountains, to take a siesta after lunch for at least one hour. Antonella always retired to her room upstairs and instead of sleeping, ploughed her way through a great mound of magazines, such as the Italian equivalent of 'Ideal Home,' whilst lying comfortably in bed - a brilliant way to relax and rejuvenate!

My room downstairs was large with a fairly high beamed ceiling. I pushed open the creaky wooden door, revealing a dark and shuttered space which smelt slightly musty though not at all unpleasant. It was reminiscent of times gone by and I loved its ambience.

I did not feel tired or in need of a siesta, so I flung open the ancient windows. During future visits to the mountains, I would get into trouble with Signora Contarini for doing this. She reasoned that during the day, I would be letting in burglars (though this is one of the safest, most crime-free areas I have ever stayed in), and during the evening, I would be letting in mosquitoes - the dreaded *zanzare.*

I have to confess that in hindsight she was right about the mosquitoes, but at the time I thought that she was being a mite over-cautious about the burglars. However, as I was a guest in her house I had to abide (for most of the time) by the rules, although I often longed to throw open the window and sometimes did when my door was closed!

The view from the window was stunning. Hazy, distant mountains were set in a background of deep blue sky. The room bounced with sunlight. In one corner was a wonderful, ancient oak wardrobe. Two simple chairs were placed near to the window and there was a typical mountain bed which was high and narrow, with a hand made mattress stuffed with wool - lovely and cosy in the winter. The headboard was constructed from iron with a small painted picture in the middle of old-fashioned boats on a lake. A delicate art nouveau lamp hung from the beams.

In Antonella's room upstairs, there were two such painted mountain beds. The other one belonged to her sister Gabriella. Their room was devoid of other furniture, save a huge stack of glossy magazines. A pretty Fleur de Lys pattern was stencilled onto the walls which resembled wallpaper but was ages old and faded in places. It was a charming room, with mountain views and a sunny aspect. Being on the second floor, it was relatively burglar proof, so Antonella was able to keep her shutters open during the day if she wanted to.

Mosquitoes were a real problem, both in the mountains and in Modena. Endless sleepless nights were spent trying to zap them before they bit us. The Italian word for this annoying insect is *zanzara* - very onomatopoeic.

Antonella and I were to stay in the mountains for about two weeks, to escape the humidity of Modena. Paolo and some other members of the family were to follow in a few days time, and other aunts and uncles would also spend some of the summer months there. The Contarini clan, like many other Italian families, repeated this pattern of living every summer, from late May to the end of August.

The women folk would stay at Casa della Fontana for the whole of the summer, but the men would come and go, as they still had to earn their living during the weekdays in the city, and the mountain house was just too far away for commuting.

Many Italian cities became ghost towns in the summer months, when all those who were not working, made either for the mountains or the seaside. August was the worst time in the city. Not only was it stiflingly hot but virtually all Italians take their holidays during this month. They do not stagger their vacation like we do - so consequently, the cities shut down. Shops close for Ferie (holiday time), and streets are eerily deserted - even some of the bars close for two or three weeks.

This culminates in Ferie Agosto on August 15, the feast of the Assumption of Our Lady. This is the greatest feast day in the Italian year, and everywhere there are celebrations, from religious processions to pagan fairgrounds.

After 21st August, there is the *'re-entra in città'* (the re-entry back to the city), and people flock back in dribs and drabs. The cities start to wake up and by the end of August they are once again vibrant, bustling and cooler.

My parents remember being in Modena towards the last week in August. My father was so surprised to see it practically empty one day and a thriving provincial municipality the next.

Teachers and children in Italy are fortunate to have four months summer holidays every year. This is great if you happened to be employed by the state and receive pay during holiday time. Being a language school teacher, I had no such concessions and every year my last pay packet was given to me at the end of May. During the long summer months, I had to support myself somehow. The Contarini family were very kind to me, and I often stayed in their mountain home, rent free with delicious food and jovial company.

In between times in the mountains, I would become an 'au pair' for a few weeks and travel to the seaside with a family, who wanted their children to learn English. Sometimes my own family would visit, and on occasions, I would return to England to catch up with friends and relations. In later years when my grasp of the Italian language was much better, I was able to take on some translation work, to keep body and soul together, whilst waiting for the language school to reopen in October.

~

Over the next few days, during that first year in the mountains, the whole Contarini family assembled at one time or another.

First to arrive was Signor Contarini, known as Pietro, a quiet Humphrey Bogart type of character. He was an industrious man, who rose at the crack of dawn to work the fruit trees and bottle his delicious wine. He must have been an extremely brave fellow, because during the Second World War, he secretly joined the partisan movement, helping prisoners of war escape at great personal risk to himself.

A few days later Signora Contarini arrived in a small white Fiat 500. She was a vivacious and emotional lady, larger than her husband, with Sophia Loren glasses perched on the end of her nose. Various aunts, uncles, cousins and Antonella's elderly and rather frail grandmother arrived, at the beginning of June. Almost the whole clan was together and there was never a dull moment.

Paolo was last to arrive on his red Moto Guzzi, roaring up the gravelled driveway at 80 kilometres an hour. Grinning and hollering 'Ciao' to all and sundry, he swung his text books off the back of the great machine, obviously preparing to spend some of the time studying.

On one occasion, I accompanied Paolo up to the higher mountains on his Moto Guzzi. It was a powerful machine, gleaming, crimson and black. These were the days before helmets were compulsory, and no one in the Modena area would dream of being seen with a 'helmet' plonked securely on their heads. We flew up the mountain-sides, zigzagging up narrow perilous hair pin bends, through glorious hilly rugged countryside, with the wind streaming in our hair.

Suddenly I felt a sharp needle-like pain at the top of my arm. A couple of wasps had flown up my shirt sleeve and had stung me several times. I tried to shout to Paolo to stop, but as the engine's roar was so loud he could not hear. When we eventually pulled to a halt, I had about four large swollen wounds on the top of my arm. I seem to remember they gave me a lot of trouble and took ages to heal.

In the evenings at Casa della Fontana, we would often trek up to the tiny village of Festa, where there was a bar with a pool table. There were enough of us young people to have a few games and then sit and chat, with beers in hand and perhaps an ice cream or two. The other young people of the area would also congregate there and it was a lively place to visit.

Whilst staying up in the mountains, my Italian improved no end. Only Antonella and Paolo spoke English. Alessandro, Antonella's boyfriend of about ten years standing, also joined us at some stage, but he spoke little English. He used to love talking about the Beatles and was impressed when he found out that I was born in Liverpool. We used to have bizarre, amusing conversations about the Fab Four, in a mixture of Italian and pigeon English.

The days were long and often hot and sunny, but not humid like the cities of the Po. Often, I would walk around the grassy slopes amongst the fruit trees, admiring the splendid views. The warm sun was exhilarating and only the constant fizz of the cicadas broke the silence. Sometimes, I would help the aunties shelling peas, making preserves, or preparing some gargantuan meal.

If we were bored, we would jump into one of the Fiat 500s and whiz down to the village of Pavullo, to do some window-shopping. The chemist shop or *farmacia* fascinated me. In the windows were various posters for identifying the numerous types of *funghi* or mushrooms that grew wild in the surrounding woods. Italians have a passion for picking their own mushrooms, and the informative posters illustrated which ones were poisonous and which of the *funghi* was okay to eat. It was also possible to take picked *funghi* into the chemist to be analysed by someone in the know. Personally, I prefer to buy mine from a shop!

There were also posters telling the general public what to do if they got bitten by a snake, and advertising the antidotes that could be bought inside. Various hardware shops, a delicatessen, cake shops and bars lined the main street. Pavullo was a wonderful little place.

In the evenings when the sun had gone down, we would often gather in groups and sit under the fruit trees to chat, watching the bright sparks of the fireflies, dancing on the temperate breeze.

Sometimes the whole family would eat together. Long trestle tables would be brought out into the courtyard, and stiff white table cloths would be thrown over them, transforming their plainness. The ladies would set the table, prepare the salads and main dishes and the men would uncork the numerous bottles of purple Lambrusco.

There were great terracotta pots around the courtyard, filled with pretty geraniums and lush oleander bushes. A couple of old deep sinks with huge copper taps stood in one corner, reminiscent of the days when the womenfolk washed their clothes outside by hand. Eating in this courtyard was a joyous occasion.

During the meal, all manner of topics would be discussed, but usually politics was the main item on the agenda. Italy was in a very unstable political situation at this time and many people in high places were corrupt. It provided great conversational material!

"Have you ever met Prince Charles?" Alessandro asked me half way through his beef steak, and changing the political discussion that we were having.

"Don't be ridiculous," giggled Antonella. "How could Clare have met Prince Charles?"

I had to confess that I had not.

Italy at that time was obsessed with the British Royal Family and followed their every move. Later when Princess Diana came on the scene, the population became even more interested, and magazines such as 'Oggi' presented continuous, slightly scandalous articles on them.

Later that summer in August, when my family visited Modena, we were all invited up to Casa della Fontana. My parents loved it, and were charmed by the Contarini family. Once more the trestle tables came out at lunch time and a magnificent meal was consumed, washed down by gallons of Lambrusco.

Speaking very little Italian, my parents somehow managed to converse with Signor and Signora Contarini through a mixture of gestures and Latin, which we all thought was hilarious. My father had once taught Latin but who would have thought that he would ever have had to speak it!

That evening, we went to eat at a local restaurant called 'The Red House' or *La Casa Rossa*. It was some kilometres from Festa - high up in the mountains, with simple, yet delicious mountain fare and local dishes. My mother was given a *focaccia*, a type of bread made with olive oil which was topped with what seemed to be a delicious spread, smelling pungently of rosemary and garlic.

"Mm what's on this bread?" asked mum sniffing it appreciatively. "It looks delicious."

"It's a sort of lard made from pure animal fat," answered Paolo.

My mother's face fell. She was at that time eating a fat free diet, and discreetly dropped the focaccia in the nearest bin when no one was looking. The idea of eating lard was abhorrent to her, however nice it tasted.

Later that same summer, after my parents had returned to England, a sad event took place at Casa della Fontana. Antonella's and Paolo's grandmother, who had been ill with cancer, suddenly died, and all the family were summoned to say their final good-byes. A group of us were about to go camping with some friends and our trip had to be cancelled.

Although it was August, the weather had taken a nasty turn and Paolo and I arrived at Casa della Fontana in the pouring rain. Great sheets of the stuff had turned the land around the house into a quagmire. Getting out of the car was difficult and slushy. Puddles were fast turning into lakes and Casa della Fontana did not seem quite so appealing.

Grandmother known as *La nonna* was laid out in an enormous bed, in a large room that I had never seen before.

"Go in and pay your last respects," said Paolo, shoving me towards the door.

Inside, the room was claustrophobic. Candles cast a shimmering glow and various relations were grouped around, or kneeling by the bed. Some were praying and some crying and wailing. It was a very moving experience.

La nonna just appeared to be asleep. She seemed at rest, with all pain gone. I edged nearer to her bedside and said some prayers. Auntie Vita and some of the other ladies were saying the Rosary and I joined in for a while.

Later that week she was buried in the beautiful little cemetery at Festa. Italian cemeteries are curious, surrounded by high walls. There are niches where the coffins are encased. On the outside of the niche is a photo of the deceased and there is a place for flowers and a votive candle.

I was amazed when I first saw a cemetery. I really did not recognise it as such, so different are they from British ones. The high, ornate, decorative, usually white walls are a mass of niches and photographs. The death of a loved one is proclaimed to the neighbourhood on a card edged with black, many of which are often pasted up on city walls, sometimes next to adverts or the daily newspapers.

By comparison, the arrival of a new life is announced with balloons and ribbons tied to the front door - blue for that longed-for boy - the Italians love having male children, and pink for a little girl.

CHAPTER 8 SPAGHETTI IN MY HAIR

That first summer in August, my parents and two of my sisters came to visit. I had returned from the mountains some time previously, as I would be moving apartments towards the end of their stay, and had to pack a lot of my stuff into boxes ready for the move. My father had kindly offered to transport my belongings from one flat to the other in his car. I do not think he realized how much paraphernalia I had amassed, during my one year in Modena.

On the day my family were due to arrive, Paolo came down from the mountains to help me prepare a meal and to welcome them. We cooked up an enormous pot of *spaghetti al tonno* - my favourite recipe. It was enough to feed everyone. We expected our visitors to arrive in the early evening, but by nightfall they had still not put in an appearance.

As we wanted our food to be fresh, we ended up eating all the pasta ourselves. We decided to cook another batch the following day.

However, this experience was repeated for three or four days running, and I was beginning to grow worried, as well as being thoroughly fed up with spaghetti.

We had no way of contacting them or they us, as there were no mobile phones in those days, and I did not possess a land-line phone in Via Paolo Ferrari. As the days went by I grew more and more worried, but as they say, 'no news is good news.' On day four, the elusive party turned up, not having realised that they had set a particular date. As we could no longer stomach the *spaghetti al tonno,* it was decided that we would dine out that evening.

"I'd like to show you a trattoria I know," said Paolo. "Lots of local people eat there. It's really authentic and the food is good."

"What's a trattoria?" asked my little sister Kate who was only ten years old at the time.

"It's a cheap, rustic eating place," replied Paolo. "Do you like spaghetti?" he asked, smiling at Kate.

She nodded. "I like alphabet spaghetti. Will there be some at the trattoria?"

Paolo laughed. "Well not exactly alphabet spaghetti, but lots of other sorts of spaghetti and other nice things to eat."

Kate seemed pleased. Spaghetti was one of her favourite foods.

We set off for Trattoria da Enzo. Some of us climbed into my father's V.W. and the rest of us squeezed into Paolo's tiny, dark blue Fiat 500. These cars are so small and light that I have actually seen people lift them up and move them when they have been parked in someone's way. They fit into tiny parking spaces and are very economical to run.

Sadly, the once ubiquitous Fiat 500 is a dying breed and has been replaced with the omnipresent, standardized Japanese and European car. It is quite rare now to see the dinky Fiat 500, known as the *'Cinquecento,'* that was once, one of the trade marks of Italy.

'Trattoria da Enzo' was situated down one of the narrow arcaded streets in the city centre. It certainly had rustic character and charm. Long trestle tables stood in rows, and wooden benches were placed around the tables, which were covered with dark blue cloths. The menu was composed of traditional Modenese food, such as pig's trotters and veal escalopes, served with a side salad. There were also the usual pasta dishes that are indigenous to the region - *tortelloni, tortellini, spaghetti bolognese* and *spaghetti alla vongole* (with whelks), or with *pomodori* (tomatoes).

We decided to go for the pasta (even though we were fed up with it!) I ordered *tortelloni alla boscaiola,* otherwise known as lovely creamy pasta with ham and mushrooms. The others also had spaghetti with various toppings. Paolo showed us how to wind the spaghetti strands around our forks, held against a spoon for easy eating. My sisters Kate and Caroline found this difficult and kept collapsing in fits of giggles, whilst trying to stuff the spaghetti into their mouths. It was unwieldy and slippy and difficult to manage.

Sitting next to our group was a lone Italian male. He had been watching us, and seemed very amused with our attempts to eat spaghetti. Quickly, he took out a pencil and began making sketches on his paper napkin of Kate, who was having the most trouble with the long stringy strands of pasta.

He sketched her looking like a Medusa, with spaghetti interwoven with her long, strawberry blond hair. When he had finished his drawing he handed it to my sister to keep. We all burst out laughing and poor Kate went bright red.

As usual we drank plenty of Lambrusco with our meal. My parents had the common reaction, exclaiming that the wine tasted 'just like pop!' However they grew to like it and were pleased when Paolo's father Berto, presented them with several bottles during their visit to the mountains, to take back with them to England.

Another restaurant that we visited on the outskirts of Modena impressed my mother in particular. It was a speciality cheese restaurant, where everything we ate was covered with delicious, different cheeses.

My family had only planned to stay in Modena for one week. The next stage of their journey would take them north to Lake Garda, and I had decided to join them on their camping trip there. Before we left, my father offered to transport my belongings to my new flat, which was in a street called Via Georgi.

The new apartment was much more upmarket than the one in Via Paolo Ferrari. Situated in a fairly new block, it had a swish entrance hall and a lift to the flat on fourth floor. I would be sharing with Monique, who had already taken possession of the apartment. I would not be living there until September, but Monique kindly allowed me to leave most of my bulkier belongings there before moving in.

My father made countless journeys across Modena from Via Paolo Ferrari to Via Georgi, with his small V.W. crammed with my things. In just one year I had accumulated a great deal of baggage. In addition to my trunk, there were boxes stuffed with books, posters, pictures, cushions, curtains, watercolour equipment and many other objects that I had brought back, on visits to England.

"This trunk weighs a ton," complained Father, as we tried to manoeuvre the great weight down the stone stairs outside the flat.

"What on earth's inside - dead bodies?" he joked.

The trunk was not my father's favourite piece of equipment. Back in September, he had given me a lift to Victoria Station with the said trunk. Originally, I had planned to take a taxi from Guildford where I had been staying with my grandfather, to Victoria Station with my huge trunk. Unfortunately, the taxi driver refused to take it on board because of suspicions at the time of frequent I.R.A. bombs being left in stations, and presumably being transported in trunks! The left luggage area was closed, because of I.R.A. activity.

Finally after much deliberation and argument the taxi driver drove off. I do not think that he really believed that I was a member of the I.R.A. but company policy dictated that under no circumstances, was he to transport a trunk anywhere. I offered to show him the contents, but to no avail! As my parents were also staying in Guildford at the time, there was nothing else to do but for my poor father to drive into central London - a thing he never did, because of all the traffic - with my bothersome trunk somehow wedged into his tiny car.

When we arrived at Victoria Station, the guard on the boat-train was equally as suspicious, and at first refused to let the trunk be loaded into the guard van. After much pleading, cajoling and assurances from us that it was just full of my belongings, he begrudgingly agreed to me opening my trunk for him to check and rummage through. This was very embarrassing, as by this time half the station were looking on.

By now, Jemp had arrived - trunkless! She had sent most of her luggage on in advance, and found the whole episode very amusing. With the help of various porters along the way, I managed to transport my trunk safely to Modena. Jemp had to wait ages for hers, as it got lost somewhere in transit.

My parents were impressed with my new accommodation in Via Georgi. The floors throughout the apartment were laid with black marble, which seemed luxurious to us, but in fact is quite normal in Italy. Although the flat was small, the two bedrooms were large with balconies, and the kitchen was big enough for a table and a couple of chairs, with a first class view over the open air cinema below.

It was in a better, leafier part of the city, and fairly close to the street where I would be working in October. However swish it seemed though, it lacked the earthy colourful character of Via Paolo Ferrari.

~

At the end of that week we began our journey north to Lake Garda. Driving through the Po Valley, the immediate scenery was flat with its endless cultivated patchwork of fields, fringed by tall swaying Poplar trees. After a few hours, the landscape started to subtly change and undulate, and soon we arrived tired, hot and thirsty at the bustling resort of Garda.

This picturesque town is situated on the eastern shore of the lake, where it broadens against a backdrop of hills covered with olive groves, palm and cypress trees, and vivid flowering bushes such as oleanders, magnolias and bougainvilleas. Vineyards which produce the famous Valpolicella grape graced the hills.

Lake Garda, Italy's largest lake is stunning. Set in the shadow of the snow-capped Dolomites which helps to create the Mediterranean micro-climate, it is lapped by clear crystal waters and edged with clean sandy or pebble beaches. We found a campsite near the lake's edge and set up home under canvas.

That evening, we walked to the pretty town of Garda and admired the graceful villas which give the resort its character. Sophisticated bars and cafés with brightly striped umbrellas, lined the traffic free promenade. Colourful fishing boats bobbed up and down on the shoreline, and we chatted to some other English people who told us that Churchill had written his memoirs there.

The following day, we drove around the lake, hugging the shoreline until we reached Sermione, which sits on a narrow peninsula jutting into the lake. The Romans were the first to discover this heavenly piece of land, and they were followed by the Goths, the Scaliges and the Venetians.

The Scaligeri Castle stands guard to this historic medieval town, and to gain entrance to its narrow streets we had to cross a sort of moat, via a bridge. Pedestrians can walk through the ancient streets which have limited traffic access, and can wander around its interesting shops, restaurants and bars.

The bustling streets eventually metamorphosed into a peaceful, luxuriant and fragrant landscape. A panoramic walk along the shoreline led to the tip of the peninsula, where the remains of the poet Catullus' grotto could be seen. The sky was a deep cerulean blue and the creamy brickwork of the ruins contrasted strongly with the misty mauveness of the mountains beyond. On the terraced hillsides, the stunted soft green olive groves gave shade, and we sat for some minutes, taking in the beauty of the landscape which seemed akin to Paradise.

"Who was Catullus, Dad?" asked Kate.

"He was an important Roman poet," answered my father, who at that time taught history and was always keen to talk about the past.

Every day at Garda, we visited one of the quaint little towns that are strung along its shores. In the late afternoon, hot and sticky from our excursions, we would stroll down to the lakeside and swim in the delicious diaphanous waters. It was the first time I had ever swum in a lake, and I missed the salt water buoyancy of the sea and the crashing exhilarating waves. Still, the mountain scenery framing the lake, more than made up for this. It was peaceful and idyllic.

One day, we drove up to Limone on the northern shores of the lake, where the mountains and olive groves rise steeply from the water's edge. As its name suggests, the pretty town nestles amongst scented lemon groves.

The narrow and colourful cobbled streets, which radiate up from the lakeside are full of character, and the old houses creak under the weight of hanging geraniums and vivid bougainvillaea. We walked around the two small lively harbours, watching the swimmers and windsurfers who were enjoying the lake's facilities.

Later, we ambled through the ancient archways which framed some of the streets. We stayed until evening, strolling around the harbour, watching the sun go down in an indigo sky. Thousands of lights were reflected in the black water, like a burst of shimmering fireworks.

It was nearing the end of August and I had planned to return to Modena, to meet up with Paolo and another friend, Madeleine, who was on her way from Liverpool to Israel. Camping again - was on the agenda! Madeline had brought a friend (whose name escapes me now), and the four of us had set off for our camping trip, by train.

This time, we were bound for Rimini on the Adriatic coast, but on the train, Madeleine's friend and Paolo had a political disagreement and the two English girls decided to return to Modena where they had been staying. Paolo and I agreed to go ahead with our camping plans but our holiday was cut short, before it even began, by the death of Paolo's grandmother. It was a sad finish to a happy summer.

The days once long, hot and sultry gradually became shorter, sweeter and fresher. The leaves were turning gold again and covering the streets of Modena with a crunchy carpet. I was heading into my second year in the City. Who knows what would happen?

CHAPTER 9 SUMMERS AT THE SEASIDE

Life in Via Georgi was very pleasant and teaching English at the Language Centre was a revelation. Terms and conditions were favourable and civilised, compared to my last teaching post. I usually taught in the mornings and a couple of afternoons, which left me free to enjoy evenings with Paolo and friends.

Rita, who was my boss, turned a blind eye to my tutoring private students and even put me in touch with some of them. She found me a job for two afternoons a week, in a small convent school, teaching English to young ladies, who were aged between eleven to sixteen years.

The girls were very sweet. One day, I arrived at the convent feeling rather tired. I had been working hard and had not slept well the night before. I arrived for my lesson and sat down wearily at my desk with my lesson plan before me.

'I'll just have a little rest before the girls come in,' I thought, as I lay my head down on the desk. I must have drifted off to sleep, because the next thing I knew was that I was being shaken.

"*Signorina, signorina, svegliarsi*!"(Miss, miss wake-up!), cried Monica, one of the little girls in my first afternoon class.

"Are you ill?" Now, she sounded alarmed.

I opened my eyes to find about ten young ladies standing around and staring at me in astonishment. Teachers were not supposed to sleep on the job. I felt very foolish

We generally had great fun in our lessons, and I learnt many Italian colloquial phrases from these girls. They were delightful and a great pleasure to teach.

Towards the end of my first year at the Language Centre, Rita called me into her office.

"Clare," she said. "How would you like to go to the coast this summer with an acquaintance of mine, and speak English with her eleven year old daughter who already speaks well? She's a very rich and well-connected Modenese woman and I'm sure you'll have a good time!"

I said I would think about it, and arrangements were made to meet Signora Luca and her daughter Natalia.

The signora was extremely chic, dressed from head to toe in the latest fashion. Natalia seemed lively and entertaining, and I decided to accept their offer which included renumeration, board and lodging. The long, penniless holidays stretched ahead and as yet I had no definite plans. They invited me to spend a weekend at their country retreat in the Veneto, in order to get to know them better.

93

We drove through the flat and marshy fertile plain of the Po valley, bounded by the Adriatic coast and the great river Po to the south-east, and by Lake Garda to the north-west. Our route took us through landscaped countryside, and we passed many Palladian villas before arriving at the Luca country residence.

Villa da Luca was the most marvellous house that I had ever seen. It was a Palladian villa of some size and set in extensive grounds. Palladio the leading 16th century architect, built numerous villas such as the Luca home all over the Veneto region, and his designs brought together the architecture of ancient Rome and that of the modern world.

He was inspired by the Pantheon in Rome, and a sense of proportion and perspective is displayed in his classical facades, loggias, pediments and porticoes. Many have domes, Corinthian capitals and graceful columns, and are a picture of classical proportion and geometric beauty.

I was given a grand and rather beautiful room in which to sleep, with a pale blue painted ceiling depicting cherubs resting on fluffy pinkish clouds. It was an enormous room complete with Venetian mirrors and a magnificent chandelier with twinkling glass droplets. The austere bathroom was as big as most people's houses, and it too boasted a painted ceiling.

We spent the weekend walking in the grounds, eating, drinking and resting. The verdant gardens were landscaped and fairly formal, with topiary bushes, sculptures, terraces and fountains. From the steeply terraced gardens, we had a wonderful vista of the surrounding countryside, as well as the different architectural areas of the garden.

The fragrance of the lemon trees and clipped cypresses, laurel bushes and herbs was powerful and heady. It was a relaxing two days and mother and daughter were charming.

It was arranged that I would accompany Natalia and her grandmother to the seaside resort of Rimini in July, where the family had a small apartment. Signora Luca would drive us there but would leave shortly afterwards on business.

The holiday started well. Natalia and I had a reasonable relationship, even though she was strong willed and opinionated for a thirteen year old, and could be difficult to manage without her mother around. She was mature for her years, and looked a lot older than she really was.

During the day we would amble down to the beach, where row upon row of sun beds and umbrellas jostled for space on the hot sand. The beaches were mostly private and divided up according to which hotel, villa or apartment, you were staying in. Our beach compartment was 'Da Silvio,' and all the sunbathing equipment and beach paraphernalia was yellow. It was very easy to identify from afar, if a little boring and regimented. Every day the same people (including us), would be sunning themselves in exactly the same place as the day before.

"*Mario, Mario vieni qui!*" (Come here) - a stout mama would shriek at her wayward two year old every five minutes, without bothering to rise from her comfortable sun lounger.

"*Mama, Mama! Mare, mare!*" (Sea, sea!) - Mario would shriek back, heading towards the blue yonder.

"Vai Patrizia! Prendere Mario, subito, subito!" (Patricia go! Get Mario, now, now!) - Mama would screech.

Poor Patrizia would unwillingly rise to her feet, and hurtle across the hot sand in pursuit of her wayward little brother.

The beach was a noisy place. Radios would be blaring. Italian families argued, shrieked with laughter or played card games. Teenagers would be kicking balls in any tiny space between the sun beds, and overhead, small aeroplanes would whiz around the sky advertising some product or other.

The sea itself was a hot bed of activity. Hardly any one swam - only the British! It was much more fashionable to just stand in the water, or skim across the top of it in a pedal, motor or speed-boat.

Around 12.30p.m. the beach would empty as people made their way back home for lunch. Natalia always wanted to return to the apartment at this time but I usually persuaded her to stay on a little longer, as I loved being on the beach when it was deserted.

Although most of the beaches were private there was always a public beach as well. Unfortunately, it was usually situated somewhere near the sewage outlet to the sea. This beach was much less regimented than the private ones. It was more open, without all the striped umbrellas and sun-lounges. People just sunbathed on towels and could choose their own place and space.

After lunch we would siesta, and then down to the beach again for more body frying. In the evening we would *'fare la passeggiata'* (walk up and down) along the main corso in Rimini. The place was lively, overflowing with street cafés and young Italians and foreigners - all people- watching and posing. Mopeds whirred up and down, gliding between the thronging crowds and groups of chatting people. There was a general air of festivity and partying.

"Let's go and buy an ice cream," suggested Natalia one evening, during our usual *passeggiata*.

We were speaking in English, as Natalia had spent some summers in England and was reasonably fluent in the language, when some Italian youths started following and pestering us.

"Do you speaka Eengleesh?" they called a few steps behind us.

"*Vada via!*" (Go away) replied Natalia in a bored tone. She then swore at them in Italian and made some rude gestures.

"Just ignore them," I advised. "They'll soon get fed up and go and annoy someone else."

Unfortunately they did not, but kept on following us making stupid, inane comments. Natalia grew furious and suddenly turned around, stuffing her ice cream into one of their faces. It was a waste of a good ice cream, but worth it to see the looks of astonishment they gave us.

Natalia was undisciplined and very spoilt. She was a little rich kid who had everything. Her poor grandmother or *nonna* was forever running after her. Natalia would shout and scream at *nonna,* if things were not to her liking. She verbally abused her grandmother big-time, and as the holiday progressed, she grew more and more self-centred. I tried to reason with her and often asked that she apologise to her *nonna*, which she refused to do. I finally decided that I could not stay in such a discordant household and gave in my notice, well before time.

I travelled back to Modena very early one morning, wandering what to do with myself. Modena is no place to be in mid summer. It is deserted and humid, with days of either glaring sunshine or searing heat.

Paolo and his family were in the mountains and I thought of joining them. However before I could make up my mind, I bumped into an old friend of mine, Cinzia, who was just about to travel to the west coast of Tuscany to a place called Punta Ala.

Cinzia, a chic young Italian woman in her early thirties, was going to camp there with her ten year old son Franco and asked me if I would like to join them. I jumped at the opportunity. Three weeks in a campsite was definitely preferable to stewing in the white heat of Modena.

~

The three of us set off in her little white *Deux Chevaux* car. I was to receive board and lodging i.e. a tent to myself and food, in return for giving Franco some English lessons. This seemed a reasonable exchange to me.

We drove through the sun flower fields of Tuscany. The bright yellow *girasole* or sun flowers, all had their heads turned skywards and splashed vivid colour into the surrounding land. The gently rolling hills were misty blue in the distance, and the rich dreamy landscape was dotted with Tuscan villas interspersed with cypress trees.

The campsite was situated in a forested pine grove, set back from the beach in Punta Ala. The trees were like great umbrellas and gave tremendous shade in the noon day sun. Cinzia and I put up the tents, while Franco checked out the neighbourhood for prospective friends.

My tent was smallish, with a camp-bed and sleeping bag. There were boxes to put my clothes in and a few coat-hangers. It was certainly different from the luxury and sophistication of Rimini, but I was my own boss and my tent was my castle, affording all the peace and privacy I required.

I tried to pin Franco down for some lessons but he was having none of it.

"Mama," he complained to Cinzia. "It's holiday time. I don't want to do lessons. I don't want to learn English!"

He rushed out of the tent like a whirlwind, looking for his pals. I felt guilty.

"Never mind," Cinzia reassured me. "You can speak English to me instead."

We had a lovely peaceful holiday. Most mornings we lazed on the beach, coming back to the camp for our lunch and a siesta. In the afternoons we would swim or visit Punta Ala, a small, elegant fishing port with a harbour, pine woods and lovely sandy beaches. Across the water was the island of Elba where Napoleon was exiled in 1815.

At the campsite we lived very frugally. Most evenings we would cook our supper on a little gas stove, and then read or chat by candlelight. Cinzia taught me several pasta dishes, and my favourite was the very simple, delicious and spicy, *olio, aglio e peperoncino* (oil, garlic and chilli peppers). The recipe goes as follows:-

- Boil water and cook spaghetti;

- Crush garlic and hot chilli pepper (not too much of the latter, unless you like it hot!);
- Fry ingredients in plenty of olive oil, on a low heat, for about three minutes;
- Mix into the pasta - delicious!

If in Tuscany, wash down with a big glass of Chianti!

CHAPTER 10 EARTHQUAKES AND FLYING PLATES

I was living in Via Georgi, when the devastating earthquake in Fruili occurred in 1976. It was a disaster of epic proportions in this mountainous part of Italy, near the border of the former Yugoslavia. I had spent the morning teaching and was riding home for lunch on my bicycle, when I noticed people running out of their apartments shouting '*Terremoto! Terremoto!*'

The after-shocks had rippled down through Italy, and were being felt in Modena as I rode my bike. Because I was moving I did not feel a thing, but the next day, I certainly felt the effects of a second earthquake, whilst visiting an office on the fourth floor of an official government building. It was a weird and surreal sensation. For a few minutes, I felt as if I were under the sea, swaying and trying to keep my balance.

In some parts of Italy, children are taught in schools about earthquake strategies, and I also gleaned some useful information.

I was told to either stand under a door frame, or get under a sturdy table or inside a bath and hope for the best!

"Has there ever been an earthquake in Modena?" I asked Paolo, on the day after the quake.

"No, Modena's built on top of a series of canals. Underneath the city it's just like Venice, and where there's water under a city, earthquakes can't happen," he reassured me.

I thought he was joking about the network of canals under Modena but apparently it is true. One of the largest streets in the historic city centre is called Via Canal Grande, which explains a lot about the history of the city. Modena fortunately, is not in an earthquake zone, as so many parts of Italy are.

People still remember those fateful couple of days, back in 1976. Many towns in Fruili, including Udine and Venzone were badly hit, but a town called Gemona suffered the most and over 1,000 people perished.

~

That year after spending Christmas with my family in England, my sister Joanna decided to return with me to Modena, for about three months.She had just completed her university degree in history and had yet to find suitable employment, so had some spare time and thought it would be a good idea to take the opportunity to visit Italy. She had various small jobs teaching English lined up, and was looking forward to spending some time on Italian soil.

Our journey back by train was fairly miserable. For some of the time we could not get seats on the Calais to Milan Express. At some stage, we even slept in the corridor lying down on the floor, whilst people stepped over us. Lying on floors in trains was a fairly common practice in those hippy days, when young people seemed to be more individual and cared less about what others thought about them. Jo and I were both small in stature and were able to find a niche, somewhere in the train's lonely corridor.

Every time the train shuddered to a halt in some deserted station in the middle of France, in the early hours of the morning, we would suddenly be awakened and wonder where on earth we were.

Early the next morning we had a moment of panic, when Jo needed to find the W.C. and went off in search of one down the corridor and into the next carriage. Suddenly the train stopped at one of the border stations in the north of Italy. I realised that the carriage that my sister was now in, was being shunted onto another train - presumably heading for the east - maybe even Austria, or the former Yugoslavia.

The carriages grew further and further apart. I could see Joanna waving frantically and I waved back feeling helpless - at the same time shouting "For God's Sake get out!"

The carriage she was in was moving slowly, and she had the sense to quickly jump out and get back onto the train destined for Milan. By this time, many of the compartments were empty and we managed to find one all to ourselves, stretch out and doze fitfully until we reached Milano Centrale.

Once safely back at Via Georgi, we organised our living space to suit our needs. As we had no spare rooms, Joanna had to sleep in my room which was very large, on a small bed borrowed from friends.

After a few days she found work, speaking English to a girl who was a university student. The girl, Maria Grazia, lived with her mother not far from Via Georgi, and they offered Joanna board and lodging in return for so many hours of English per day.

This started off as a wonderful arrangement, but as time went by, Joanna grew weary of the pair who argued every meal time in Italian, hurling plates and insults at each other. Eventually, Joanna quit this job and found another one as a sort of housekeeper cum babysitter for a wealthy, aristocratic woman, who lived in one of the grand *palazzi* in the centre of Modena.

However this post was short-lived too, as Signora Milandi was a complete control freak. Every day, Joanna had to make sure that the curtains were drawn to exactly the right place at the windows, that the cushions were plumped to exactly the right height and width, and that the chairs were placed just so! After a couple of weeks of this, she was a quivering wreck, and decided that she would just stay with me and take on a few private students. There were always people in Modena who wanted to learn English from an English person, on a one to one basis.

One weekend in February, we decided that we would visit Urbino, an ancient town situated in the region of Marche, next to Emilia-Romagna. Marche a central province, together with Tuscany, Umbria and northern Latvium forms a link between the north and south of the country. Much is known these days about the beauty of Tuscany or Chiantishire as we like to call it, and many Brits now live there. The other regions around Toscana or Tuscany, such as Umbria are just as beautiful, although maybe a little wilder and much less known.

Setting off one damp chilly morning, it seemed strange to be sight seeing in the winter and we wrapped up well. I do not remember how we travelled to Urbino, but I do recall seeing the town for the first time up on the ridge of a steep hill, surrounded by a circle of ramparts. It was straight out of the pages of a fairy tale. The town was built on the site of a former Roman settlement, and was later dominated by the Byzantines and Lombards, until the Franks gave it to the Papal States.

The town flourished under the famous Montefeltro family, who ruled between the 12th and 16th centuries. It then came under another important family, the Della Rovere, until 1631. In 1860, it was annexed to the Kingdom of Italy. Raphael the great Renaissance artist was born there and we were able to visit the little 'Casa di Raffaello.'

Urbino is an interesting place, and we enjoyed walking around the palatial buildings dating from the 15th and 16th centuries. We visited the Palazzo Ducale, a magnificent fairy tale building with twin towers, which was once the seat of the powerful Montefeltro family and is an important example of Renaissance architecture. Inside, there is a large museum, The Galleria Nazionale delle Marche, with paintings by Raphael, Titian, Piero della Francesca, Uccello and many others. I remember that inside the palace there were some fabulous marquetry doors, which were made up with pictures, inlaid with various pieces of different varieties of wood.

The palace is located on a high cliff and after looking around the gallery, we were able to find a place to sit with an excellent panoramic view of the picturesque surrounding countryside.

It was far too cold to *fare la passeggiata* that evening and anyway the streets were deserted. Instead, we contented ourselves with visiting a bar and drinking hot chocolate topped with a dollop of whipped cream, before turning in to our modest *pensione* and having an early night.

On the way back to Modena, we stopped off at San Marino - a tiny, independent republic with its own coins and postage stamps. Perched high up on a precipitous cliff, this little principality has wonderful views of the surrounding hilly countryside. We decided that it would be a grand place to visit in the summer. Now it was cold and deserted, with a mysterious, eerie atmosphere.

~

Once back in Modena, we decided that we had enjoyed our short break to Urbino so much, that we wanted to travel somewhere else the following weekend.

"Where would you like to go?" I asked Joanna.

"I'd love to visit Rome, or maybe Venice," my sister replied.

She had spent some time previously in Venice as part of her university course, and thought she would enjoy seeing the city again. However, after much debate we settled on Rome, the Eternal City.

We travelled south by train. The weather was still only a few degrees above freezing, so we were well clad with hats, scarves, gloves and boots. In those days, it was not necessary to book a hotel in advance - especially in winter, and we found a reasonable *pensione* very near the station.

Rome was hectic and very noisy. The traffic was a nightmare and the drivers all seemed to be completely mad. It was touch or go as to whether they would stop on a zebra crossing or not, or even at the red lights. Italian drivers have incredibly quick reactions and just as you think they are going to mow you down in cold blood, they break abruptly, slamming their cars to a stop, millimetres away from your quaking body. They then wave and grin and call *'ciao bella'* before roaring off, as if they have done you an enormous favour!

Our first place of call was the Vatican - that great seat of Catholicism and trove of art treasures. We entered St. Peter's which was vast and warm and glowing in the candlelight. It was a refuge, after the chilly outside February air.

We wandered around in awe. There was so much to look at.

"It's strange," I said to Joanna. "Italy was such a cultured place, but there doesn't seem to be much culture any more. There used to be so many wonderful artists and writers like Dante and Pirandello, but where are they now?"

Joanna shrugged. "I suppose there are some amazing film directors like Fellini, Visconti and Bertolucci. Perhaps film has overtaken painting as an art form."

"Italy is renowned for design and fashion," I added. "All their artistic talent and ideas must've gone into that side of it. Also the Renaissance was a time when artists were paid by rich patrons to paint their families and create wonderful cities and buildings. I suppose since the invention of photography, there hasn't been the same urge to paint representational things like people and landscapes. Aren't these floors fantastic?" I continued.

We admired the beautiful, marble tessellated shapes and the intricate floor patterns that were coloured in muted reds, greens, blacks and whites. The floor undulated slightly, worn in places by generations of feet.

"I think we should go and see the Sistine Chapel ceiling," said Joanna. "After all, it's not everyday that you can see paintings by Michelangelo."

I agreed. When we arrived at the pay desk, we were dismayed to find that it cost about 12.000 lire to enter, the equivalent in those days of about £8, which was a lot of money when we were trying to see Rome 'on a shoestring.' In 1976, I only earned about £120 a month, so £8 was a huge chunk of this. We deliberated and debated, and in the end decided that we could not come all this way and not see the most important work of the great artist Michelangelo. After all when would the chance present itself again!

The vaulted ceiling of the chapel was magnificent. We stared up at the brooding energy of the figures painted in the early 16th century. There was a feeling of classical grandeur, drama, and a powerful moody atmosphere of foreboding.

The ceiling is divided up into sections, within which are contained numerous figures illustrating the story of mankind, from the Creation to Noah and the Great Flood. The theme is divided into three areas. The central part is made up of nine panels, depicting the origin of the world, of humanity and of sin and its consequences. The next area encloses the central part, and illustrates the story of the prophets who announce the coming of Christ. The final area which is composed of triangles, tells the story of Christ's predecessors and the salvation of Israel. Michelangelo wanted to represent the anguished, heroic struggle of man against the physical adversities that opposed his freedom of spirit.

We came out of the huge chamber feeling subdued. The painting had had a powerful effect on both of us. We agreed that the money we had parted with had been well spent. We also had painful cricks in our necks, from looking up at the ceiling for so long.

Our return to Modena was planned for Sunday afternoon, so we spent the morning of that day at the Forum, enjoying the pale winter sun that had broken through the clouds. This lovely quiet place full of ruins was almost deserted. We felt immersed in history as we sat on rocks amongst the long grass.

Looking over to the Palatine hill, there were the remains of former Emperor's palaces, and we gazed in fascination at the beautiful columns from the temple of Castor and Pollux. The Forum had once been the hub of the Eternal City, a busy market place trading in all things, including slaves. It was extraordinary to think that this place was right in the centre of one of the world's capital cities. It was the antithesis to the rest of Rome.

Another weekend took us north to Venice or Venezia - city of lagoons or 'La Serenissima,' as the Italians affectionately call it. I had always wanted to arrive in Venice by moonlight as my mother did years before, but instead, I caught my first glimpse one chilly and grey early February day, when the canals looked dank and the buildings sad forlorn and closed.

It had a mysterious, melancholy, unreal and at times slightly sinister atmosphere which brought to mind a fairly recent film - the psychological thriller 'Don't Look Now,' starring Julie Christie and Donald Sutherland and set in an eerie, psychically charged Venice. I have since visited this city many times, but usually in the summer when it is a completely different place - sunny, friendly and throbbing with tourists. On that grey February Saturday, it was wrapped in an odd ghostly quality.

Joanna and I chanced upon a small *pensione* in the Santo Stefano area of the city, fronting onto a canal. We spent the rest of the day exploring, traversing the hundreds of tiny bridges and canals that radiate like an intricate spider's web all over the city.

The place was wonderfully deserted. Even St Mark's square, nicknamed 'the greatest drawing-room in Europe' by Napoleon, was pleasantly empty and we were able to gain access to St. Mark's Basilica without having to join an endless queue, that often leads to frustration in the summer months.

We stood spellbound inside the great Basilica, which was modelled on the Byzantine churches of Constantinople. The interior is studded with gleaming mosaics which date from 1071, and were created by craftsmen from the east in Constantinople. Many more mosaics were added over the years until the early 18th century. These wonderful mosaics are made from marble, glass and porphyry and they tell the story of the Bible. The predominant colour of the Basilicas is a rich overwhelming gold - glinting, glistening and sparkling. Charles Dickens is said to have commented, on a visit to the Basilica: 'Opium couldn't build such a place.'

The following day it was damp and misty. The city seemed blanketed in gloom and monotonous greyness. It felt like a private city, ethereal, closed and silent. Only the distant clanging of church bells reminded us that it was Sunday morning, and that people actually lived here. We had risen early, hoping to make the most of the day and we strolled along the empty canal sides in anticipation.

Eventually we came upon quiet back water, which we later found out to be the Jewish quarter. It was more run-down and less colourful than other areas nearer to the glitzy centre, but somehow it seemed more real, a place where Jewish people lived and worked - a place that tourists probably often missed. It had its own great charm and character and I felt privileged to have stumbled upon it.

This ghetto still remains the heart of Jewish life in the city, with synagogues and Jewish workshops. Many of the men in this area were dressed in traditional Jewish attire, and kosher bakeries offered unleavened bread. The place was unexpected and a welcome surprise.

In subsequent visits to Venice, I have always preferred to seek out the less well-known tourist tracks - the hidden secret Venice, such as the Zattere, the Campo della Maddalena and the peaceful lush island of Torcello.

Noticing that all the shops were full of dazzling, Venetian masks we realized that we were just about to miss the annual *Carnevale* or the great Venice carnival, which we were sorry about.

Originally in medieval times, masks had allowed the nobility to mingle incognito with the ordinary folk of Venice, but nowadays it gives the city an excuse for an extravagant party, where the citizens dress up in fancy dress costume, complete with mask. Costumes can be traditional, historical or fantasy based. The masks are usually made from papier mâché, or thin leather or even china, with papier mâché being the cheapest and most popular.

"I've got to have a mask!" I said to Joanna.

We entered one of the little artisan shops that line many of the canals and inner streets or *calle.* It was stacked from floor to ceiling with masks. There were so many to choose from - gold and silver ones, glittery ones, patterned and bejewelled ones - all representing the theatricality of Venice and promising mystery and romance.

"I think I'll have a blank one and decorate it myself," I said.

Rummaging through the hundreds of masks, I found one that fitted perfectly. Joanna also purchased one.

"What a shame, we'll miss the carnival," she said wistfully. "It must be an amazing experience."

"Mm yes, we should have visited Venice next weekend instead." I said regretfully.

We had not realised what we would be missing. It promised to be a dazzling spectacle from the preparations that were starting to take place.

Before returning to the railway station *Ferrovia St. Lucia*, on the edge of Venice to take the train back to Modena, we decided to visit St. Mark's for a final look. It really was like a stage set, with grand arches bordering it on three sides. The arch ways were framed with theatrical and flouncy canvas Austrian blinds, some of which were raggy with age. What other city actually has curtains in its main square? Lively music came from the celebrated bar 'Café Florian,' and a couple of people were dancing to it, waltzing over the patterned, uneven flagstones.

There are two famous cafés in the Piazza - Quadri and Florian. We would have liked to have sat down and had a coffee but the prices were exorbitant, so we contented ourselves with just watching the crowds go by. Behind the arcades that line this elegant square are small individual shops that sell things like lace and silk scarves. Facing us was the Basilica of St. Mark and the Campanile or bell-tower.

In Venice, east meets west. Images of the east are everywhere. The Venetians took much from the Arabs and Turks, and this is really evident in the architecture which is a mixture of Byzantine, Gothic and Renaissance.

We had spent a couple of wonderful days in *La Serenissima*. I could not wait to return to Venice again - the city of lagoons.

CHAPTER 11
SIENA AND THE PALLIO

The second summer of my Italian sojourn also saw the return of my parents and youngest sister Kate. This time they did not stop off in Modena, but drove down to Siena where they had rented a villa for a couple of weeks, I was to join them there.

Siena in Tuscany is the city of the famous Palio - a horse race, run in honour of the Virgin Mary. The medieval city has seventeen historic quarters, which fiercely compete with one another for the trophy, an immense flag bearing the image of the Virgin. Much to the excitement of my family, in particular Kate who loved horses, the Palio was to take place during our visit.

Our rented villa was just outside the city walls, overlooking seductive dreamy countryside. From the house, it was a short but hilly amble up to the ancient gateway to the city, and on our way we would catch glimpses of Siena's magnificent silhouette, crowning three hills, with the black and white striped cathedral and the town hall towers, starkly outlined against the deep blue of the sky. Once inside the walls most of the city is given over to pedestrians and it has completely retained its medieval character.

Siena had a turbulent past. In medieval times, the city was often at war with its hated rival Florence and in 1290, the latter was defeated at the Battle of Montaperti. Later the proud Sienese were beaten by the Florentines at the Battle of Colle Val d' Elsa. Many Sienese died in 1348, in the Great Plague which ravaged the area at that time, and the city never fully recovered.

The spectacular Romanesque-Gothic cathedral which was built around this time was to have been the largest church in the Christian world, but because of the plague it was never finished. In 1555, Siena was incorporated into the Medici Duchy of Tuscany, and was forced into a secondary position to the great Renaissance centre of Florence. The Sienese who are proud people have never really forgotten this act, and to this day enmity still runs deep.

Wandering around the narrow medieval streets of this beautiful city, one feels the power of history. Symbols of the Roman she-wolf adorn the place and legend has it that Ascius and Senius, the sons of Remus who was one of the famous twins of Rome, were forced to flee from the Eternal city from their uncle Romulus. They fled to the hills of Etruria and founded the city of Siena there.

The winding streets and Renaissance buildings open up on to the main piazza, Piazza del Campo - a dramatic and sloping theatrical place of immense proportions. We stood and stared at the beautiful enormous space. '*Campo*' means 'field' in Italian and like many Italian piazzas, it seemed surreal. We felt like players on a stage.

Only in Italy do I ever get this sensation of unreality, of fantasy, and of being in a dream world. I thought I had loved the city of Florence but I loved Siena even more. It was truly a magical place.

Pigeons swooped and dived. Around the square's circumference were tall medieval palaces, most of which were at least five storeys high. Many windows were shuttered to the rising sun but some were open, their inhabitants leaning out and surveying the scene before them. Some were waving and shouting greetings to friends and neighbours below. These houses were built of lovely mellow brick and all the shutters were painted brown, giving a dignified uniformity to the façades.

The square itself is composed of red brick and is divided into nine sections. Other lovely buildings, such as the Gothic Palazzo Pubblico or Town Hall, and the Torre di Mangia or Mangia Tower which is lit up at night piercing the velvet nocturnal sky, also surround the piazza, where in a few days time the great Palio was to take place.

The day of the Palio arrived. It was bright and scorchingly hot. An ever increasing crescendo of tension and excitement had been reverberating around the walls of Siena for some time, and today it was to reach fever pitch. This great horse race has occurred every summer in August since the 17th century. The city's seventeen historic quarters or *contrade,* fiercely compete with one another for the honour of winning the Palio flag or trophy.

A Sienese citizen is born into a *contrada* and he remains a member of this community for his entire life. Each *contrada* has its own churches, meeting places, bars, colours, costumes and flags. A very tight-knit bond exists amongst its clan.

On Palio day, each quarter of the city dresses up in medieval costumes of rich velvet and sumptuous satins, in the glorious colours of their *contrada*. The men resemble Renaissance princes and the women could be mistaken for beautiful, fairy tale princesses. Before the Palio gets under way, a procession of flag wavers, hurl and twirl their stunningly colourful flags up into the air. The music resounds. The parade has started.

It is the greatest honour to win. Families are often torn apart during this time, when a husband might belong to one *contrada* and a wife and her family to another. Preparations for this great event go on for weeks beforehand, and by Palio day, intense tension hangs in the air.

There are two Palio days every year - July 2nd and August 16th. The Piazza or Campo, large though it might be, is too small for all seventeen *contrade* to race each other at once, so ten are chosen in a draw to participate in each Palio. The seven who did not run in the first race, then compete in the second race, as well as another three whose names are drawn again. The horses are also picked in this way, although the jockeys are professionals brought in from outside.

Before the beginning of the race, the horses and their riders are blessed in the churches of whichever *contrada* they are competing for, and if a horse happens to pee in the church it is considered to be a good omen!

On that August day, excitement was mounting minute by minute. The great piazza was starting to steadily fill up around the edges with hundreds of people, all eager to watch the spectacle. It reminded me of a football stadium. Italians were hanging out of every visible window, and the more adventurous souls were even sitting on high up ledges and on top of lamp posts in order to secure a good view.

The atmosphere was electric. The crowd grew bigger and I lost sight of my family. There was barely enough space to breathe, and being stuck in the middle of a tightly packed crowd in the searing noon day sun, with no one to talk to was starting to feel claustrophobic.

Suddenly the event had begun, with some practice runs and an historic festival parade. Then the real Palio commenced which only lasted about a minute. Ten horses and their riders were stampeding around the piazza at break-neck speed. I held my breath. Would any of the horses fall? They had done so in the past, with both horse and jockey suffering horrible injuries. The crowd was frantically shouting and cheering. This was a ruthless race, with the honour of the *contrada* at stake.

The crowd was so dense that I could not move my arms - they were pinned to my side in the squash. I swayed with the throng, first this way and then that. On several occasions I even felt my feet being lifted off the ground. I desperately wanted to get out and find my family.

Suddenly, a squirt of lemon tea jetted out of my handbag and hit me between the eyes. The crowd was so tight, that a small sealed carton of iced tea that I had bought previously, split in the crush, and the force of the crowd caused it to spray like a fountain in an upward direction. That incident was the last straw for me and I managed to tunnel an exit, and to my relief find the edge of the Campo.

I went to recover in a nearby bar and ordered a shot of brandy. A large white umbrella offered shade, sanctuary and sanity. After scanning the crowd for several minutes, I finally spotted my family on the other side of Piazza del Campo. By now, the merry crowd had started to disperse.

I do not remember which *contrada* won that year, but there was great jubilation and celebration within that quarter of the ancient city. The festivities went on until the early hours. Great mounds of rubbish drifted into street corners and confetti and party poppers lay abandoned in ever growing piles. The piazza was starting to look dishevelled.

Cafés and bars were overflowing with festivity. For the Sienese the day had been the culmination of many months of hard work and there was much embracing, crying, shouting and laughing amongst friends. The triumphant contrada paraded through the narrow Sienese streets, with the Palio flag - their prized trophy - held high, and celebrations continued well into the night.

~

Often in the evening, we would take a stroll around beautiful Piazza del Campo, and drink an aperitif in one of the numerous bars around its rim. The Mangia Tower would be illuminated against the indigo sky, where a million stars would spangle in a canopy above us. The Sienese sky at night is a rare colour, a gorgeous dark turquoise, deep and alluring.

For a short while, Paolo joined us from the mountains. My family had their favourite eating place called 'La Lupa,' and most nights we went there to eat some of the delicacies of Tuscany.

Each region in Italy has its own delicious specialities and in Toscana, wild boar could be found on most menus. This came in many shapes and forms such as sausages, ham, roast boar or salami. *Bistecca* or beef steak features heavily in the region, and soups made with *fagioli* or beans are very popular, especially in the cold winter months. Often, we just ate spaghetti as this was a favourite. It was cheap and tasty and a variety of mouth watering toppings could be added. This would be washed down with several carafes of Chianti - or sometimes Orvieto, if we fancied white wine.

One evening, we were gathered at 'La Lupa.' Paolo was talking animatedly with a burly Italian sitting at the next table to us, who apparently came from Sicily. He told Paolo that he was travelling north to find a good Alsatian dog. The Sicilian, whose name was Giuseppe, told us, that the best Alsatians are bred in the northern regions.

"How much would you be prepared to pay?" asked Paolo.

Giuseppe named his price and Paolo looked pensive. He jumped up, grinning at Giuseppe.

"Just a minute! I'll be back soon," he said, making his way to the phone booth, on the wall near the entrance.

Paolo returned a few minutes later with a big smile on his face.

"I've found you a fantastic Alsatian!" he exclaimed ecstatically, slapping Giuseppe on the back. "An acquaintance of mine in Parma breeds them. I don't think you'll be disappointed. The dog in question is a pure bred puppy - only born a few weeks ago, so you'll be able to train him as you like!"

Paolo handed Giuseppe the address of his friend and the two men shook hands beaming at each other. We all toasted the new Alsatian with another bottle of Chianti.

Another evening, after Paolo had returned to the mountains, we decided to be a little more adventurous and change our eating venue. We found a pleasant little *trattoria* tucked into one of the tiny medieval streets near the ancient walls of the city.

As usual we ordered spaghetti; it was becoming our staple diet. Once ensconced inside, Kate decided that she needed to use the W.C. Suddenly there was a scream and my sister came bursting through the door, her face ashen and her eyes large.

"There's a rat in the toilet!" she shrieked "There's a rat!"

"Calm down Kate," said Dad. "Are you sure?"

"Of course I'm sure," said Kate shivering. "It's huge with a horrible, disgusting, long tail!"

Caroline and I started to giggle. The proprietor came over to speak with us, alerted by the noise and agitation in our corner.

"*Buona sera signore,*" (Good evening) he said looking alarmed. "Is everything alright?"

Everyone looked at me expectantly, as I was the one with the best command of the Italian language.

"I'm sorry to have to say this," I said "but my sister has seen a rat in the toilet."

"Nonsense!" replied the proprietor looking horrified. "This is a clean establishment. We do not have any rats here. Come, show me!"

"I'm not going back," said Kate looking terrified.

"Oh, I'll go then," said Dad, wanting to get the matter settled.

Needless to say, the rat had disappeared. The proprietor was adamant that no rats lived on his premises. We were obviously not happy finishing the rest of our meal so we left and decided to return to 'La Lupa,' where we would be sure of a good reception and wholesome, hygienic food. The proprietor there was very jolly and always wanted his customers to have a good time.

Although many Italians had wonderful bathrooms in their houses during the 1970s, the actual toilets in most restaurants and bars left much to be desired! More often than not they were the sort of toilet that consisted of a ceramic surround with a scary hole in the middle. The unfortunate person using this W.C. had to crouch over the uninviting hole and hope for the best! Pulling the toilet chain was a bit of a hit and miss affair and it was always best to open the door for a quick get away, to avoid being drenched!

~

Whilst staying in Siena, we visited many beautiful towns in Tuscany and Umbria, including San Geminiano with its surreal collection of towers, and Gubbio where we bought brightly glazed traditional pottery, painted with intricate patterns. Gubbio seemed unchanged since the Middle Ages, and we were intrigued to discover that along the narrow twisting streets were secret narrow doorways called the *Porte della Morte* (doors of death).

Another day took us to Assisi, home of the famous saints - St. Francis and Santa Chiara or St. Clare. We journeyed down to Umbria through fertile rolling plains, and eventually arrived at the walled city proudly situated on a spur of Mount Subasio.

Nowadays, Assisi is known as the city of Peace and is the ecumenical meeting place of world religions. However, like many walled cities in the region, it has seen troubled times and has had a violent and bloody history, with its fair share of sieges, pillages, occupations and turmoil including earthquakes.

It was a glorious day for sight seeing and we decided to visit the Basilica di San Francesco first. This massive church was built between the years A.D. 1228 - 1253, and is one of the most visited Christian shrines in the world. As we entered the Basilica, we remarked to each other on the feelings of peace and harmony that pervaded the air.

St. Francis who was born in 1182, and who founded the Franciscan order of monks is buried here. He is the first known Christian to have received the 'stigmata' or bleeding wounds, on his feet, side and hands, corresponding to those of Christ on the cross.

St. Francis shunned his privileged background and embraced a life of poverty, looking after lepers and animals and immersing himself in his love of nature and God. He is supposed to have great power in Italy. Apparently in the 1940s in Sardinia, when bandits were rife, a group of them prayed to the saint to help them with their next planned criminal activity!

The magnificent church of St. Francis contains priceless frescos by Giotto, Cimabue, Lorenzetti and others. In the autumn of 1997, disaster struck when an earthquake rocked central Italy, causing widespread havoc. Assisi was badly affected. The Basilica inner roof collapsed, causing tremendous damage and killing two people. There were thirty other people inside at the time, but most of them rushed out of the building before the vault came crashing down. Many of the frescos seemingly perished but have since been carefully restored.

We wanted to see the church of Santa Chiara next. This saint is often associated with St, Francis. She was born in Assisi in 1193, and was received into the Franciscan order where she founded the Poor Clares, an order of nuns devoted to the Franciscan ideal of poverty. The church was beautiful and contained many Giotto influenced frescos.

I have always taken an interest in St Clare as she is my own name sake saint. The Italians consider the day of the name sake saint almost as important as a birthday, and celebrate it accordingly. It is called an *Omnastico* and people often receive cards from their loved ones on this day.

Around the narrow streets of Assisi, there are many shops and stalls selling religious icons and other paraphernalia. These tourist shops are the mainstay of this little central Italian town.

We returned to Siena, with images of St.Francis and Giotto's frescos filling our heads. It had been a very fulfilling day, and we were still discussing all that we had seen when we turned up the drive way of our rented villa.

In the distance, the lights of Siena twinkled and the Mangia Tower was lit up in all its glory. We had had an enjoyable but exhausting trip and we looked forward to turning in. Tomorrow was the last day of our holiday. I would soon be returning to Modena, and that night, I dreamt that I had been locked in the Ghirlandina and when I looked out from the top floor window, all I could see was the swirling mist and swathes of thick white fog!

CHAPTER 12
SEE NAPLES AND DIE

In the 1970s, I hated flying and nothing would induce me to step on an aeroplane and fly in comfort to Bologna - a mere two hours away via the sky. I took the tougher option and always travelled to Italy by train, a journey which often took between twenty-two and twenty-four hours from London, and involved changing at Calais, sometimes in Paris and for the third time in Milan.

I mostly journeyed alone. Occasionally I had travelling companions such as friends or family, who were accompanying me to Italy for a holiday or a long visit. My journey south would start at Victoria Station, where I would board the old battered boat-train for Calais. In winter time the seas would surge and swell, and the boat would be practically empty, giving me a great choice of seat. The crossing could be choppy, and I remember one voyage where almost everyone on board was seasick. It was a relief to reach the French shore.

At Calais I was always slightly apprehensive, in case I boarded the wrong train and ended up in some strange and unknown city in the centre of Europe. Usually the train for Milan was easy to locate, standing forlorn and silent, a large black dusty locomotive with ridiculously high boarding steps. I would heave my luggage on and then follow, being careful not to fall down through the enormous gap between steps and platform.

Once in the corridor I would try to find an empty compartment, so that when night fell, I would be able to stretch out on the brown plastic seats and hopefully catch some sleep. Sleeping was a precarious operation posing many threats. I had to lie with my handbag under my head. All my valuables were enclosed, things like passport, tickets, keys and money. I was wary of thieves and always slept with one eye open.

If the train was packed, as was so often the case in late summer, I would sleep sitting up, my handbag carefully tucked under my coat. Sleep was fitful and by the time I arrived in Modena, I was totally exhausted.

On one occasion, I paid extra for a couchette or sleeping bunk. I was sharing the compartment with five other people and I was lucky to acquire the top bunk. During the night, the other occupants in the compartment were robbed of some of their belongings - only the top bunks were spared. Rumours abounded, of bandits entering trains heading south and committing such dastardly crimes as cutting people's fingers off whilst they slept, to acquire valuable rings. Of course, all this was fictitious nonsense, but it made travellers wary and less trusting.

On another memorable occasion, my friend Teresa and I were travelling back to Modena together. Teresa, another college friend, of whom you will hear more about later, came over to Italy to teach English and share a flat with me in my third year there. On this occasion that I am thinking about, we met up for the journey together, in Victoria Station. There had been all sorts of hold-ups in London with British Rail and the ferry was also late. Consequently we missed our connection at Calais, and the next train was not for another ten hours. We wondered what to do and decided to travel down to Paris and try to catch a connection there, as trains to Italy were more frequent from the Gare de Lyon.

We arrived in Paris at about 10 o'clock in the evening, tired and irritable after a taxing day. Our train for Milan would be departing at around 11.30 p.m. and we had one and a half hours to kill. As we were very sleepy, we made for the waiting room in order to get somewhere quiet to rest.

According to Teresa, I fell asleep immediately. I was inelegantly slouched on a chair, grouped with others in a sort of central island, when apparently a fight broke out behind me, between two men and flick-knives were produced. The police eventually arrived and marched the two offenders away. All the other inhabitants of the waiting room had fled to the outer limits of the chamber near to the exit, for a quick get away should the need arise, leaving me stranded in the centre of the room, blissfully unaware of the danger around me. Teresa had been worried that I would be caught in the cross-fire.

During the later years of my time in Italy, Teresa and I would usually travel together by train. We would often meet fascinating characters on our journeys. The Italians we encountered journeying back to their homeland would always offer us food and sometimes wine.

I remember one elderly gentleman who had a whole crate of wine balanced precariously on the luggage rack above him. Every time the train lurched, the crate would wobble menacingly. He continually offered all in his company, plastic glasses of the homemade stuff. Needless to say the whole compartment was rather merry by the time we reached Milan.

The train from Calais would cut through France, juddering to a stop in the dead of night at some station or other. Numerous carriages would be shunted off and maybe other new ones added, and the noises and screeches often awoke us from our fitful slumber. Eerily deserted platforms, presented just the odd person boarding or descending from the train in what seemed to be the middle of nowhere, at some unearthly hour. The brightly lit, empty stations threw dazzling light through the train windows, cutting further into our intermittent sleep.

Next morning we would awake to the splendour of the Swiss countryside. Magnificent snow capped peaks whizzed past our windows. Eagerly, we would rush out of the stuffy compartment into the corridor to view the fairy tale scene before us, happy at the chance to stretch our numb legs and excited that our journey was nearing its end, and was becoming more visually stimulating.

The pristine little chalets perched on the mountain sides were very picturesque. Many would have colourful quilts hanging and airing from upstairs windows, and in the summertime, balconies would sing with cascades of brightly coloured, crimson geraniums. The scene was rural, idyllic and in apple-pie order. I found it fascinating, being used to more mundane northern climes.

As we neared the Italian boarder, the chalets would become a little more dilapidated and the terrain less perfect, but the hospitality and gregariousness of the Italian character permeated the landscape. The bed-linen hanging from the shuttered windows was less colourful, but the warmth of the people in the countryside as they waved and hollered at the speeding train, was heart warming. It was a lovely feeling to be on Italian soil and I felt as if I had come home.

The countryside north of Milan, is similar in some respects to southern Switzerland - the Italian-speaking Ticino region. The train would criss-cross the Alps, with rugged panoramic vistas of craggy peaks, chestnut groves and spectacular waterfalls. Alpine meadows nestled amongst the wooded and glacial landscape, and as we made our way further into Italy, the meadows gradually gave way to terraced olive groves and vineyards.

Eventually, the long snaking train would reach its destination - Milano Centrale. On approach to Milan the aspect of the countryside changed dramatically. The fields and woods were replaced with high-rise apartments, huddled together in an ever growing mass. Space was at a premium. At this point the train would reduce its speed, weaving its final path slowly, though the bustling and industrial business-like city.

The apartment blocks were multi coloured, some strung with flowers, some with gaily coloured washing. The streets revealed avenues and boulevards, punctuated with tree-lined piazzas, where old men like those everywhere in Italy, sat and discussed politics and football.

Most northern Italians joke that Milan, home to the fashion and football industry, is really the capital of their country. Walking through its chic designer shop-lined streets, it is easy to agree with them. In the fashionable Montenapoleone district, there is a bar that sells designer sandwiches named after Moschino and Versace. Milan is quintessentially a northern city, cosmopolitan in its outlook, threaded with arcaded galleries and peppered with beautiful buildings.

In the station, the train would snort to a halt and its weary passengers disembark, each to go their separate ways. We always meandered through the thronging crowds to the notice-board, which had the *'I treni in partenza'* (Departing trains) timetable glued upon it, and looked up our *binario* or platform for Modena. These timetables were exceptionally easy to read and could often be found in glass cases under the arcades in city centres. I seem to remember there was one in Via Emilia in Modena.

Often we would have an hour or two to wait, and we would hunt out the station restaurant and treat ourselves to a big bowl of spaghetti, before boarding the train for Modena. Sometimes we would wander around the vast station, known to be one of the most splendid in Europe, taking in its mosaics and marble, and luxuriating in its opulence. If we had more than a few hours to spare, we would venture out into the Milanese sunshine and explore the surrounding area.

Sometimes we would visit the Duomo or cathedral, which is a triumph of Gothic, fairy tale engineering. The cathedral was begun in 1386, but until this day remains unfinished. Flying buttresses, gargoyles, soaring towers, pinnacles and dreaming spires pierce the ever changing sky. The statue of the Madonina clothed in gold, stands on the highest pinnacle, protecting the city and all who walk down her streets.

Often we would sit in the immense Piazza del Duomo in the very heart of the city, looking at the beautiful cathedral built from white marble, which fronts onto the *piazza*. The square bustles with commuters, tourists, old and young, and a great flock of pigeons who wait hungrily for people to feed them. Around the square there are grand *palazzi* and the arcades are packed with cafés, where one can enjoy an aperitif and indulge in that favourite of Italian sports – people-watching.

The Galleria Vittorio Emanuele is an imposing and beautiful meeting place for the Milanese. It is known as the drawing-room of Milan, and is a masterpiece of arcaded architecture, with complex patterned marble floors and a wonderful iron and glass cupola. We would wander around, gazing at the expensive speciality shops and sophisticated cafés that line the gallery.

Milan has many other attractions, including a castle known as the Castello Sforzesco surrounded by English gardens. Inside is an art gallery, with works by Bellini, Titian, Correggio and Michelangelo. Other interesting places include the canal quarter, the Brera quarter and the Quadrilatero or the fashion district. Often on our journeys back to Modena, we would only have time to explore one aspect of the city and Piazza del Duomo was our favourite place.

Once ensconced in the Modenese train, we would watch the familiar flat landscape speeding by, totally belying the fact that beautiful medieval cities were somewhere hidden in those low lying lands - jewels in the Emilian crown.

~

Another memorable journey occurred during the time when my sister Caroline came to stay with zia Vita for a couple of months, to help her daughter Portia with her spoken English.

Caroline had taken a year's break from her university course and as she was reading history and European studies, thought a short stint in foreign parts would be good experience. Caro was also very politically motivated and was intrigued by the left wing leanings of northern Italy. She also hoped to learn some of the language.

One long week-end at the conclusion of her visit, the two of us decided to take our lives in our hands and visit Naples - 'See Naples and die,' my grandfather used to say, quoting an old proverb, which in time became a sort of family joke.

Our journey down to the south was fairly straightforward. The return journey is the one that sticks in my memory.

Naples is a fascinating place – like the Italy I had always imagined, before actually going there. The narrow streets in the centre were strung with layers of washing, the daily laundry probably forever fluttering between neighbouring balconies, giving the streets a festive air.

Sights and sounds were vigorous. Neopolitans gesticulated animatedly and voices rose and fell dramatically. Singing mingled with television broadcasts emanating from open windows, and everywhere, people shrieked and greeted each other.

It was much dirtier than Modena. We could smell the sea and the garbage at the same time. Impromptu market stalls were set up in unlikely places, selling *cocomoro* or watermelon. There was movement everywhere and lots of vivid colour.

We kept our bags close to our chests, as the fear of being robbed in this notoriously crime ridden city was great. There is no other place in Italy that has the same reputation as Naples and stories of being conned, robbed and taken for a ride, abound. Many years later, Caroline and my mother went on a short trip to that beautiful but dangerous city and both had their luggage, bags and passports stolen on the same day, but in two different incidents.

On our first evening in Naples, Caro and I walked along the promenade that frames the Bay of Naples. There was a tremendous sunset, and Mount Vesuvius loomed in the background in all its beauty. The evening sky was streaked with shots of purple and pink, and a luminous half moon rose in the heavens, casting glints and slivers of silver on the sea below. The sheer beauty of the scene took our breath away.

We decided to find somewhere to eat along the sea front. Naples is a port and fishing is a vigorous industry, so sea food dominated most menus. It is also the city where pizzas originated, and we decided to order pizzas with sea food toppings. A hefty blanket of octopus, squid, shrimps, prawns, whelks and other dainty morsels covered the pizzas and they were delicious.

On our first full day, we visited Pompeii - the beautiful lost city, covered with lava from the eruption of Vesuvius in A.D.79. During the last two centuries, the town was restored as much as was possible, and has provided an insight into how life was lived in those far off days. It is a fascinating and evocative place.

Caroline and I walked down the silent stony streets of Pompeii in the sultry heat and thought about those poor people of long ago, who were killed in an instant, their last actions preserved forever in petrified stone.

"Can't you just imagine the Romans wandering around in their togas before the disaster struck?" I commented.

"Or lying on a Roman settee in one of those houses, with a big bunch of grapes," Caroline added, pointing to one of the villas.

"I'd love to have a glimpse of life in those days," I said. "To mingle with the people in the market place or taste a Roman meal."

We wandered around the place, the scorching sun making our pace quite slow and leisurely. The setting of Pompeii is idyllic - rural and away from the accoutrements of modern surroundings. The grassy slopes surrounding it are covered with beautiful wild flowers, and the intrinsic interest of the ruins makes it a fascinating site.

Just the year before the eruption of Vesuvius, Pompeii was given a warning of the impending disaster, by an earthquake of fairly large proportions. However nothing happened at first and the town continued to flourish, the inhabitants taking no heed. On the 24th August A.D.79, the famous eruption occurred. Pompeii was covered with a layer of tiny fragments of pumice stone called lapilli and afterwards by a covering of ashes. Some fled the city, but many died in the collapse of the buildings, and by breathing in poisonous fumes and the accumulation of volcanic debris.

Pompeii was buried under lapilli, molten flaming lava and ashes, and only the upper parts of some buildings protruded through the debris. Many centuries later these served as an indication of where the lost city had been, and excavations began.

We wandered into the Pompeian houses, through the atriums or inner courtyards which were surrounded by roofed arcades. Many rooms were intact, with painted frescoed walls and wonderful mosaic floors. The walls were divided into three horizontal bands consisting of the dado, central zone and frieze, and were brilliantly coloured, mostly in yellow and red.

The city itself appeared to be designed on a grid system, not unlike New York, which made it easy to walk around, although the cobbles were very uneven. Besides the numerous dwellings, shops and market place known as the Forum, there were temples and theatres and workshops of great interest.

"I think it's such a sad place," remarked Caroline. "All those people who died covered in stone. What a horrible way to go!"

Many of the inhabitants were cloaked in lapilli as they went about their everyday jobs, and have been perpetually preserved in stone like a piece of sculpture. It really is a sobering experience to see these figures in the museum at Pompeii.

The following day we decided to head out of the city, and took a coach trip to the seaside town of Amalfi. The coastal scenery was sensational along the serpentine cliff-top road, and we held our breath and covered our eyes, as the coach swung exhilaratingly up the hair pin bends and up the soaring limestone cliffs. The view was awesome. The clearest greenest sea lay far below us, and lemon scented hill side villages clung to the slopes.

All along this coastline, mountains rise sharply from the sea and tortuous roads zigzag for miles, leaving the passenger either with a feeling of euphoria or with a sense of quivering unease and impending doom.

"I'll be glad when this is over." The elderly woman sitting behind me, said nervously to her companion.

I silently agreed with her, but could not keep my eyes away from the mesmerising view below.

We passed the resorts of Sorrento and Positano, keeping to the coast road in a wild desolate and uninhabited landscape. We had dramatic glimpses of tiny villages, clinging haphazardly to the hill sides, seemingly about to plunge into the indigo bays beneath, surrounded by terraces of vines, fruit and vegetables. Positano seemed to be the stuff that dreams are made of, with colourwashed houses piled in random fashion upon the terraced hill sides. The steep mountains behind were carpeted with pines, cypresses, olive groves and wild rosemary.

Below us, lay a panoramic vista and the small town of Vettica Maggiore. The domes of the church of San Gennaro glistened with a million mosaic pieces. The SITA bus threaded its way along winding roads, alongside olive groves, vines and lemon orchards to Amalfi, where we finally scrambled out, thankful to still be alive after our roller-coaster trip.

Clare Stimpson

Walking along the promenade, we admired the pale coloured houses piled higgledy-piggledy upon each other. It was blisteringly hot, so we made our way past the sedate palms to the small beach, resplendent with colourful umbrellas and reminiscent of a bygone age. It was an exceptionally charming place. Caroline and I had had a very busy couple of days so we opted to stay on the beach and soak up the sun before returning to Naples

Eventually it was time for me to return to Modena. Caroline was travelling to the east coast of Italy to Brindisi, in order to catch a ferry to Greece where she would meet up with some of her friends. Caro's train left at 10 o'clock p.m. The Modena train was due to depart at 10.30 p.m, but it was two hours later when the huge locomotive shuffled to a stop on Napoli station.

The north bound train was packed. There were soldiers on their way to their military service in the north - this is still compulsory for young men in Italy. There were old people, juveniles, and all sorts of characters spilling out of compartments into corridors where they were pressed up against the windows. I, like many others tried to board the train but failed miserably. I decided to spend the night sleeping on the station and to wait for the next train to Milano, which would pass through Modena on its way to the great industrial north.

I found a rather uncomfortable seat on the station platform and tried to settle down for the night. There were plenty of young people doing the same, as most of the trains rolling into the station were full. It was difficult sleeping there, noisy, cold and smelly, and I was always aware of the danger to my bag and money.

In the morning, I awoke after a semi-sleepless night, bleary eyed and in bad humour. I still had the long journey to make north to Modena, which would last for about eight hours or so. In those days trains ran twenty four hours a day and it was possible to travel through the night.

The next train was due at around 8 o'clock a.m. so I found a wash-room and made myself presentable. The 8 o'clock train was late - around two hours in all and when it finally drew to a halt, it too, was packed to the brim. There were even people sitting in the toilets and many of them were holding live birds - hens and chicks. The pungent smell was dreadful.

I had to get on this train. I was obliged to be in Modena for Monday to teach and it was now Sunday morning. I pushed my way on board with others doing the same, and found a small space in one of the corridors. I was shoulder to shoulder with fellow travellers - absolute bedlam! Once past Rome the train emptied a little but I had to stand the whole way to Modena. When I arrived home, my ankles were swollen to twice their normal size with all the standing and heat.

However I soon recovered and had many other happy memories of that weekend to fuel me through the next few weeks, when life in Modena became prosaic, and teaching many hours a day left me feeling tired. I was looking forward to the long summer vacation, even if it was unpaid.

CHAPTER 13
PENNY AND HER PUPS

The time had come to move out of Via Georgi. Monique had decided to move in with her Greek fiancée Spiros, who had travelled from Athens a couple of years before to study law at Bologna University. The owners of the apartment in Via Georgi also wanted their property back for their son who was shortly to be married.

My college friend Teresa had written saying that she would like to spend a year or two in Modena, and it was decided that I should look for an apartment that we could share together. This was easier said than done. Eventually, after trawling around many unsuitable habitats, I found the perfect place in a quiet little street near the northern confines of the city. The street was called Via Zattera.

Teresa and I were to have the top floor of a family residence which belonged to an elderly couple - Signor and Signora Zampini. I was shown around the apartment which had pretty pink marble terrazzo floors.

The flat was self-contained with its own entrance. There was a roomy kitchen and biggish bathroom complete with bidet - very swish! The rest of the apartment consisted of three large rooms and a spacious entrance hall. It seemed like a palace compared to the other Italian places I had lived in. One of the rooms had French windows and a small balcony with a lovely view over red tiled roof tops, interspersed with cypress trees. It was the first apartment I had viewed in weeks that I felt any affinity with. I signed the lease straight away.

"There's only one problem," I said to Paolo later that evening. "It's unfurnished."

I had been so excited at the prospect of living in Via Zattera, that I had completely overlooked the fact that there had been no furniture in any of the rooms.

"What will you do?" he asked, looking thoughtful.

"I have no idea," I replied. "Perhaps we'll have to sleep on camp-beds. I haven't got any spare cash and I don't suppose Teresa has either."

"There's just a small possibility that you might be able to borrow some furniture from Casa della Fontana - I'll ask my parents."

On the day I was due to take possession of my third flat since moving to Italy, Paolo arrived on my doorstep, with a van full of beautiful antique furniture from the mountains.

I was overwhelmed by his family's generosity. Paolo had gathered together some of his friends, and we spent the day hauling furniture up the three flights of steps of Casa Zampini. The old couple peered anxiously out of their door way at the comings and goings on the stairs which were made of marble and had great acoustics.

One piece of furniture, a huge old mirrored wardrobe which I was to have in my room, just would not fit up the stair way.

"I think I'm going to have to take it back," puffed Paolo. "It's not going to fit."

"Please, please try," I begged him. "I really love it!"

But it was no good. The wardrobe would not fit. Then Paolo had a brainwave.

"I know!" He shouted. "We'll haul it up on a pulley through the French windows!"

I thought that he was mad but I had seen Italians hoisting heavy furniture in and out of upper floor windows before, particularly in Florence where many of the medieval *palazzi* do not have lifts, and stair ways are narrow.

After much shouting, shoving, encouragement and pulley shifting, the beautiful wardrobe was finally placed along one of the walls in my room. Paolo provided Teresa and me with a small kitchen table and chairs, an ancient fridge and cooker, two beds, chests of drawers and tables where we could teach our private students. There was a week towards the end of September before Teresa was due to arrive, and I busied myself trying to make the flat look homely with rugs, curtains, cushions and pictures.

By this time I was the proud owner of a little *motorino* or moped. I still had my bicycle, but the moped gave me much more freedom to whiz around. Two panniers attached to the rear enabled me to transport my shopping home easily. Being motorized gave me the possibility of teaching private students, in the outlying villages around Modena.

We now lived on the periphery of the city and the moped facilitated travel into the centre of Modena. Italians buzz around everywhere on these natty little machines. The legal age to ride one is fourteen, so most teenagers own one and often ride them dangerously with two or three perched on the same moped - one on the seat, another sitting on the handlebars and the third standing up somewhere in the middle - life threatening but fun!

Old and middle-aged men and ladies gaily ride on *motorini*, their shopping and other transportable objects strategically placed around them. Italy is a nation of mopeds and the scooter or *motorino* is a way of life. When it rains, people just ride with umbrellas up.

Teresa arrived towards the very end of September, and settled down to the Italian way of life as if she had been born into it. She learnt Italian quicker than I had done, as she was plunged into an Italian speaking set of friends straight away - even I spoke the language now! At first she was rather bemused by *'la dolce vita,'* but quickly settled down and grew to love the pace of life. Many people we met thought she was Italian, as she had big brown eyes, long dark glossy hair and an Italian name.

After a few days of being in the country she met her non-English speaking boyfriend Claudio, who was one of Paolo's friends. The four of us would hang out together, go for meals, or to the Luna Park or cinema, or even to Viareggio on the Tuscan coast where Claudio's family had a small seaside villa.

Viareggio is the gateway to Versilia, a stretch of coastline north of Pisa with glorious white sandy beaches. Surrounding the area is the largest marshland region in Tuscany, which is the habitat of more than 250 species of rare nesting birds. This used to be a swampland, rife with malaria until it was reclaimed in the 1890s, when swimming became fashionable and the area was cleaned up.

Claudio's family were the proud owners of a small whitewashed house, sitting alongside others in a pleasant tree-lined boulevard, framed by palm trees and bougainvillea. The Duchess of Bourbon, Marie Louise, was responsible for the layout of Viareggio, and her good taste resulted in many tree-lined avenues set out in a grid formation. It is now a fashionable seaside resort and is the capital of the Italian Carnival scene. Viareggio is also the place where our own great poet Shelley tragically drowned.

Just up the coast and a little inland, are the towns of Massa and Carrara famous for their creamy white marble. Marble roads run parallel to the coast up into the mountains composed of this valuable commodity, the main ingredient of which is calcium carbonate. In my first year in Modena, one of the other English girls and I had spent a week in Marina di Massa. We swam in a pellucid green sea with a quilted white mountainous backdrop.

Often in Modena, the four of us would go to the cinema which was a great experience, as Italian cinema in the 1970s was a phenomenon. Every street corner was blessed with a picture house, rather like we used to have local pubs in England. There were also open-air cinemas during the summer months, where one could watch a film in the cool of the evening, under a velvety night sky studded with stars, after a sweltering day.

Italy has a wealth of famous film producers - Fellini, Bertolucci and Antonioni to name but a few and all of them from Emilia-Romagna. One film that made a big impression on us during this time was entitled '1900,' directed by Bertolucci and set in Emilia-Romagna, charting the rise of Fascism in the region at the beginning of the 20th century. Italian film directors are well-known for being influenced by their environment.

Fellini who was born in Rimini became famous for his acclaimed films '*La Dolce Vita*' in 1959 and for '*Amacord*' in 1974, meaning 'I remember' in Emilian dialect. This film is set on the Adriatic coast, during the Fascist dictatorship and is based loosely on Fellini's own childhood.

Italian T.V. was not very exciting in the 1970s and I have reason to believe that it is even worse now. The cinema was a much better option, with viewings running almost continuously and well after midnight.

Italian citizens did not seem to mind if they missed the beginning of the film. They came in at any point, even near the end and then stayed for the next viewing, watching the part that they had missed. I found it bizarre to see the end of a film before the opening scenes, but I soon got used to it. Apparently this was quite normal in England during the 1930s and 40s.

The cinema was a hive of activity, with comings and goings throughout the film. People could stay there all day if they wanted and watch the film over and over at no extra cost! There was no rustle of sweet papers, slurping of ice creams or chomping on pop corn as Italians did not eat in this setting. It was a cheap way to spend the evening and as films changed regularly, we went often.

~

One day Paolo arrived on my doorstep looking very excited.

"I've rescued a dog from the gutter," he said. "She's in a dreadful state. I don't think she's eaten for months. She's like a skeleton."

"Well, where is she and what sort of dog is it?" I asked looking around thinking he might have the poor creature with him.

"That's the problem," said Paolo seriously. "I've taken her home but when my mother finds out, there'll be trouble. She won't let me keep the dog but I really want to cure her. I've already bought some tablets and a course of injections. Please, please," he pleaded "can she stay here with you?"

"Paolo, I don't think so," I said horrified, thinking that a flat was no place for a dog to live in. "There's Teresa to think of as well. I don't even know if she likes dogs!"

"Well there's really nowhere else," stated Paolo flatly. "I can't just throw her back onto the streets."

I agreed with him on that point at least, but my heart sank. I loved dogs but did not really have the time to look after one - especially on the third floor of an apartment block with no garden. Also, I wondered what sort of state the poor dog was in.

"What kind of dog is it?" I asked, feeling my resolution ebbing away.

"She's a beautiful red cocker spaniel. You'll love her," Paolo enthused.

"Well I'm not sure."

I was wavering. I could see that I would probably be the one to look after her, as Paolo was studying to be a vet in Parma and could not keep a dog in his digs. I would be the one to take her out for her morning, noonday and evening walk, clean up her mess, feed and groom her etc, etc.

During my teen years, my family had owned a lovely border collie called Dylan. We had pleaded with our parents for a long time for them to buy us a dog. They did not really want to, knowing full well that our hankering for a puppy was probably a whim, and that they would be the ones to end up caring for him, once he was a dog. This is exactly what happened and Dylan really became my mother's dog and close friend.

"Paolo I'll have to ask Teresa," I said weakening. "After all, she lives here too."

"Come over to my house now and see her," Paolo suggested "I'm sure you'll love her."

We sped off in Paolo's little Fiat 500, to his house in the northern part of the city. His parents had recently purchased a new apartment for their retirement. It was elegant, with a grand marble entrance hall and lifts. The interior contained a couple of good sized balconies and spacious rooms.

As Paolo turned the key in the lock, I could hear a whining and growling sound from within the apartment.

"I think she must be scared," said Paolo. "I reckon she's been really badly treated and doesn't trust humans."

The spaniel was sitting in a cardboard box, padded with cushions, inside one of the baths. She was very thin and looked malnourished and neglected. I felt sorry for this poor, shivering, emaciated creature.

Paolo lifted her out of the box and stroked her.

"I think she's got fleas," he said grinning, "but we'll soon sort that out!"

'Oh great,' I thought. "Well make sure you do before she comes to live with us," I said.

Thank Goodness we did not have many rugs or carpets in the flat.

"Who on earth would leave a dog in this terrible state!" I continued.

"Oh, I 'm sure she'll love living with you and Teresa," said Paolo jubilantly. "It's only for the winter months. In the summer she can live up at Casa della Fontana in the mountains."

"Well what shall we call her?" I asked.

"Let's give her an English name, as she'll be living in an English household," Paolo answered. We decided to call her Penny. It seemed to suit her.

Teresa was horrified when she found that we would be sharing our flat with Penny.

"We can't have a dog here!" she cried. "There isn't room!"

"I know," I said. "I'm really sorry. Let's tell Paolo that we'll have her for a week and then he'll have to find somewhere else for her to go."

In fact, Penny stayed with us for nearly a year. She grew as fond of us as we were of her and requested our attention full time. When friends came around she grew very jealous, and sat in her wicker basket in the kitchen sulking, her little face turned away from us, staring at the wall until the friends had left. Penny was a real character.

A few weeks after Penny had settled in, Paolo dropped a bombshell.

"I'm going to mate her with another spaniel - one with a pedigree," he casually informed us. "I want Penny to have puppies."

"What!" Teresa and I gasped together.

"Where exactly is she going to have them?" I demanded.

"Well I was hoping that once she's pregnant, she can have the puppies here" said Paolo in a hopeful tone. "I'll come and deliver them of course."

"No way!" exclaimed Teresa. "It's one thing to look after a poor beaten up dog, but quite another to look after a litter of puppies too. You must think we're mad!"

Teresa and I were adamant, but Paolo would not give up.

"I'll take Penny away with me today," he said "and when she's pregnant I'll bring her back. I promise you, you won't have to do a thing. I'm sure you'll miss her."

And we did. We had become used to her daily walks. Either Teresa or I did the morning shift and the other the evening one. It was difficult getting Penny down the stairs to the road, as the steps were made of a highly polished marble and her poor little paws could not grip the surface, so she would slither and slide all the way down to the bottom. Getting back up was easier.

Penny had to have her long silky ears washed and brushed regularly. They were so long that they trailed in the road and picked up all manner of things.

The marble floors in Italy look beautiful, but need a lot of care and attention. Italy is all about presentation and floors are no exception. Hours are spent with a special polishing machine which buffs up the surface of the marble, and makes it so shiny you can almost see your face reflected in it. Visitors to most homes, are expected to slip their fully clad feet into a contraption that is a cross between a felt slipper and a duster, enabling them to further polish the floors as they walk around their host's or neighbour's house.

Teresa and I were very industrious and kept our flat as shiny as a new pin. Before living in Italy, I had not been particularly meticulous about cleaning and tidying up, nor have I been since returning to England. However while I was living in *la bel paese*, I found myself becoming very house-proud and I felt as if I was turning into an Italian *signorina* who has to have everything just so. Housework was taking over and I had no time to read, sew or paint. I still enjoyed the buzz and adrenaline shot of teaching, but maybe looking after a once sickly dog and her little pups would give more purpose to my life.

Luckily Teresa agreed and when Paolo brought back a pregnant Penny a few weeks later, we were overjoyed to have her back.

"The puppies should be born in about eight week's time, give or take a few days," said Paolo. "You'll have to phone me as soon as you think she's in labour. I'll try to be in Modena that week."

"But what if it's in the middle of the night or if they come early?" asked Teresa uneasily.

"I'll give you a number in Parma to phone as well as Modena," said Paolo. "And I'll talk you through the delivery procedure!"

He laughed at our horrified faces. "Only joking! I'll obviously leave the number of the local vet - but don't worry, I'll be here!"

"You better had," I muttered darkly.

As the weeks went by, Penny grew fatter and fatter and more and more lazy. The poor creature could hardly get up and down the stairs, and most of the time we had to carry her down to street level in her basket.

One evening whilst out for a meal, Paolo and I encountered a couple with whom we became friendly. Lena was Norweigan and Matteo, her husband, Italian. Home for them was a small villa, newly constructed on the outskirts of Modena. They invited us over to meet their bulldogs.

Alba, one of the dogs was also heavily pregnant and when the puppies were born prematurely, Matteo phoned Paolo to ask for his help in assisting with the birth. I also tagged along hoping I might learn something. Nine puppies came into the world, but sadly, only three survived and they were poorly. Alba was not producing enough milk, so we had to feed the hungry pups every two hours or so, from tiny bottles that Paolo managed to procure from somewhere.

I will never forget the feeling of a miniscule baby bulldog in my palm. It was so tiny; his frail vulnerable little body fitted easily into my hand and his soft furry being, quivered and shook. A miniature tongue reached out for the milky bottle, and his doggy eyes remained closed. All three survived and grew up to be fine strong bulldogs.

151

Penny's confinement was drawing to a close. We were all excited at the prospect of the puppies' imminent arrival.

"What will you do with them Paolo?" asked Teresa.

"Well, I'm hoping to sell most of them and keep one for myself," answered Paolo. "The father has a good pedigree and I should be able to get quite a bit of money for them. I may even go into the business of breeding dogs," he added mysteriously. "No seriously, I just want to see them go to good homes."

Teresa and I looked at each other and rolled our eyes upwards. So long as the breeding program did not take place in our apartment!

A few days later Penny started behaving strangely, and we knew the births were imminent.

"Paolo get down here now!" I ordered over the phone. "I think the puppies are about to be born!"

It was quite a respectable hour, about five o'clock in the evening. Paolo arrived almost immediately. He was carrying his black vet's bag and various other bits of equipment.

A few days before, we had moved Penny upstairs to a sort of attic called a *solaio*, which is standard in most Italian apartments, and situated at the very top of the building. Ours was just above our flat. The *solaio* is a communal area where people hang their washing when it rains, and where there are extra rooms for residents to store their junk. It was darkish and quiet and few people rarely ventured up there - perfect for Penny who needed peace and rest.

Paolo went up to attend the birth. I put on the kettle to boil up some hot water, just in case! At any rate, we all needed a good strong cup of tea.

"Clare and Teresa get up here quickly," shouted Paolo excitedly. "The first pup has been born."

We raced up the stairs two at a time. Penny was lying on her side and Paolo was briskly rubbing down her new born, who was completely black in colour. Eventually two more black puppies and one ginger coloured one, in the image of Penny, made their entrance into the world. All four were soon noisily slurping milk and thriving well.

Paolo sat up with them all night, but was so confident that they were doing well that he returned to Parma University later that week, to sit one of his many exams, leaving Teresa and me in charge, with strict instructions to ring him should anything go amiss.

Day by day, the little pups grew. They were very labour intensive and had to be litter trained. They constantly yapped in unison and people in the building started complaining. Although they were adorable, Teresa and I both felt that it was time for their departure.

Paolo had already found some prospective buyers for the black spaniel pups and he decided to keep the ginger one for himself. He called her Florence and sneaked her home one day when Signora Contarini was out. Of course she discovered his secret, but in time she grew very fond of Florence, and like my mother had with my dog, became her keeper. The two enjoyed many happy years together.

Florence loved to go up with Penny to Casa della Fontana every hot summer, where she frolicked with the fireflies and snoozed in the long, lush grass.

CHAPTER 14
LEAVING LA DOLCE VITA

All good things come to an end. Over the three years that I had lived in Italy, my relationship with Paolo had been on and off and I was desperately yearning to return to England, for some time to assess the situation and perhaps make a new life for myself.

At this time Paolo was not even living in Modena but had taken up residence in the beautiful historic city of Parma, where he was studying to be a vet. Parma is about thirty kilometres north of Modena, and as neither of us possessed cars at that time and our working hours were complicated, we saw very little of each other.

During this time, I made various journeys to Parma by train. It is a charming city, on the main railway route going up to Milan. In the 1970s, like Modena, it was a bastion of Communism. The hammer and sickle motif was ubiquitous, and copies of Communist and Socialist newspapers were glued to notice-boards all over the city.

During the Second World War, it was a centre for the Resistance Movement and this is commemorated in Parma with statues of these brave fighters. In fact, it was the last city in Italy to succumb to the Fascist regime back in 1922. Parma was badly bombed during the more recent allied raids, but fortunately the medieval centre was spared.

Despite its Communist connection, the Parmigiani always appeared affluent, well-heeled and contented with life - very similar to the characteristics displayed in Modena.

In the heart of Parma is the Piazza del Duomo, a fine cobbled square, bordered by the cathedral, bell-tower, exquisite baptistry and Bishop's Palace. This is guarded by marble lions, similar to those sleepy stone creatures standing sentinel outside Modena cathedral. The Duomo, like that of Modena, is Romanesque and its cupola is covered with a painting of the Assumption by Correggio. The interior was actually damaged by an earthquake in 1117, but was restored to its former beauty in 1130.

Correggio who lived from 1489 - 1534, was a self-taught artist and he influenced Parmigianino, who was one of the most important painters in Italy in the first half of the 16th century. Parmigianino, so nicknamed because of his birth in Parma, was the founder of the European Mannerist Movement, excelling in his use of colour and his graceful figurative compositions.

The baptistry in Parma is a memorable building, being octagonal in shape and five stories high. It is Romanesque-Gothic in style and its galleried interior is adorned with the most beautiful frescoes imaginable.

Parma is famous for its tasty, finely cut slivers of ham and Parmesan cheese. The pigs that are bred for the ham are fattened on chestnuts and whey, which is the milk left over from the cheese making, and they are bred only for salami and hams. Often these meats are hung up to cure for about a year. The delicatessen or *salumerie* in Parma, are awash with hanging hams and pungent smelling salamis.

Other mouth watering treasures such as stuffed tomatoes and peppers, little meatballs spiced with garlic and rosemary and roast chicken and quails, adorn the shop windows. Like its sister cities, Modena and Bologna, Parma is a gastronomic delight.

My main memory of Parma is of its shoe shops, selling wonderful, soft leather foot wear. Like Modena, the city has a plethora of small individual shops tucked away in the city's historic alleyways. These fascinating little businesses are often passed down through the generations, and some of them have hardly changed over the centuries. I loved to visit Parma but it did not feel as comfortable as Modena did.

One day in Modena, I was walking along Via Giardini, a long tree-lined, arterial, traffic laden road leading to the city centre. It was a bright, crisp, September morning and the dried gold and red leaves crunched and crackled under my feet. Long edged shadows flickered through the overhead canopy of trees and filtered into every corner.

It was a beautiful early autumnal day, but I felt weary at the thought of another winter in fog bound Modena, and the fact that my life seemed to be going nowhere. At that moment I decided I would return to England.

Teresa was shocked when I told her my plans.

"But you can't go," she cried. "Please won't you stay? There's so much we can still do together!"

I was adamant. I phoned up the language school and told Rita that I would not be returning in October. I asked her if Teresa could take my place and as she already knew her, she agreed. I pulled out my faithful trunk and each day packed away some of the treasures I had accumulated. It was not an easy task and my resolve almost weakened.

I spent some days visiting the Contarini clan to say my 'good-byes.' It was to be the hardest part of my leaving. They had become my surrogate family in Italy, and I wondered if I would ever see any of them again. Signora Contarini agreed to take care of Penny and Florence.

"You are always welcome to stay with us," said Signora Contarini with tears in her eyes. "Please come and stay with us up in the mountains any time during the summer."

I assured her that I would love to.

Back at the apartment, my lovely room looked bare, and I had to repaint all the walls as there were marks around the pictures that I had put up and had now taken down. Paolo assured me that sometime he would return all the furniture to the mountains. My trunk was packed and despatched.

I almost changed my mind a hundred times about returning home, but I felt that I had become Italianised and needed to touch base with my roots. I walked for the last time down Via Emilia, through the elegant arcades, into Piazza Grande where I was confronted by the wonderful cathedral and Ghirlandina. All around me were the characteristic ochre coloured buildings and faded green shutters. People were riding bicycles and mopeds, chatting to friends or busying themselves with the daily shopping routine.

The elderly men, sombrely dressed, were gathered in groups, animatedly discussing politics or football. It was a typical scene of Modena that I would treasure forever. I walked on through the vegetable market and mingled with the women looking for the freshest greens of the day. The aroma of percolated coffee wafted down the narrow street.

At last, the sad day of my departure arrived. I had said all my farewells - my *arrivederci*. I felt that I had fulfilled my dream. I had lived the Italian life - *'la dolce vita.'* It had been everything I had expected and more. I had loved every minute of it but now it was time to go back.

Life in England was grand for a while, but day after day, the dream came back to haunt me, until I could ignore it no longer. I knew that I had to return to Italy.

Modena's Romanesque Cathedral with its stunning
rose stained glass window

Clare Stimpson

Piazza Grande with the beautiful Duomo or Cathedral in the
background

The grinning lions outside the Duomo

The Gothic façade of Modena Cathedral

Piazza Grande on a Monday morning, filling up with men

The Ghirlandina surrounded by birds

The Modenese chatting in Piazza Grande

Kate aged about ten years, tucking into a plate of
spaghetti whilst staying in Siena

My lovely green and red bicycle

Casa della Fontana nestled amongst the Apeninnes

Penny at Casa della Fontana.

Mum, Kate and myself, somewhere on Lake Garda

Kate and Dad sitting in Catullus' grotto

Boats on Lake Garda

Having a rest in Sermione

Pallio day in Siena

Basking in the sun near Naples

Florence's magnificent skyline

Discussing plans in a Florentine street

In Venice, with the Bridge of Sighs in the background

Venice 'La Serenissima'

Somewhere along the Amalfi coast

Pompeii

PART TWO

ITALY REVISITED

CHAPTER 15 SAN REMO

'*La bel paese*' came back to haunt me so much that I could only stay in England for a couple of months. It was fine at first being in the old country. I met up with friends and found a temporary post teaching art at a girls' school where my father worked, but the pull of Italy was always there, always somewhere in the back of my head and always pervading and colouring my dreams. Trying to get back to Italy became an obsession.

While I lived there, I was often discontented with many aspects of the Latin way of life, and I was becoming seriously fed up with the political situation, and the fact that every time I visited Bologna, I seemed to become involved in some minor terrorist activity or student unrest.

I was often irritated and infuriated with the endless bureaucracy that bogged the country down, but I loved the people, the language, the art, the food, the wonderful mesmerising countryside and the fact that there was very rarely a dull moment. The Italians live life to the full and having experienced a slice of their *joie de vivre* it was impossible to not want more. Stendhal wrote that living in Italy is 'akin to that of being in love' and I totally agree with him. After leaving I felt sad and restless, and was determined to go back and start again.

I also felt an affinity with the Italians - in fact, far more so than with the British. Even though many northern Italians were Communists, most were born into Catholicism and as I was also a member of this faith, it held no mysteries for me.

During my convent schooldays I was brought up on miracles, appearing Madonnas, feast days, holy days of obligation, rosaries and novenas and it was always comforting and familiar to chance upon a niche set in a wall, complete with a statue of Our Lady surrounded by candles and flowers. She is to us Catholics the mother of all mothers, and is particularly venerated and adored in Italy; this could be one reason why Italian motherhood commands such important status. Mama is usually much more exalted than Papa. Mama is often put up on a pedestal.

Italians are a paranoid nation in the loosest sense of the word. They observe lots of suspicious rules and regulations, for example, the belief that if one does not leave at least four hours before swimming after eating, then, one will surely drown. There are many such idiosyncrasies. I found this way of thinking suited my mentality much more than the phlegmatic British approach to life. Mystery and intrigue was much more interesting.

As each new day approached, I longed to return to Italian soil. In mid November, when the days were chilly and bleak, I noticed an advert in one of the national newspapers for an E.FL. teacher in San Remo, on the Ligurian coast of Italy.

"Oh you'd really love it there," said my father, who had probably had enough of me hogging the one and only bathroom every morning.

"It's fantastic in November - warm like an English summer. The Riviera's a very nice part of the world. I wouldn't mind teaching English there myself!"

I mulled over the situation, and within a week I was southward bound on the Calais to Genoa express, heading for a new Italian adventure. As usual, I travelled overnight complete with masses of luggage. Next morning feeling dishevelled, I struggled out of the high old-fashioned train, onto a platform dappled with sunshine and brimming with tropical flora.

I found the much smaller local train for San Remo, and we chugged our way along the ravishing, Ligurian coast. Faded pastel coloured apartments and villas with verandas clung to the steeply rising cliffs and the Mediterranean was a deep indigo, edged with pure white lace along its shoreline. Colourful fishing boats bobbed on the water and picturesque villages huddled amongst the nets and lobster pots.

Eventually we reached San Remo, and once again I hoisted myself out of the train carriage onto another pretty flowery platform. Palm trees rustled and people moved about leisurely. I took a taxi to the International School of English where I would be working for the next few months.

The owner of the school was a pleasant, vague, middle-aged gentleman called Charles. He appeared a tad disorientated and disorganised. His slightly long hair was tinged with grey and his glasses kept slipping down his nose.

"Good afternoon," he shook my hand. "Oh, er um you must be......
Who do you say you are?" he asked with a quizzical expression on his careworn face.

He pushed his spectacles onto his forehead and scrutinised me absent-mindedly.

"I'm here to teach English." I replied, smiling. "My name's Clare."

"Oh yes, yes of course. Did you have a good journey?" He rustled some sheaths of paper and frowned.

"We weren't expecting you until tomorrow," he said. "But never mind, you're here now. Maria, my secretary will take you to your apartment after I've shown you around the school."

We had a guided tour of the classrooms and then I was handed the key to my flat.

"Oh by the way," added Charles. "I forgot to tell you. Two evenings a week, you'll be teaching in Ventimiglia on the French border."

My heart sank. "How will I get there?" I asked. There had been no mention of Ventimiglia in the job description. I was beginning to be less than happy and my confidence was starting to slip.

"Oh there are lots of trains. It's just up the coast," he explained waving his hands about vaguely.

I was not impressed and found it hard to hide my disappointment.

"Well let's see how it goes," he said, trying to placate me.

However I did not feel appeased and later learnt that two of the new teachers who had only started in September had already left and returned to England. Somehow I was not surprised.

I was introduced to Maria who was to be my chaperone for the afternoon. She was a young, pretty Italian girl in her early twenties, a similar age to me and during my stay in San Remo we became firm friends. We piled my entire luggage into the back of her tiny Fiat 500 and set of through the imposing looking town and along the winding coast road.

"Maria, isn't my apartment in the city centre?" I asked wondering how I was going to travel back and forth. I could have done with my lovely bicycle and moped but they were both in Modena.

"No it's a few kilometres outside," smiled Maria. "There's a bus and the service is reasonable."

I complimented her on her command of the English language and she told me that her mother was Irish, but that her parents were divorced and her mother had returned to Dublin.

We left San Remo far behind. The coastal road was wild and windswept with giant cacti, palms and other exotic fleshy plants, punctuating the narrow verges. Below the turquoise sea glistened and shimmered enticingly. It really was a stunning place.

After driving uphill for a short while, Maria pulled to an abrupt stop, outside what seemed to be a solitary block of apartments, the ground floor of which revealed a bar, a restaurant, a hairdressers and a florist shop.

"Well this is it," she said. "I'll come up with you and help you with all your bags. It's not actually this block," she continued "but the one behind."

We passed through a small tunnel linking the two buildings. The second set of apartments seemed closed up and forlorn. There were no lights in any of the windows and it emitted an eerie, sinister presence.

"It looks a bit deserted," I commented to Maria.

"Well," she looked very uncomfortable. "No one actually lives here at the moment. These are all summer holiday flats."

I was speechless for a moment. "I'll be the only person living in this enormous block of flats? I don't think I can stay here on my own. I'm afraid the whole idea's horrible and scary!"

I was upset and nervous at the idea of living alone in a huge deserted building. No wonder the other English teachers had fled!

"I'm really sorry," said Maria gently. "I've told Charles that the teachers don't like living here - but really there's nowhere else in San Remo. Rents are terribly expensive in the city centre. This flat belongs to the school and it's nice and cheap. Come and have a look. Anyway there may be another English teacher arriving soon, who'll probably live next door to you."

We pushed open the door and the inside revealed spacious accommodation, with a balcony overlooking the lush vegetation and the sparkling sea. It would be fine during the day but how would I feel once night fell?

"Let's see how it goes," said Maria who had obviously learnt that phrase from the ever optimistic Charles.

"I'll leave you to do your unpacking and then call back at 7.30 p.m," she called, exiting. "We'll go and eat a pizza or something."

The flat was bare - institutionalised even, with white walls and the minimum of furniture. I thought longingly of my last place in Via Zattera, and wondered why on earth I had left. I felt alone and did not want to be in San Remo.

By the time Maria arrived back, I had unpacked. I did not have all my belongings with me as my trunk was in transit, but I had remembered to include my Indian bed spread and some large Japanese prints and these instantly cheered the place up.

"Ciao," Maria greeted me. "Oh, you have made the flat look homely."

We chatted for about ten minutes and then clattered down the stairs to the ground floor, calling into the nearby Bar Jolly for an aperitif.

"How long have you worked at the school?" I asked.

"About six months," she replied. "To be honest, I'm thinking of leaving as it's a bit disorganised. As you know two teachers have already given up and a few left last year before their contracts were up."

This was not what I wanted to hear.

We finished our drinks and drove along the spectacular coast road down to San Remo, the largest resort and self-styled capital of the Italian Riviera di Ponente, which is the stretch of coastline between the French border and Genoa. It seemed very elegant and glamorous and had a cosmopolitan atmosphere.

Ravishing art nouveau villas and hotels lined the streets, with views of the surrounding hill sides. Although it was November, the climate was indeed mild and many people were enjoying an early evening drink in the outside bars.

San Remo is situated on a broad sweeping bay, nestled between twin headlands. Its popularity as a classy place to be, reached a peak from about 1850 to the outbreak of the Second World War. The wonderful winter climate, genteel atmosphere and beautiful art nouveau Liberty style architecture, attracted the nobility of the era, particularly the British and the Russians. The Empress Maria Alexandrovna became one of the most famous residents of the town and exerted a lot of influence over the place. The palm-lined promenade, Corso Imperatrice, is named after her.

It must have been a very beautiful place at the beginning of the 20th century, but Maria and I noticed on our drive to the centre, that some of the splendid villas around the station area were dirty and grimy, and could do with a spot of restoration. In the more classy districts however, the villas were beautifully presented, some decorated with ornate brickwork in the form of swags and floral patterns.

We parked near the palm-lined promenade. Dusk was just falling, and a thousand tiny lights lit up the bay like a string of twinkling diamonds. A crescent moon floated in the indigo sky and dropped its shafts of light on the unruffled sea below. It seemed perfect.

We decided to forgo the pizzas and made instead for a small, centrally located trattoria that Maria was fond of, called 'Nuovo Piccolo Mondo' which had a lovely family atmosphere. I learnt that it had first opened its doors in the 1920s and had been run by generations of the same family who still owned it.

As usual I could not resist a plate of spaghetti and there were so many Ligurian specialities available, that I found it difficult to choose which sauce to have with it. Apparently Liguria has the longest life expectancy of any region in Italy and the healthy fishy Mediterranean diet contributes to this.

After eating our fill, we ambled back to the car. It was pitch black by now and the drive back to my apartment along the coast road, seemed lonely and forbidding. I tried not to think about it but I was not looking forward to spending the night alone in an eerie building, with no neighbours in the immediate vicinity.

However my journey had exhausted me so much that I had no trouble sleeping that night. The next day, I was to report to the school and receive my timetable for the coming months. Charles informed me that I would be teaching mainly in the evenings - three in San Remo and the other two in Ventimiglia on the French / Italian border.

I was still not happy with this latter placement, and did not relish the thought of travelling by train along the Ligurian coast in the late evening hours. Even after I had arrived in San Remo from Ventimiglia, I would still have to catch a bus to my lonely apartment. The whole idea seemed impossible.

I had one last day before teaching was due to begin, so I decided to explore the old medieval part of San Remo, called La Pigna. This intriguing part of the town is reached by steep lanes to the north of the more commercial seaside resort. This historic quarter is a warren of tiny alleyways, many of them with flights of steps and vaulted ceilings, reminiscent of somewhere like northern Africa and very much in marked contrast to the wealth and glamour of the modern town below. This neglected part was really picturesque. It was where the old people and the working folk lived and had been doing so for generations.

After exploring La Pigna, I climbed up to Piazza Castello, where I was rewarded with a stunning, panoramic view of the town below. I then sauntered back to the modern part, taking in the Giardino Ormond en route. This wonderful garden is filled with date palms, bougainvillea, jacaranda, olive trees and even yuccas as well as other exotic species. The heavy scent was glorious.

San Remo is really famous for its flower markets, the most notorious of which is the *Mercato dei Fiori*, Italy's most important wholesale and cut flower market, open only to traders. Carnations, mimosa, roses and other beautiful blooms are shipped from here all over the world. Sometimes the town centre revealed evidence of the early morning traders, with flower heads and greenery littering the place

Towards the end of my first week on the Rivirea, some friends that I had made at the school drove me along the coast road to Monte Carlo for the day, and I noticed that much of the landscape around San Remo was dedicated to the flower raising industry.

The terraced hillsides were covered with row upon row of cultivated blooms, many under plastic tarpaulins, or in greenhouses which gleamed and shimmered in the distance like a thousand humped-back bridges of glass. I thought that these plastic domes spoilt the beautiful landscape, with its lush vegetation of oleanders, citrus trees and tamarisks.

Four kilometres east of San Remo is Armea, home to the lively, early morning wholesale flower market of the region. This small town springs to life at around 4.00 a.m. when there is great hustle and bustle amongst the dawn traders. Vans and vespas are adorned with boxes, which will carry the sweet smelling produce to their export destinations. By the time most ordinary folk are up and ready for their day's work, the trade at Armea is done and dusted until the next morning.

The hinterland of San Remo remains hilly and the landscape contains silvery olive groves. Herbs such as lavender, rosemary and thyme are cultivated in the lush surroundings.

After a relaxing stroll in Giardino Ormond and admiring the exotic blooms there, I decided to pay a visit to the Gothic cathedral of San Siro. I learnt from some other English tourists that the wonderful façade of this late Romanesque cathedral was restored around 1900, and it looked glorious with 12th century bas reliefs above its side doors. The interior was serene, with luminous pools of candle light brightening dim corners - an oasis of calm in contrast to the clamour of the Ligurian streets.

I had heard about the Russian Orthodox, onion domed church called San Basilio which was built in the 1920s, another legacy of the Empress Maria Alexandrovna and which served the Russian contingent of that time. I thought it sounded interesting and decided to take a peek. However its exterior with its bulbous shaped towers and ornate crosses and wedding cake façades, was much more impressive than the inside.

Having seen enough of churches for one day, I continued my exploration of San Remo, by walking down Corso Imperatrice which lines the sea-front and is named after that ever popular Russian Empress.

In the 19th century, numerous wide, palm-lined avenue*s* were created to facilitate gentle and healthy strolling for the newly arrived foreign travellers. These elitist visitors loved coming to San Remo, particularly in the winter because of the mild climate and romantic setting.

Tchaikovsky and Edward Lear the nonsense poet both lived in Corso Imperatrice, with its charming, floral, Liberty style architecture. Nearby, is the sophisticated Art Nouveau Casino, a white Liberty style palace with distinctive turrets and sweeping staircases, designed by the French architect Eugene Ferret and built during the early 1900s. Outside this imposing building there are shady palms and gently flapping flags.

The modern part of San Remo seemed very classy and chic. I wandered towards the Mediterranean and down to the small, sea-scented beach. I was surprised to see a few hardy souls sunbathing in the mild November weather.

I had arranged to meet Maria in a sea-front bar at about 5 o'clock. I caught sight of her dark, shiny head and waved.

"Ciao! Have you had a good day?" she asked.

"Yes thanks. San Remo is a fascinating place and I'm sure I've only seen parts of it."

"Well there's plenty of time to see the rest. What would you like to drink?" asked Maria beckoning the waiter.

"I think I'll have a Cinzano," I answered settling back in my seat.

The late November sunshine beat down on us and was surprisingly hot and pleasant. It would probably be raining in England right now, I thought to myself. Really, San Remo wasn't so bad after all!

However my euphoria soon evaporated after spending another lonely night tucked away in the 'House of Horrors.' Luckily Maria had given me a lift home that evening and I retired to bed early, as tomorrow would be my first day teaching at the International School. I shut my eyes and tried in vain to think of pleasant thoughts, but every little creak and night-time noise woke me with a start and I failed to feel comfortable or reassured.

Next morning I arose early feeling wan with tiredness, and pottered around the apartment trying to make it feel like home. I threw open the large French window and drank my coffee on the veranda. I thought wistfully that it could be idyllic if only it were not so isolated. By day light, the apartment lost its menacing feel and I loved the spectacular view along the coastline.

My first class was scheduled for 5 o'clock that evening, so at around 4 o'clock I sauntered down the marble stairs and out into the mild winter sunshine. My first task was to find the bus-stop which was fairly easy, and after a couple of minutes an old 1960's automobile rumbled into view. The journey down the coast road was breathtaking. We hurtled around very tight bends without slowing down. I had to hold on tightly to the seat in front, or I would have fallen out onto the floor. The landscape was exotic, and the air coming through the bus's open windows was warm and fragrant.

~

My first class went well. The students were all fairly young. Advanced English conversation was the order of the day. They were eager to practice their English and wanted to discuss life in Britain.

"Is it true that all Englishmen go to work wearing bowler hats and carrying umbrellas?" asked Simonetta.

I laughed and dispelled this very popular myth that exists amongst Italians. It was not the first time I had heard this assumption. The 1960's T.V. programmes 'The Avengers' had a lot to answer for ! It reminded me of my own preconceptions of Italy before I actually came to the country.

We talked for a while about English customs and work, and then settled on the topic of English food which usually sends every Italian into a frenzy of negative expletives.

"English food is really disgusting," said Fabio a young man of about 18 years. "When I visited London last year, I didn't eat anything I liked. Luckily I brought lots of Italian food with me - and your coffee - ugh!"

I had to agree with him about the coffee. In the 1970s, typical English food was rather dire and unimaginative and of course Italian food was delicious. But how times have changed! Now Britain boasts some of the most cosmopolitan cooking in the world and its restaurants are second to none, whist in my opinion, Italian cooking has remained static - it always was good and it still is!

My evening finished at 10 o'clock. I packed my bags and wearily made my way to the door. In my opinion, teaching E.F.L. requires a lot of stamina as the conversation teacher is constantly standing or walking around, directing questions and correcting answers. It is enjoyable but there is no let up. The emphasis is on the spoken word and concentration has to be absolute. Students expect the teacher to correct their every word. It is a little like being on stage!

I had enjoyed my evening, but no one had stayed behind to chat or go for a pizza as they used to do in Modena. Maria worked during the day, so she was not there. The whole place was deserted apart from Charles who was waiting to lock up, keys in hand.

"Well how did your first day go?" He asked, jangling his bunch of keys.

"Not too bad thank you. I enjoyed it," I replied.

I bid him good night and made my way down the street to the bus-stop. After about 15 minutes, the old vehicle arrived and transported me up the coast to my unwelcoming little home. Looking out of the bus windows, all I could see was darkness with the odd twinkling light on the horizon.

In the dark I was not quite sure where my stop was and panicked for a while, until I saw the brightly lit neon lights of Bar Jolly in the distance. The bus stopped with a jerk and I tumbled out, thankful to be on familiar ground.

I fumbled my way through the pitch black and in through the front door of the apartment block. Breathing a sigh of relief, I pressed the timer switch just by the door and the place was flooded with brilliant light. This bright new world would only last for three minutes. Italian condominiums usually have these annoying three minute lights, which give people just enough time to rush up the stairs to their flats before the switches go off. Too bad if you are old, or tired, or have a bad leg - you have to find another switch and press that if you want more light!

I awoke next morning with a thumping headache, and a feeling of depression swept over me at the thought of having to go to Ventimiglia. I spent the day preparing my lessons for that evening, and reluctantly left the apartment at around 3 o'clock, to be at the frontier for a 5 o'clock start. I was not sure how long the train journey would take, and I did not want to be late on my first day.

The train for Ventimiglia was a *locale* or local one, and fairly basic. It was already standing at the platform when I arrived at the station, and did not appear to be going anywhere in a hurry. I settled myself down inside, and twenty minutes later, it slid noisily along its tracks and out into the early evening sunshine.

The 10 mile journey was scenic enough, sometimes passing through tunnels hewn through the rocky coastline, sometimes running parallel to the aquamarine sea. We stopped at Bordighera, which glimpsed from the train window, appeared similar to San Remo. Date palms and *fin-de-siecle* architecture predominated, and the station was well kept and full of tropical plants.

We sped on to Ventimiglia, and I was surprised at the size of the station there - it was enormous - perhaps because it is a border station. The town looked like it had seen better days, although the scruffy buildings did have a certain charm with tall dark houses jostling together and gaily coloured washing strung from windows, recalling southern Italy rather than the Riviera.

The International School of English was situated in one of the main streets radiating from the station, and was relatively easy to find. I introduced myself to Bruno who was in charge there, and received my timetable for the two evenings that I would be working in this unknown place, each week.

Most of my students were office workers or civil servants and very amusing. Soon it was time to board the train for the return journey at 10.15p.m. Unfortunately on this particular evening, the San Remo train was over an hour late, and by the time I reached my destination I had just missed the last coastal bus up to my apartment.

I wandered out of the station and into the darkness. In Italy, I have rarely felt unsafe alone at night - not like I do in England. Often, when I lived in Modena, I would ride home from a friend's house late at night on my bike or *motorino*, without feeling the slightest bit worried. In the three to four years that I lived in Modena, not a single person had to my knowledge, been attacked - let alone murdered. I felt reasonably safe in San Remo too, but I was not prepared to walk the couple of miles up the coast road alone at midnight.

I did not have enough money for a taxi, and the only alternative was to go back into the station and phone Maria for advice. It was reassuring to hear her voice amid the darkness and she promised to drive down to the station and give me a lift home.

I was very grateful to Maria, but obviously this was a situation that could not be repeated too often. I decided that next morning, I was going to tell Charles that I was only prepared to work in San

Remo. This did not go down too well but I stood my ground and would not be manipulated. Charles lost no time in telling me that he was going to advertise straight away for another teacher and that if I did not reconsider the situation, I was in danger of losing my job.

I had a lot of thinking to do. I was not really happy in San Remo, but looking back now, I do not think I was really prepared to be. I wanted to be in Modena. After deliberating for a while, I decided to give Ventimiglia another try - after all the students there were really nice - it was just the journey that was precarious and unpredictable. I decided that if I did stay, I would definitely look for another flat, preferably in the centre however difficult and expensive that appeared to be.

It was already December. The next Ventimiglia day dawned bright but a little colder. The warm balmy days of November had passed and there was a decided nip in the air. I tried not to feel apprehensive about the coming evening, but my pessimism was justified and as I had mentally predicted, the train for San Remo was late again, leaving me without a bus and having no option but to take a taxi.

All these fares were costing me a fortune and taking up a lot of my salary, leaving me with very little cash. Buying a car was not an option as I could not drive then, and a moped would not get me to Ventimiglia as it was too far away. I decided to give in my notice and either return to Modena, or go back to England.

The next day I rang Paolo. We had remained friends and he was surprised to hear that I was back in Italy. He promised to come to San Remo at the weekend and take me back to Modena, to stay with his family until I had made up my mind what to do.

I said my good-byes. It seemed to be becoming a habit with me. Charles had already found another gullible teacher who was to take my place. I felt sorry for the students, never seeming to have any continuity and I knew I would miss Maria. One last job remained to be done before heading off to Modena - I had to see if my trunk had arrived at the station and decide what to do with it.

Each day, the weather was growing colder and there was a decided nip in the air when I arrived at the Dogana or customs section of the station. The tropical potted plants seemed a little wilted and incongruous, and their colours had faded in the cool clear atmosphere. I made my way to the wooden counter and asked the man in charge if a trunk had arrived from England.

"*Si, si Signorina. È arrivato ieri – ecco lo.*" (Yes, yes Miss. It arrived yesterday - here it is).

Beaming from ear to ear, he pulled my familiar trunk from under the counter.

"Please will you sign for it," he thrust a pen into my hand.

"I'm sorry," I said "but I don't want to take it. Please could you send it back to the address in England that's on the side."

"You can't send it back," he shrieked, horrified at the idea. "It's only just arrived."

"Yes I know," I explained sheepishly. "But I'm not staying here. It needs to go back to England."

"Very well but it will cost you!" he added hoping I would change my mind and thus avoid all the bureaucracy and red tape that was obviously going to ensue.

I had to rewrite the address on the front, and pay about 20.000 lira - the equivalent of roughly £13 which was a lot in those days, but I was happy that the matter was settled. My parents probably would not be quite so ecstatic when the scruffy, well travelled, battered old trunk arrived on their doorstep, but it would not fit in Paolo's Fiat 500, and I did not want to burden the Contarini household with its bulky presence.

CHAPTER 16 MODENA REVISITED

Skirting the coastline, and weaving the car around tiny coves and secret grottoes, we left the sparkle and colour of the Mediterranean far behind, and headed through the mountainous terrain of the Apennines, towards the flat lowlands of the Po and the ethereal misty city of Modena.

The Contarinis were surprised to see me and kindly suggested that I should stay with them until I had sorted myself out, which would probably be sometime in the New Year. I was immensely grateful for their hospitality. They fixed up a bed for me in the study which became an impromptu bedroom at night and a work place by day. I contacted some of the private students that I had been teaching in the summer before I had left, and the Contarinis allowed me to tutor them in their study, which was very generous.

On the Friday before Christmas, Antonella and I wandered into the city centre, with a view to visiting the busy morning market. We walked through bustling Via Emilia, and the familiar landmarks gladdened my heart. As usual, the centre was a hive of activity, with ubiquitous orange trolley-buses gliding alongside the seemingly ever increasing number of timeless bicycles, shiny mopeds and revving Vespas. It was a cold day, shrouded in mist - typical of Modena. The shop windows were brightly lit like beacons, inviting and warm against the dimness and the stark bitter chill of outside.

We dawdled on our way to Piazza Grande, looking in the shop windows as we went. They were not particularly Christmassy - not full of gaudy decorations as they would have been in England, but they held their own charm. Some of them exhibited a nativity crib or crèche, displaying a miniature stable with statues of Mary, Joseph, donkeys, angels and the three kings with the Christ child at the centre of the scene.

The nativity crib was introduced to Italy by St. Francis of Asissi. One Christmas, the saint asked a certain Giovanni Vellita to create a manger scene, in front of which he said mass. This made such a lasting impression on all who witnessed it, that it was repeated year after year.

That year, Christmas Eve was cold and wintry, but instead of the usual nebulous writhing mists, the sky was a deep blue and the day sparkled and danced under the azure sky. In the evening before midnight mass, a simple supper of fish was consumed.

Christmas Eve is not as exciting for Italian children as it is for their English counterparts. In Italy, the main exchange of gifts takes place on 6th January or the feast of the Epiphany, and the celebration is in remembrance of the Magi's visit to the baby Jesus.

On this night, children await a visit, not from Father Christmas, but from the *'Befana'* a sort of white Epiphany witch who comes down the chimney on a broomstick, bringing toys to the good children and pieces of coal to the naughty ones. The children leave an orange and a glass of wine for the old woman, and some of them believe that she is Father Christmas's wife, who lives at the South Pole while he lives in the north.

According to an ancient myth, three wise men stopped during the long journey they were making and asked an old woman - *La Befana,* for food, drink and shelter. She refused and so they continued on their way. However after a few hours, the women had a change of mind but the Magi were long gone. *La Befana,* so the legend goes, still searches the earth looking for the baby Jesus.

At eleven o'clock that evening, we ventured out with the purpose of going to midnight mass in the Duomo. We underestimated how many others had the same idea and the medieval Duomo was packed, long before midnight. The 12th century doors were flung open so that the faithful outside could at least hear the choir, and catch glimpses of the enticing candle lit interior - a haven of warmth on that cold, clear night. We were wrapped up well against the freezing air and as midnight approached, Piazza Grande filled with Modenese of all shapes and sizes, all of whom were hoping to find a place in the cathedral.

The pungent, spicy smell of incense wafted through the doors, and the heavenly voices of the singers also reached us. Above, the illuminated Ghirlandina soared upwards towards Heaven, and a liberal sprinkling of tiny stars was tossed at random throughout the clear, dark blue ether.

We were a merry party as we drove homewards, laughing and joking. We were looking forward to Christmas Day, when we had all been invited to zia Vita's Modenese house for lunch. The next morning we surfaced later than usual, and the entire Contarini family including Gabriella who was by now living in England and on holiday in Italy, drove eastwards through the city to be welcomed by zia Vita and her family.

"*Buon Natale, tutti!*" (Happy Christmas, everyone). "Venite, venite!" she exclaimed as she hugged and kissed us.

A huge, fragrant smelling Christmas tree took pride of place in one corner of her dining room. The table was set for about sixteen people. A heavy snowy white damask cloth bordered with intricate lacy edges, was draped over the table. Silver cutlery, delicate china dishes and sparkling glasses were laid and in the centre, numerous bottles of Lambrusco were lined up intermittently with baskets of home-made bread, sauces and elegant Christmas candles.

I had been warned beforehand that this would be a marathon meal, with many pasta and meat courses and I will always remember it as one of the most delicious dinners that I have ever eaten. Conversation flowed and glasses clinked. The *primi piatti* consisted mainly of filled pastas that melted on the tongue. This was followed by a variety of roast meats and vegetables and then we indulged in a *zuppa inglese* - a sort of trifle soaked in liquor. Next, the *panettone*, or Italian version of Christmas cake, which is totally unlike our rich fruit cake was on the menu.

Panettone comes in a big colourful cardboard box with a sweet little looped ribbon on the top for ease of carrying. Trust Italian designers to think of such a tiny, but nevertheless important detail! The box is as chic as a handbag and looks great. *Panettone* is manufactured by different companies - Motta and Alemagna being the biggest and most famous.

Italian tradition has it, that people exchange these cakes with each other during the festive season and present them as gifts, when making their Christmas visits. The cake itself is rather like very light bread with some crystallized or dried fruits dotted about its mixture.

Finally, after taking our fill of *panettone* we attacked the cheese and fruit, which was followed by numerous *digestivi* and zia Vita's famous *Nocino* - a particularly potent and delicious *digestivo* made from nuts and of course, alcohol.

We were all stuffed with food and stayed at the table for the remainder of the day, chatting and sipping our *digestivi* and enjoying the Christmas ambience. Television was not considered an important festive accessory in this household, and instead of sitting glued to the box - I did think nostalgically for a moment of Morecombe and Wise and wondered what tricks they would be performing this year - we played cards and Monopoly, complete with famous Italian landmarks, and thoroughly enjoyed ourselves.

Twilight fell early and soon it was time to depart into the cold crisp night. Tomorrow would be Santo Stefano, the next important feast day on the Italian Christmas calendar. New Year's Eve was looming and a tradition in Italy on this day is to eat *zampone* or pig's trotters with lentils. According to my father who grew up in Liverpool, pig's trotters was a normal dish there in the 1930s and 40s and so was tripe. Funnily enough the Italians love tripe and it can often be found on menus. Although the *zampone* was delicious cooked with garlic and onions, I found the concept of eating this part of the poor pig's anatomy, slightly disturbing.

After supper, we ventured out into the city centre where a crowd had congregated to watch a spectacular firework display. On the stroke of midnight, the pyrotechnic event lit up the heavens. Dazzling colours shattered and exploded against the night, fragmenting into a million luminous pinks, greens, blues and purples.

Little orbs of flashing light dropped down to earth, illuminating the surrounding buildings and people. Vibrant streaks and pulsating flashes of every tone and hue, rent the dark New Year sky, taking us into 1978 with loud sizzles and bangs.

~

One cannot live in Modena for nearly four years without mentioning the fact, that in the winter months many of the cities' youth, go up to the nearby mountains to ski at the weekends. When my sister Joanna had visited, we experienced one such weekend, with Paolo and some of his friends. Neither Jo nor I had skied before, and we were excited at the thought of whooshing down the slopes, little realising that it takes time to learn how to stop and how to turn.

We had all piled into a couple of Fiat 500s one Sunday morning, the skis precariously balanced on what seemed to be tiny roof racks. Our destination was Monte Cimone near Abetone, the nearest resort and a drive of about one and a half hours from Modena. We headed off into the mountains south of Casa della Fontana, on the Emilian-Tuscan border.

It had started snowing. Large white silent gossamer flakes surrounded us, turning the countryside into a snowy winter wonderland. Paolo jumped out of his car and rummaged in the boot producing a number of chains, which he deftly secured around the wheels of the car, to prevent us from skidding and being stuck in the snow. Apparently all Italians carry such equipment in winter, and would never venture out into the wild, mountainous snowy landscapes without them.

Joanna and I looked like a couple of refugees dressed in jumble sale gear, as we had borrowed our jackets, boots and leggings. Only our hats and gloves were our own. Laura one of the Italian girls in the party looked like a fashion plate about to be photographed for Vogue, and most people on the slopes were clad in the latest designer gear.

My sister and I spent most of the day falling over, accumulating a number of bruises and gradually becoming more and more disillusioned as the day wore on. At first Paolo tried to teach us how to stop and turn, but we were so hopeless that after a while he gave up. He and his friends were excellent skiers and wanted to head for the black runs, so they left us to our own devices. Sometimes we would collapse in a heap of giggles - sometimes in heaps of frustration. It looked so easy!

After a morning of being vertically challenged, we decided to head for the bar and drown our sorrows with a glass of wine or two. Surprisingly enough, we felt braver after this and even managed to reach the bottom of the nursery slopes once or twice, without hitting the ground. However dusk came early that day, and towards three o'clock we were feeling decidedly chilly and wanted to return home. Unfortunately there was no sign of Paolo and his friends, so we decided that the warmth of the bar, more wine and a big plate of spaghetti was what was needed.

I have skied many times since that day and I have a 'love-hate' relationship with the sport. I love the fabulous mountain scenery, the endless blue skies that are often found in these regions and the feeling of euphoria when a run is completed without a tumble, but I hate the feet-numbing experience as the unforgiving boots clamp around my ankles, and the knowledge that I will not feel my toes for the next couple of hours. I hate all the bruises and sprains that inevitably accompany a skiing trip.

At the beginning of 1978 whilst living with the Contarini family, my friend Monique rang me one Saturday morning and asked me if I would like to accompany her for a day's skiing to Monte Cimone.

Paolo had returned to Parma and I was feeling bored, so I eagerly accepted her invitation. By then, I owned my own skis which the Contarini family had stored in their garage for me, when I returned to England the previous September. Monique lent me some of her clothes and we set off in a jubilant mood. The little *'Deux Chevaux'* that Monique still owned, bumped along as we climbed up into the mountains, the skis rattling on the roof-rack.

'"This will be my last year in Modena," Monique informed me.

"Why Monique? Are you returning to Paris?" I asked.

"No, Spiros and I are going to live in Greece after he gets his degree in the summer," She replied. "We'll probably get married in a few years time."

"Oh Monique, I'll really miss you!" I exclaimed.

She had been a good friend to me. I doubted I would see her very often if she intended to live so far away. We were quiet for a while pondering this fact.

"Spiros is returning to Greece at the end of June," said Monique. "I'll follow him later. I'm actually going to take my car and drive there, although it'll probably take a couple of days!"

I wished her all the luck in the world. I too had been thinking about my own precarious future and had heard through the grape vine - in fact through Rita at the language school, that there was a young couple who lived near Via P. Ferrari, who would like an English girl to live with them rent free, plus food, in return for English conversation.

I felt that I could not stay with the Contarini family forever. There were just Signor and Signora Contarini at home, as Paolo had returned to Parma and Antonella had recently been married to Alessandro, and had moved out to a very swish, new penthouse apartment that her wealthy in-laws had bought the couple as a wedding present.

To my disappointment, I had missed Antonella's wedding, as my own sister Joanna was married on the same day. Antonella gave me a set of beautiful earthenware dishes as a present for Jo and her husband Robin, and I remember lugging them back to England, via various trains. She still uses them to this day and whenever I catch a glimpse of the terracotta dishes, my mind fills with memories of Modena.

Antonella still lives in her wonderful apartment, and the once new block of flats is now softened with trees and landscaped shrubs that have blossomed and bloomed over the last twenty five years, lending it an even more elegant appearance. I remember in 1978, being extremely impressed as she showed me around.

The apartment is set out on two floors and it boasts two bathrooms and a fabulous kitchen. The eating / dining area is open plan with gorgeous antique furniture, Roman blinds keep out the heat and pictures hang on every wall. Antonella and Alessandro are seasoned travellers, and bring back treasures from far off lands, giving their apartment an eclectic appeal.

Antonella had been wonderfully untidy when she lived at home with the Contarini's. I used to marvel at her bedroom, where she seemingly tossed her clothes at will, until a small mountain of designer gear lay in gay abandon around the room. The beautifully elegant, immaculate clothes she always wore bore no resemblance to the stuff I used to see in big piles around the place. I think she must have spent a lot of time ironing!

The feast of San Gemignano came and went. By February, I had decided to accept Daniella and Roberto's offer of a room. It turned out to be another study, but I was grateful for anywhere to lay my head and keep my few belongings.

It was strange being so near Via Paolo Ferrari again. I would walk along Corso Emanuelle II, and memories of my first term with Jemp in our old flat with character, came to mind. The place still looked dilapidated from outside, the shutters tightly closed against the nebulous February air. I wondered if it was still rented out to English girls and if so, were they encountering the same problems that Jemp, I and the others had experienced.

One day, out of curiosity, I knocked on the door of the flat in Via Paolo Ferrari. A tall English girl called Sally invited me in for a coffee and a chat. Her flat mate Mary was there and the couple chain-smoked and drank black coffee after black coffee, as they discussed their latest diets - non-stop. The flat was still decorated with the glorious red paint, but the rooms looked uncared for and messy.

Daniella and Roberto, the couple that I was staying with, were very nice and allowed me to teach my pupils in their apartment. However I soon started to feel guilty, as they were hardly ever at home and I did not feel that I was fulfilling my part of the bargain. Also, I was only just making enough money to live comfortably on.

Each week I had to save for a ticket home should the need arise, and although I did not have to pay for rent or food I still had to buy petrol for my *motorino,* pay for any pizzas or meals that I went out for and buy clothes, stamps, phone calls and cosmetics.

I had recently assessed my wardrobe, and decided that most of my clothes had seen better days and that I needed new ones. Unfortunately, I had a weakness for Italian shoes and boots and was determined to buy a few pairs before returning to England.

The question about whether I should return to England or not, was constantly being pushed around my brain. I had tried returning to 'good old blighty' before, and my attempts to put down roots there had failed. I felt as if I were in Limbo, in no-man's land, and it was very unsettling. I knew I either had to make a commitment to the Italian way of life and find myself a proper, secure job with a salary, or return to my home country and settle down there.

I scoured the newspapers for job advertisements, and spied what seemed to be an excellent one, in a ceramic factory painting designs on tiles. This would be perfect with my artistic background. I had taught art for a year in London, before setting foot in Italy and I realised that I missed the creative part of my life.

An interview was arranged, and I set out for the factory on my little *motorino*. It took me two hours to get there and a further two hours to return. The job had sounded exciting in the advert, but in reality, it required painting the same design over and over again. It was not for me and I put it down to experience!

There were no vacancies in any of the language schools in Modena or any of the nearby towns, but the possibility of teaching English in a *Scuola Statale* (state school) was a possibility. However this too fell through, because I was not an Italian citizen and complicated bureaucracy prevented me from obtaining a post.

By this time I was thoroughly dejected, and even contemplated opening my own language school with a loan from a British bank. One day when I was wondering where my next step would lead me, a letter arrived from my aunt in Southampton, with the news that a temporary vacancy had arisen in the children's home, where she and my Russian uncle were the house-parents. I had worked on many occasions at 'Greenfields' as a student, and loved the challenge and fun it presented. There and then I decided to return to Britain once more.

I felt relieved that I had made the decision to quit. I knew that part of my heart would always remain in Italy, and that it was impossible not to be touched or seduced by her beguiling ways. I knew that I would miss so much; the gregarious, vivacious people and their kindness; the wonderful mouth watering food; the art, culture and beautiful presentation; the medieval cities, rolling hills and fields of sunflowers. But in my heart of hearts I knew that for me it was all an illusion.

I felt as if I had been wandering on a stage for four years, taking part in a spectacular drama that had no real place in ordinary life. It had felt like a dream and now, unfortunately, I had to wake up.

CHAPTER 17 FROM ONE COAST TO ANOTHER

The next time I returned to Italy was in 1980. It had been difficult returning to England, but I knew deep in my heart that I had made the right decision. By now, Teresa had also returned to Britain and both of us were feeling nostalgic for *la dolce vita,* and decided to spend a couple of weeks there during our summer vacation.

We choose Catolica as our destination, as it was on the coast yet in the familiar territory of Emilia-Romagna. Situated on the Adriatic, along an eighty mile stretch of white sand, Catolica is a holiday paradise for Germans, Swiss, English and other Europeans, including the Italians themselves. In fact, the Italians joke and call the summer crowds who go there and to other places along the coast, the Third Gothic Invasion; the first being the fifth century conquest by the Barbarians and the second, the Nazi occupation during the Second World War.

Rimini is the most well known of the string of gaudy seaside resorts along the Adriatic coast and has dedicated itself to tourism since 1830, when the area was developed in response to the new craze for sea-bathing. We thought about staying in Rimini with its historic centre and vibrant beach culture, but decided that it was too popuar and would be heaving with holidaymakers in August.

We chose Cattolica instead - a much smaller, quieter and more family orientated place, situated in the lee of the hills that surrounded it. Cattolica is a border town, the gateway to La Marche and near the tiny principality of San Marino. Like all the other Adriatic seaside resorts, it is well-manicured with tree-lined promenades, and it has a bustling outside café life. It sounded just the place for Teresa and me to unwind after a hectic and stressful teaching year.

As usual, we met up in Victoria station and boarded a series of trains which would carry us to Milan. It felt strange not to be encumbered with tons of luggage - trunks, suitcases and baskets full of necessary junk. Instead we travelled light with rucksacks and some hand luggage. How liberating that felt!

Our journey from London was fairly uneventful, although at one stage we did have to share a compartment with two very smelly men. They insisted on taking off their shoes and Teresa and I nearly fainted at the stench. Teresa whipped out a perfume spray that she had in her handbag, and when they dozed off to sleep, she liberally squirted it around the compartment, much to the amusement of another fellow passenger who obviously did not share our acute sense of smell.

The two smelly folk had no luggage - only a huge radio which they insisted on playing very loudly, throughout the night. They did not take the hint when Teresa and I moved out into the corridor for some peace, but continued to blare out the music. We stared morosely from the window at the passing blackness of the night. If we had retained our Italian qualities we probably would have told them to turn it off, but as we both had been back in England for a couple of years and had metamorphosed back into Brits with stiff upper lips, we did not have the heart to spoil their enjoyment.

Milano Centrale was as familiar to us as Victoria Station, and we found our way through the crowds, to the *Treni in Partenza* notice board, to elicit what time the Cattolica train would be departing. Soon, we were speeding through the urban conglomeration of apartments that constituted the outskirts of Milan. We had to change trains in Bologna and that meant passing through the landscape of Emilia-Romagna and the cities that we knew and loved, like Parma, Reggio Emilia and of course Modena

As the train slid into Modena station we moved into the corridor and stuck our heads out of the window, straining to see if there was anyone we knew standing on the platform. I had telephoned Antonella from Milan, to let her know roughly what time we would be passing through. She promised to try to be there, to say '*ciao*' and wish us on our way.

I craned my neck scanning the platform for her elegant slim figure and sleek dark hair, and just as the train was about to resume its journey, she ran up the steps waving her arms excitedly, shouting "*Ciao Clare, ciao Teresa, ci vediamo presto!*"(We'll see each other soon!)

"Ciao Antonella," we chorused in unison, amazed that she had made it to the station.

After spending a week at the sea, Teresa and I had resolved to return to Modena for our final week. She would visit Claudio and his family and I was to head for Casa della Fontana, and meet up with the Contarini clan.

We conversed with Antonella for about thirty seconds about our forthcoming return to Modena, before the train started up its engines to gather speed for Bologna. We waved and shouted from the window as Antonella receded into the distance, a minute figure against the grey Fascist architecture of the station building.

Most railway stations in Italy were built under Mussolini and have a uniform square modernist appearance, complete with lots of grey concrete or creamy ornate marble. Some are more decorative than others and the coastal stations are often the prettiest, softened with shrouds of climbing plants such as bougainvillea and potted palms.

Spilling out of the train at Bologna, we had a wait of about two hours before the coastal Adriatic train was due. It was time for lunch and we devoured a big plate of *spaghetti bolognese* in the station restaurant. Little did we know that in just under a week, this would be the tragic crime scene of the Fascist P2 Bologna bombing of 1980. On that terrible day, eighty four people died at 10.25a.m. The clock in Bologna station is permanently stopped at that hour, to commemorate those who lost their lives in the blast.

Recently, the station authorities wanted to restore the clock, but there was such a local outcry that they reconsidered their plan. A permanent memorial has now been erected to the dead, consisting of a glassed-in, jagged gash through the restored restaurant's window. The names of those who died are etched into it. It is a very poignant reminder to the thousands of passengers who use this enormous station every day.

Blissfully unaware of the tragic events of the following week, we boarded our train for Cattolica, and whizzed through such places as Imola, Forli, Cesena and Rimini, skirting the Po Delta to the north, an expanse of polluted marshlands and lagoons. As we drew nearer to the coast, the scenery changed and lush gentle valleys covered with fig and chestnut trees and dotted with ancient hill top towns, could be spied from the train windows.

Before reaching the coast, we glided into Santarcangelo di Romagna just west of Rimini. This walled hill top settlement with an ancient castle, looked intriguing from the train. As we rattled on past Rimini, gathering speed, we gazed contentedly out of the windows at the countryside and caught alluring glimpses of a Madonna blue sea glinting in the distance, and silky beaches covered with colourful umbrellas and sun beds. After a while, however, the resorts all seemed to blur into one another.

The train stopped at Riccione, which was more up-market than the other places. I remembered from a previous stay in Rimini with the spoilt little rich kid Natalia that nearby Riccione was a sophisticated town, attracting the wealthy second home owners from the hinterland. It boasts designer shops, chic cafés and bars, a beautifully laid-out beach and lots of pretty flowering shrubs, such as the ubiquitous pink oleander bushes with their delicate perfume, and bright splashes of bougainvillea along its promenade and gardens

Reaching our destination, we began to grow slightly apprehensive, as we had not booked anywhere to stay. These were the days before the internet and we had not wanted to commit ourselves to a package deal, preferring to devise our own itinerary and go where the will took us. We began to feel that this was slightly foolhardy as we tumbled into Cattolica station, along with hundreds of other backpackers and young people such as ourselves.

Teresa and I had often holidayed together, rarely booking anywhere in advance. We had always been lucky, and in a way it made the holiday more fun - less predictable. A memorable three weeks had been spent in Greece when we were students together. We stayed for a while in Athens with a friend of Teresa's. Midway through our vacation we decided on the spur of the moment, to travel to the Peleponese Islands and landed on Mykonos, without a clue as to where we would spend the night. If all else failed we could have slept on the beach, as many students did in those days.

On disembarking from the boat, a group of old Greek women, dressed from head to toe in black, vied for our custom as potential lodgers. We attached ourselves to one, and she led us to a single-roomed apartment, which we had to share with two other unknown English girls, some old wall mounted photographs of previous Greek generations, and some rather hard, dubious looking beds.

This luxurious pad cost us about 30p a night. It was somewhere to lay our weary heads, although in retrospect, I think the beach might have been more comfortable! If I remember rightly, we washed in the sea and brushed our teeth with bottled water, as Mykonos was dry that year

However, this was Cattolica. We could speak reasonable Italian, so things, we reasoned, should not be too difficult. After trudging around for a few hours and being turned away from numerous overflowing hotels, we decided it was time to hit the tourist office. Maybe they could find us a place to stay.

Having accomplished this, we were given details of a small two star hotel, not too far from the beach and the centre of the town. By now we were very tired, and all we wanted to do was to flop down on our beds, rest and shower and find a good place to eat.

Lazy days were spent, roasting ourselves on the beach. When that became unbearable, we gingerly picked a path, past prostate bodies, hardly daring to tread in the scorching hot sand on our way to the sea. The water was like a warm bath, salty and buoyant - a dream to swim in.

Overhead, small planes buzzed around advertising soft drinks, whilst water sports were being practised all around us. When we were tired of sunbathing, we would hire a pedal boat or retire to the nearest bar for a *cappuccino* - if it was in the morning, and a *bombola* or doughnut filled with creamy custard.

Italians are funny about drinking *cappuccino*. It must be done before 10a.m. or they consider you to be ever so slightly mad. After lunch or dinner a shot of *espresso* is the right coffee to throw back, but we found this to be too small and bitter. *Caffellatte* or *caffe macchiato*, with just a drop of milk is O.K. to drink in the afternoon but not in the evening. So many coffee rules and regulations! Teresa and I liked to break them and drink *cappuccini* when we liked!

The beach emptied between 12 o'clock and 1.00 p.m. People went back en masse to their hotels for lunch and a siesta. Often Teresa and I would linger, even though the noon day heat was enervating. We loved having the beach and sea to ourselves. We would sit under the shade of a big umbrella and stare as if in a trance, at the dancing turquoise sea. The golden sand would shimmer and the scene was tranquil and soporific. We realized that the only other souls on the beach were British, and we laughed as we recalled the song by Noel Coward that only 'Mad dogs and Englishmen go out in the mid day sun.'

One day we contacted our Canadian friend Lisa, who lived in Modena and arranged to meet her for the day. We were quite excited at this prospect as we had not seen her for nearly two years, and it felt like we had a lot of catching up to do. We arranged to meet her half way between Modena and Cattolica. The day started well, but the series of events that were to unleash themselves that morning, will never be forgotten by many people. The day we had chosen to meet Lisa was the day that the P2 bomb ripped through Bologna station at 10.25a.m.

We arrived in Forli at around 11 o'clock, totally unaware of the chaos just a few kilometres down the line. We sat on the station in the shade. The place had a dusty, desiccated look, and appeared to be a bit of a dump as far as railway stations go. In an attempt to brighten up the place there were some flowers in pots, but even these had died in the cruel heat. The station was practically empty and Teresa and

I stared up and down the line, wondering where all the trains had disappeared too.

"It's strange," I said to Teresa, "there hasn't been any traffic on the line for about half an hour."

"I know," she answered, "But the trains are always late. Maybe Lisa will arrive soon. If the train doesn't come in the next 10 minutes I'll go and ask the guy who sells the tickets what time it's due."

We waited and waited. At around noon, we trundled into the station hall and made for the ticket kiosk. The railway official had a small transistor held up to his ear and a striken look of horror on his face.

"A che ora arriva il treno da Bologna?" I asked politely,

"Haven't you heard?" asked the railway employee aghast. "There's been a huge bomb on Bologna Station. They won't let any more trains through today - or tomorrow - or the day after. Lots of people have died." His eyes filled with tears and he made the sign of the cross, as he turned his attention back to the radio where up to the minute details were being broadcast.

"My God!" exclaimed Teresa. "Lisa was travelling through Bologna."

We stared at each other in dismay. We both felt sick. These were the days before mobile phones. We had her home number and rang it immediately. To our relief, Lisa answered and told us that on her arrival at Modena Station, the atrocity had already occurred and she had obviously been forced to return home.

Stumbling out of the station, we wondered what to do next. Both of us were in shock, but obviously the horror of the situation did not really hit home until later that afternoon, when every bar television flashed images and news accounts, and the evening newspapers portrayed graphic descriptions of the carnage, on the front pages.

The whole of Italy was in shock, reeling from the horror of this cataclysmic event. Teresa and I were presented with a problem, which seemed tiny by comparison but was nevertheless a problem. We had travelled to Forli by train - how on earth would we return to Cattolica if the line had been closed? We decided to venture out into the place and investigate the situation.

Forli was like a ghost town, boiling and simmering under the midday sun. The hot white light was undiluted, and we walked in silence through the dusty streets, surrounded by Fascist architecture. It seemed different from the other Italian cities, more modern and less historically interesting, unless you like Fascist buildings. Obviously, it was siesta time, so we headed for the nearest open bar. It was also August and many businesses were closed down for the *ferie agosto* - or summer break.

Inside, the bar was dim and deliciously cool. We felt we needed a stiff drink each and ordered brandies. Once our eyes had become accustomed to the darkness and then the diffused light, we noticed a small television set, high up on a wall shelf. Details of the Bologna bombing were being transmitted. The barman was silently staring at the T.V, unable to comprehend how this could have happened. After a while he started swearing, crying and gesticulating wildly, with many *'porca miserias.'*

At this point we thought it was time to leave, and decided to find a church or cathedral where we could light some candles, pray for those who had been killed and stay in the shade until the city woke up. We finally made our way back to Cattolica by bus.

The next morning we felt uneasy about going to the beach as the disaster had been right on our doorstop. However everyone else appeared to be going about their daily business, although conversation was only about one topic. On the beach there were more newspapers than usual, as many folk needed to read accounts of the horrors and know the details of the tragedy.

Radios are part of the beach culture in Italy and at 11.00 a.m. the radio suggested a 3 minute silence in respect for the dead and the whole beach drew to a halt. Those swimming stayed still in the water - the ball players stood lifeless - even the planes were grounded. It was a surreal experience and very powerful and poignant. All of Italy was grieving.

Our week at the seaside drew to a close. It was time to return to Modena and go our separate ways for a while. Fortunately the railway line opened up again and as the train drew into Bologna, the awfulness of what had happened really hit us. Platform one was in complete disarray. There was rubble all over the floor and a huge gaping hole in what used to be the waiting room and restaurant. It was simply horrifying.

Antonella was on the platform to meet me at Modena. We said our good-byes to Teresa who was being met by Claudio. On our way back to Antonella's penthouse apartment, we discussed the Bologna situation. At that time it was thought to be a terrorist attack by the Red Brigades, but we now know that it was the Fascist P2 group.

The next day promised hot and sultry weather. I had forgotten how humid Modena could be. We left early for the mountains, weaving our way past the river Panaro and up hair pin bends until we arrived at Casa della Fontana.

It was wonderful to be there again. Penny and Florence rushed out to greet us, yapping, barking, running around in circles and wagging their stumpy tails. After hugging and kissing everyone in sight, I took my luggage to my room. It was the same old room that I'd always had and it felt like home. I threw open the shutters and leant out, taking in the familiar gorgeous scenery and feeling the faint breeze on my cheeks.

"Don't let Mama see that window open," chuckled Antonella. "She'll skin you alive!"

I laughed and half closed it. The thought of burglars coming in through my window was ridiculous, and it was too early in the day for mosquitoes.

The rest of the week passed in a haze. Paolo came down from Parma and was ill with flu, and spent most of his time in bed eating oranges. Gabriella and her English husband were also there, and in the evenings we often ate out in the courtyard, dining *'al fresco'* at the huge table covered by the usual pristine cloth and groaning under the weight of all the home-made *Lambrusco* and *Nocino*. La zia Vita and all her family joined the party, plus other aunts and uncles too numerous to mention.

All too soon it was time to return to Modena, and then the long journey back to London beckoned. I was sad at leaving the tranquillity of Casa della Fontana, and this feeling was even more tangible when I realised that this might be the last time that I would stay there.

~

The following year, Teresa and I planned another holiday in Italy. This time we opted for the Mediterranean coast and decided that we both liked the sound of Sestri Levante, on the Ligurian Riviera Di Levante.

Although we were intrepid travellers by this time, neither of us were great fans of flying, so we took our usual mode of transport - the train, from Calais to Genoa, where we caught a local train to Sestri.

Again we had been foolhardy in thinking we could just find a room in a hotel without booking, and after a tiring trudge around all the hotels and a tourist office which yielded nothing, we were left wondering what our next step was.

We decided to ponder the situation in a café with a glass of wine or two. We did not really want to sleep on the beach and were considering a move to nearby bigger La Spezia, when a middle-aged gentleman at the next table to ours approached us.

"Are you looking for a room?" he asked. We replied that indeed we were.

"My sister often takes in tourists when the hotels are full," he informed us "Would you like me to accompany you to her house and find out if she has a spare room?"

We replied that we would and followed him down the main street. We must have looked an incongruous three some; an oldish Italian chap with a care worn, sunburnt face, dressed in black complete with hat, followed by two very white English *signorine* clutching their luggage.

The sister's house was located a few streets away, and after buzzing the bell and intercom and holding a lengthy conversation with her, which seemed to be conducted in dialect, he led us upstairs.

"*Ecco ci siamo!*" (Here we are)! He said with a beam. "This is my sister, Signora Bruni. She says that she does not have a spare room but if you want you can stay in her bedroom, and she will sleep in the living-room."

We did not want to turn the poor woman out of her sleeping quarters, but she insisted. Renting out rooms was a good source of income for many people on this seaside coast. Obviously she did not seem to mind the inconvenience.

"*Venite, venite,*" she called, waving her arms.

Signora Bruni led us into a large sunny room with a double bed, a couple of chairs, its own sink and a balcony which was full of shady, glossy plants.

With a swish of her aprons, she left Teresa and me to unpack. In Italy most double beds are actually single ones tied together, so as soon as she had departed we pulled them apart, and improvised with the sheets and covers.

A few minutes later there was a knock on the door.

"*La cena sarà pronta tra cinque minuti!*" (Dinner will be ready in five minutes!) she called putting her smiling head around the door. She did not seem to mind that we had disassembled her bedroom and she even offered us some more sheets and towels. We felt that this was going to be better than staying in a hotel and definitely cheaper.

She assumed, without asking us, that we would be eating with her in the evenings, and as we did not want to hurt her feelings, we agreed. That evening, we dined on *spaghetti al pesto*, a speciality of the region. It was delicious. The simple ingredients of pine nuts and basil were skilfully cooked with garlic, to make a memorable sauce.

Signora Bruni's recipe is as follows:-

- Take a large bunch of fresh basil, pine nuts, two cloves of garlic, a pinch of salt, some Parmesan cheese and some olive oil;
- Grind the basil leaves, pine nuts and garlic together in a mortar, with a little salt - if you don't have a mortar, use a blender;
- Add the cheese and when the mixture is the consistency of a thick puree, start adding the olive oil, a little at a time, until the sauce has the consistency of creamed butter;
- Prepare the spaghetti and add topping;
- Enjoy with large glass of vino!

~

The next morning we wandered down to the beach. Sestri Levante is a charming, peaceful seaside resort. This coastline was certainly not as frenetic as the Adriatic, and there was plenty of space on the sand to stretch out and arrange our belongings.

During our last holiday in Cattolica, each person on the beach had had about six square feet to rest their heads, and actually getting to the sea for a swim was an obstacle course. Here in Sestri we did not feel so hemmed in. Gaily coloured fishing boats were moored on the beach and families played ball, picnicked under fluttering umbrellas or frolicked in the crystal clear waters of the Mediterranean. Behind the beach was a long promenade extending the length of the bay, with the romantic name - the Bay of Fairy Tales! (*Baia delle Favole*)

At lunch time we would saunter into the old centre, which had a traditional Ligurian feel to it, to buy bread, cheese and fruit and then we would find a shady palm to sit under while we ate our tasty fare. Sometimes we would rest in the shade for a couple of hours, chatting or reading.

On our way back to Signora Bruni's we would walk along cobbled streets and gaze into the shop windows at the lovely shoes and bags on sale. Often we would pass cafés, where large groups of elderly men sat under umbrellas playing cards.

Once home we would flop on our beds for a couple of minutes and then sit outside in the cool shade of the potted plants. It was a pleasant spot to write postcards or read before dinner. The only downside to Signora Bruni's, was the fact that there was no hot water and we had to grit our teeth every time we showered or washed our hair.

In the evening after our spaghetti meal, we would stroll down to the bay, and watch the sunset turn the sky from turquoise to tangerine and then to indigo. The moon, a great round orb, would rise into the heavens, first yellow and then changing to a diaphanous white, hanging heavy and suspended over the dark water, throwing a shimmering bouncing light over the Bay of Fairy Tales. Sometimes we would take a bottle of wine down with us, and once or twice we had a moonlight swim. We had the whole sea to ourselves. The mainland sparkled with a thousand twinkling lights and more lights appeared in the sky above when the stars came out.

One day we decided to venture further afield, and on a whim took the train to Portovenere. From there, we planned to take a boat to one or more of the Cinque Terre which consists of five picturesque villages, clinging precariously to cliff edges and tumbling down steep hill sides, to rocky little bays and coves.

The villages are called Levanto-Monterosso al Mare, Vernazza, Corniglia, Manerola and Riomaggiore. They seem suspended in time, each village a huddle of sorbet coloured houses which look as if they are in danger of toppling into the sea. Tourism has not yet really made its mark here, because these places are virtually inaccessible by land or rail, and most roads leading to them are only open to the inhabitants. It is possible to walk from village to village and the trip takes about four hours.

On arrival at Portovenere we were so taken with its picturesque appearance, that we almost abandoned our plan to visit the Cinque Terre. We decided to spend about an hour in the small fishing port and we eagerly explored its medieval lanes dotted with boutiques and designer shops.

Beyond the port the hills rose as a back-cloth covered with a rich blanket of cypresses, chestnut trees, pines and palm trees. There were stunning views of the Cinque Terre, strung like a string of jewels along the coast. The houses by the waterfront were painted in rich tones of terracotta, yellow ochre and coral and this contrasted with the deep green of the wooden shuttered windows.

This stretch of coast will forever be linked with the romantic poets, Shelley and Byron. In the early 19th century Byron lived in La Spezia and apparently loved swimming in the waters around Portovenere. There is a grotto dedicated to him called 'Grotta Arpaia,' also known as 'Byron's Grotto.' One fateful day, Shelley was sailing from Livorno to Lerici when his boat 'The Ariel' capsized, and he was drowned aged only thirty. Eventually his body was brought back to the mainland, and rumour has it that Byron cut out his heart and sent it back to England in a box to be buried, whilst burning the rest of his body on the beach.

We boarded a boat for the Cinque Terre, and were soon sliding past rocky inlets and tiny inviting looking coves. Sometimes the cliffs plunged sheer to the sea, only punctuated by miniscule bays. The water was emerald green and deep turquoise in places. We soon spied the Cinque Terre, perched perilously on the hill side above, and decided to disembark at Vernazza, which is supposed to be the prettiest of the five villages.

It was certainly a place that dreams are made of. We wandered through the winding alleyways studded with craft shops, and found a restaurant with a beautiful terrace where we dined on freshly caught fish and salad. We then made our way down to the breathtakingly picturesque port with its clusters of pastel coloured houses, natural harbour, tiny beach and medieval round tower. We sat on the beach for a while and dipped our toes in the sparkling Mediterranean, before hopping on board a boat that would take us back to Potovenere.

All too soon our Riviera holiday was at an end. We thanked Signora Bruni for her kindness, and she cried and hugged us and begged us to return the following year.

A few years further on, Teresa and her husband Tom did return. They stayed with Signora Bruni and experienced the sort of holiday that you cannot find in a travel brochure.

CHAPTER 18 THE GRAND TOUR

A couple of years passed. I was delighted one evening when three friends of mine suggested that it would be fun to drive down to Italy that summer. We spent hours pouring over maps, deciding whether to drive down to the east or west coast, and where to eventually head for.

Our mode of transport was to be 'Doris,' a beautiful 1970's bright red V.W. and we started our journey one breezy late July morning, not knowing what adventures lay ahead. Fiona was our driver, and wherever we ventured she caused quite a stir, with her cheerful Geordie accent and her curly, luxurious Kate Bush style hair that was dyed a brilliant aubergine. The other passengers besides me were my cousin Michele and my close friend Suzanne.

Michele was very interested in politics - in particular those of the left wing variety and she enjoyed a good political debate. Both she and Fiona were feisty and outspoken and tended to team up together. Suzi and I had known each other for a long time and felt comfortable in each other's company. She was a down to earth, lively sort of girl who was good fun and easy to talk to. Suzi also possessed a stubborn streak but her sensible and caring nature won her many admirers. I was the absent-minded, slightly eccentric member of the group, who was always loosing or forgetting things. However, we all shared a similar sense of humour and the ability to be able to laugh at our short comings.

We knew each other reasonably well and by the end of our three week trip, had become close allies. Doris was not a big car and we were all squeezed in together, but this didn't bother us. We joked and laughed as we sped along, enjoying the varied countryside unfolding before our eyes.

It was to be mainly a camping holiday, interspersed with a few hotel stops. So besides carrying us four girls, poor old Doris had to transport all the camping gear, including a massive tent, cooking and sleeping equipment, plus our personal luggage. Our aim was to travel to Italy as quickly as possible, stopping maybe for one night in France and one in Switzerland, before hitting the Italian border. From there, we would go right down to Gargano in the region of Puglia, before traversing the country and visiting Rome.

On our journey through France we stopped frequently for coffee breaks. Fiona had to have a caffeine shot every few hours or so, and it was pleasant to stretch our legs and listen to the mellifluous sounds of the French language. At one café we took our drinks outside, placing our cups on a table that was almost the same height as ourselves. Not one of us was taller than 5' 2", and we burst into a fit of giggles at the huge table with the four small people around it.

We were in a silly mood and for some unknown reason started calling each other Doris. This habit stuck and we became known amongst ourselves - V.W. included - as 'The Five Dorises.' We did indeed receive some very strange looks, and some of the people that we met on our way, could not understand how we could all be called Doris - including our car. We tried to tell them that it was a joke - the English sense of humour! I think most people thought we were slightly, if not completely mad.

That evening we found a pleasant camp site somewhere in the heart of France. It was quite a lot of effort to erect the tent for just one night, but none of us wanted to linger in the area. We were all adamant that we should push on to Italy, and decided that the effort involved in assembling and dismantling our canvas home, for only one night, was worth it.

In France, the countryside was gloriously varied and soon we found ourselves up in the mountains and over the Swiss border. Here the scenery was stupendous, and the snaking serpentine roads threading their way around the mountains, afforded wonderful breathtaking views of towering pinnacles and peaks. The grassy verges were clothed with wild flowers and pretty well-kept chalets were dotted over the landscape.

Fiona was terrified of heights and kept her eyes firmly on the road ahead, not daring to even glance once, at the vertiginous spiralling drops on one side of the car. She chewed gum furiously to keep herself focused on the road ahead and to stop her mind wandering towards the great chasms below. The rest of us, although also slightly apprehensive at the view of the yawning gaps to the right, thought that this was very funny and at the same time very scary. One false move and we would be over the edge!

Just outside Geneva, Doris the V.W. started behaving badly, giving us a bumpy ride, and every so often veering over to the right. On entering Geneva we decided to look for the nearest V.W. garage. Little did we know, but that particular day was a national holiday and 90% of all garages were closed. After a frustrating trip around the city, looking for V.W. signs and querying the local inhabitants as to the whereabouts of the nearest garage, we limped into one just in time. Doris had had enough!

We all piled out, much to the astonishment of the mechanics. They were especially taken with Fiona's hair and could hardly take their eyes off its glowing glory. I think the sight of a red V.W. bearing a British number plate and full of young giggly ladies was an unusual sight for them, to say the least.

The chief mechanic, once he had recovered, approached us with a sorry expression on his face, tutting as he walked around Doris the V.W. examining her body work and gazing at her wheels,

"This car - she is a grandmother," he said admonishing us. "You should not be driving her. She should be in a museum - you understand? She is an old lady." He shook his head sadly.

"She is not an old lady," retorted Fiona indignantly. "This is the first time I have ever had any trouble with her." She then turned around so that the mechanic could not see. "Cheek!" she muttered pulling a face.

We hung around while the men in blue prodded poor old Doris, decided upon her problem and put her to rights. Suddenly Fiona looked panic stricken.

"Oh my God," she wailed "I haven't got any Swiss francs!"

None of us had any Swiss money, except for Suzi who had a few francs in her pocket. In the end we paid over the odds with Italian lira, and spent the francs on a couple of Coca Colas and then proceeded on our way.

The national holiday was creating chaos. A procession with banners caused havoc with the traffic making us creep along. We were all slightly nervous, as we needed to find a camp site before dusk fell. It was bad enough having to put up a tent in the light of day - but in the dark by moonlight would certainly be another matter!

We forced our way out of the city and were soon speeding southwards along the motorway. Suddenly Michele gave a squeal.

"There's a hand bag on the bonnet!"

We all looked and sure enough there was my brown leather bag bouncing up and down on Doris' bonnet. Inside was my passport, money, insurance and other belongings.

"Oh no!" I groaned. "I must've forgotten to put it back in the car when we stopped at the garage!"

It was such an incongruous sight that we burst into laughter which was becoming a habit with us in tricky situations.

"I'm sorry," spluttered Fiona, trying to keep a straight face "but I can't stop on the motorway. You'll just have to wait until we get off. I'll try'n drive carefully."

We watched the bag with bated breath and suppressed laughter. It was dancing rhythmically to the hum of the engine. I prayed that it would not fall off. Once off the motorway, I retrieved it and mentally promised myself that I would try to take better care of it in future.

The next day we reached the Italian border, travelling through the Great St. Bernard Pass. Once we were on Italian *terra firma* we felt as if we could stop and explore any of the towns that took our fancy. Driving through some of the highest peaks in the Alps, we wound our way across Italy's oldest national park called the 'Val d'Aosta.'

The beautiful rugged scenery, besides being dramatically frightening and necessitating lots of chewing gum for Fiona, while she kept her eyes firmly on the road ahead, was also uplifting and very picturesque, with green carpeted valleys peppered with castles. On several occasions the rest of us shut our eyes to the precipitous drops surrounding us, leaving Fiona and her chewing gum in sole charge.

The Val d'Aosta is the least Italian of all the country's regions and French is often the language spoken in these parts. Recovering from our awe-inspiring ride, we took some time out and stopped in the lovely old town of Aosta and explored its attractive cobbled streets. The town stands at the junction of two important trade routes from France to Italy, and was originally built by the Romans, who constructed the streets in a grid style and wrapped the city up with a Roman wall, which is still well-preserved to this day. The air in this region was bracing, and the shops sold a variety of Swiss cuckoo clocks and other mountain themed paraphernalia.

We found our way to the main square, Plaza Emilio Chanoux, and settled down in a café to do a spot of people-watching and coffee drinking - two of our favourite pastimes! Whilst we were there, I telephoned Paolo whom I had not seen for a couple of years

Paolo suggested that we pop into Parma that evening, on our journey down south. He told me that we were all welcome to stay at his flat for the night, so long as we did not mind sleeping on the floor. We were cheered by this prospect, as we were disillusioned with erecting and dismantling the tent and other equipment every day. We were longing to reach a more permanent base somewhere in the south, probably in Puglia and settle down for a while.

After much deliberation, we agreed to drive to Parma on the motorway rather than take the scenic route, as we had a fair few kilometres to travel. The majestic scenery softened into hills, and flattened out into a patchwork of well-cared for fields with orchards and vineyards, as we reached the suburbs of Milan. From there, we sped through the plains of the Po and down to Parma, catching fleeting glimpses of the Pianura Padana - the northern flat land, bordered by poplar trees and home to isolated square built terracotta coloured farmhouses. It was familiar scenery.

On arrival in Parma, we headed for a bar with a telephone and some hot strong coffee. We had been on the road for most of the day and were dishevelled and tired. Paolo came to meet us and led us back to his apartment. It was good to see him after all this time and he did not seem to have changed at all. He filled us in with lots of news

"I'm sharing my flat with an English guy called Pete," he told us. "He teaches English at one of the language schools and he's looking forward to meeting you all as he hasn't spoken to a proper English person for ages."

When we arrived at Paolo's flat, his latest girlfriend was also there. Apparently, when she had discovered that four young English ladies were expected, she had rushed out to the nearest beauty salon to tart herself up. Really she need not have bothered. We all looked a mess!

"This is Doretta," said Paolo introducing her. The four of us tried not to catch each other's eyes and had to suppress our bubbling laughter. Doretta means 'little Doris' in Italian and is by all accounts, an unusual Italian name. Michele and I started chuckling, much to everyone's embarrassment and we had to explain about our Doris nicknames. It was obviously a real coincidence that her name was also practically Doris and she did not understand the joke. There was a decided chill in the air amongst the ladies and I think she thought that we were potty.

We spent the evening chatting and discussing politics. Pete seemed pleased to meet us Brits and to have the opportunity to converse in English once more. Even though Paolo could speak almost perfect English, they rarely spoke the language together.

Doretta did not appear to understand our jokes and laughter and Paolo had to translate every conversation, until she became bored of the whole performance. I felt sorry for her as I remembered how I felt when I first arrived in Italy, and everyone around me was gabbling in Italian and I could not understand a thing.

Our merry party continued talking well into the night, and at about two o'clock, reluctantly realised that we had better get some sleep if we were to continue our travels the following day. We spent an uncomfortable night on various floors and headed off stiffly the next morning, for the Adriatic coast and the *Mezzagiorno.*

Our final destination on the Adriatic was to be the Gargano promontory, some five hundred kilometres further south. In the 1980s, this region was virtually unknown as a tourist trap, and we looked forward to visiting Apuglia or *Puglia* - the gateway to the south. We had heard about the *trulli* or strange igloo shaped houses that many people dwelt in, and we knew that the landscape would be compelling, wild and beautiful. Apuglia an ancient land is situated on the heel and spur of Italy's boot shaped coastline. We gathered that it would be very different from the sophisticated north.

A few stops had been planned on route. On our return journey we had high hopes of visiting Rome, Florence, and Siena where my parents had rented a house. We also intended to visit Modena where we had been invited, by Paolo, to stay in the Contarini family apartment for a night.

Our first stop after leaving Parma was San Benedetto del Tronto. Driving to it through stunning hill towns, with steep twisting hilly roads and deep lush green valleys, we greatly admired this picturesque region. Soon, we reached the coast near Ancona.

The little seaside resorts sprinkled along the Adriatic, were similar to those further north but retained a more old-fashioned charm - a slightly forgotten air. I remembered my holiday with Jemp at Sirolo all those years ago, and felt nostalgic for the good old days.

The white cliffs of Monte Conero, which plunged straight into the sea, rose south of Ancona providing a tantalising panorama. The road followed stunning spectacular coast line scenery. Doris the V.W. wove her way around the coast, giving us fabulous and scary views of the turquoise Adriatic.

Fiona's fear of heights returned to haunt her, and much chewing gum was consumed – this time by all of us, as we held our breath and dared to glance at the shimmering sea below.

We arrived safely in San Benedetto del Tronto, with its six kilometres of beach, and its reputation for possessing some five thousand palm trees. We reckoned that it would be as good a place as any to pitch the tent for a few nights and recuperate after the long drive from Parma.

We were becoming proficient at erecting our tent. Fiona directed and delegated as the tent belonged to her, and we had it up and habitable in less than half an hour, amidst much shrieking, laughter and fooling around. Next, went in our soft mats and sleeping bags and out came our clothes, which of course were all crinkled and had to be hung up at various points around the framework of the tent, to ease out the creases.

I had brought my heated hair rollers with me – I rarely went anywhere without them in those days, and the others teased me mercilessly.

"Well you won't be able to plug them in here – there's no electric point," said Suzi, grinning at me.

"Michele won't be able to use her travel iron either," pointed out Fiona. "It was a waste of time bringing both those things."

I tried to justify the heated rollers as I often woke up with a 'bad hair day,' and as I explained to the others, they only took a second or two to use.

However the teasing continued so I only tended to tame my unruly locks when it was really necessary

Generally, we took turns at cooking each evening, but on this day we decided to eat out and explore the town's nightlife.

Because of its excessive number of palm trees, San Benadetto is also known locally as the *'Riviera delle Palme.'* As dusk was falling, we sauntered along the promenade and found a convenient eating area, where we ordered seafood and spaghetti with fish sauce. This was washed down with the local wine. To finish our fishy meal we tucked into various different flavoured *gelati* (ice cream).

The next day dawned bright and clear, with azure skies filled with fluffy white clouds. We all awoke late and agreed that yesterday's drive had exhausted us. Voting to have a lazy day, we pottered around the camp site and thought about going for a swim. Fiona decided that her stunning aubergine curls needed re-dying and she tottered over to the shower room to do the honours. The rest of us washed out some of our clothes and settled down on our sleeping mats in the sun, to have a good read or a snooze.

"Look at the sky," I murmured lazily looking up from my book. "It was blue a minute ago. Now it looks grey!"

"I think we may be in for a storm." Michele answered.

"Well," joined in Suzi, "I hope the tent withstands it. Continental storms can be very fierce."

As she was speaking, great splatters of rain fell on us and we scrambled our belongings and flung ourselves into the tent. Camping is not pleasant when everything gets wet and mildewed. A vivid flash of lightning rent the sky and thunder pealed ominously. Great drops of rain sloshed down and beat a rhythm on our canvas roof. Water appeared to be entering the tent, and when we peered out, the terrain around us was flooded. I could see Fiona in the distance with a towel draped around her head.

"Oh great," I said. "Let's get the sleeping bags off the ground and everything else for that matter."

The tent unzipped and Fiona fell in. The rest of us burst out laughing as she looked a sight. I do not know what sort of dye she used, but it had not set properly and purple streaks were dripping all down her face, over her white top and onto her arms. She resembled Alice Cooper or someone from 'The Rocky Horror Show.'

"Oh my God, Dorises, I hope it washes off!" she shrieked in dismay. "I haven't brought many tops. Ugh! What a mess!"

Her towel was striped with purple and her white shirt had taken on the appearance of an abstract expressionist canvas.

The thunder and lightning cracked and hissed and threw dramatic lights over us for a while, and then suddenly it wore itself out. When we peeped out of the tent, the sky had resumed its brilliant blue colour and any rogue clouds had disappeared. The shrubs, flowers and grass around the tent seemed new and sparkly.

We stayed in San Benedatto for a few more days, chilling out, sunbathing, swimming and eating good food. The urge to push onto Gargano was always present One morning after packing up all our stuff in record time, we waved good-bye to friends we had made on the camp site, and continued on our adventure.

~

The five Dorises headed into Abruzzo, a sparsely populated, mountainous region that marks the divide between north and south Italy. We hugged the coast road, as we had read somewhere that the interior landscape was wild, with abandoned hill villages and vast untamed mountain plains. This could be a problem if we wanted to stop for a coffee, or if Doris the V.W. broke down.

To our left as we bumped along, was the ubiquitous ribbon of sand, studded with beach umbrellas and bronzed sun worshippers, and the ever alluring Madonna blue Adriatic, shimmering under the glorious sun. To our right were gently undulating hills planted with soft green olive trees - a rolling, hilly version of the more inhospitable hinterland.

We stopped in Pescara for lunch, and then drove on to Vasto where we pitched our tent for the night. Tomorrow we would be heading into Molise, a much gentler and poorer region than Abruzzo and one prone to earthquakes.

The following morning we set off bright and early, stopping at the coastal town of Termoli for a coffee break. The long sandy beach was empty and we sat for a while musing on our journey so far, with the old walled town guarded by a castle behind us. On the horizon we could see the ferries, making endless trips to the Tremiti Islands. It was a good place to while away the time.

Molise soon gave way to Apulia, and the previous hilly terrain metamorphosed into vast inland plains. The region is four hundred kilometres in length and stretches from the spur of the Gargano peninsular to the heel of Italy's boot. We passed through diverse landscapes, some with an indented rocky coastline, some with beaches and lagoons. In 1991, the whole area became a national park, giving it protection against the ravages of a new found and future tourism.

After consulting the map, we decided to head for Peschici, a pretty fishing village. Doris bore us proudly down the rocky peninsular. We flew past craggy limestone cliffs topped with scrub pine and wild rosemary, and alongside wide sandy beaches and clear limpid waters.

Peschici perches on top of a rocky vantage point overlooking a wonderful sandy bay, lapped by the clearest cleanest waters. It was originally built in 790, as a garrison against the Saracens, and the town boasts a labyrinth of winding alleyways and whitewashed houses with domed roofs, which give it a very Arabian feel.

We set up camp and decided that this would be our base for the next week. Our tent was ensconced in a lovely little olive grove, and we could smell the wild rosemary growing in abundance nearby, mingling with other wild herbs which were indigenous to the region.

The washing facilities were rather basic with out door sinks and only a couple of primitive showers and toilets at our disposal, but the setting was so beautiful we decided to put up with a few inconveniences. That night we dined on *spaghetti al tonno* (with tuna) and drank our fill of the local wine.

The next day feeling refreshed after a good night's sleep, we ventured down onto the beach. To gain access to this lovely stretch of sand we had to traverse the steep cliffs, by means of a narrow stair way cut into its plunging sides. The steps were made of stones and cobbles and afforded a spectacular view of the bay below. We were armed with a picnic lunch, and spent a glorious day sunbathing and swimming.

This beach was very different from its northern counterparts - there were no lines of parasols, sun beds or even deck chairs. We sunbathed lying on our towels, the silky sand soft beneath us, and when we could no longer suffer the heat, we would race into the sea, splashing, kicking and swimming in its warm, embracing limpid waters. From the sea, the view of the coastline was spectacular.

As we soaked up the sun we spoke lazily of our future plans for the remainder of our holiday. Michele was amused by the amount of make up and jewellery the Italian women wore on the beach. It was as if they could not be seen anywhere without a full face of glossy mascara and lipstick. I explained to the others that this was all part of the Italian culture - the love of beautiful presentation - *la bella figura*!

"Anyway, you can talk Clare," laughed Michele. "Fancy bringing heated rollers on a camping holiday."

It seemed that I was not going to be allowed to forget this misdemeanour.

"Well fancy bringing an iron!" I replied. "You haven't used it once! At least I used my rollers in Parma!"

At that, we fell silent and closed our eyes to the glaring sun, happy to be relaxing on a beautiful, fairly deserted beach.

There seems to be an unwritten rule in Italy that it is safe to leave your belongings unattended on the sand whilst you go for a swim. I have done this many times and never once had anything stolen

These languorous days formed the pattern of most of our time in Gargano. In the evenings we would explore the maze of tiny streets, dropping into bars, restaurants or discos as the whim took us.

One evening at a particularly noisy disco, we met a guy called Enrico who promised to visit us the next day and drive us to Vieste, a particularly lovely town along the coast. It was a wonder that we understood anything that he said, because he could not speak English and we had to keep shouting "What?" in his ear every five seconds, because of the loud music. When he arrived the next morning, only Suzi and I were awake and raring to go. Fiona and Michele were dead to the world, and sleepily declined the offer of an interesting tour with a knowledgeable local.

We set off in Enrico's Fiat 127, passing through fragrant countryside, stopping every so often along the coastline which was indented with grottos, to admire the scenery. We had brought our swimming gear and all three of us went in for a splash at one of the particularly inviting looking grottos, where the water was an iridescent green and as clear as glass.

On arrival at Vieste, a charming whitewashed town with tiny winding streets paved with uneven flagstones, we stopped for a simple lunch of *orecchiette* - ear-shaped pasta with a tomato and basil sauce. As we strolled around the town, we admired the canopies of drifting bougainvillea and iron-work balconies, tumbling with vivid blood red geraniums, which looked stunning against the brilliant white of the buildings. Old ladies dressed exclusively in black, sat and crocheted or made intricate lace outside their bright homes. It was seemingly timeless, and very reminiscent of Greece.

Our Gargano holiday came to an end all too soon. Fiona and Michele were eager to rush on to *'Bella Roma.'* I was less enthusiastic as I knew the city would be deserted - all its inhabitants either holidaying in the nearby mountains, or lying in rows at the seaside. There are few people in the 'Eternal City' in August and hardly any of them are Romans.

We loaded up Doris who was beginning to groan a little at the weight we expected her to carry. During our week in Gargano, we had purchased gifts and souvenirs to remind us of our holiday. In Vieste, I had bought a gorgeous Etruscan looking pot with a jug and mug to match. It was glazed in cream earthenware with small blue repeated motifs.

"Where on earth are you going to put those, Doris?" demanded Fiona.

"In my kitchen of course," I responded. They would look a treat with my blue wallpaper.

"No, silly - I mean where are you going to put them in the car?"

"I'll stick them behind my feet," I said, ignoring the pained expression on everyone's faces.

"I don't think they're going to fit in," groaned Michele, who was going to be sitting in the rear of the car with me.

"Don't worry," I said. "If the worst comes to the worst, I'll travel with them on my knees or balance them on my head." I was determined not to leave my lovely pottery behind.

Our journey to Rome took us from the east to the west coast, not a typical route for most tourists, as we had to traverse some very inhospitable terrain. We edged into the mountains of Abruzzo, sprinkled with hill top villages, surrounded by high desolate ranges where wolves, chamois, bears and red squirrels roam free and eagles and woodpeckers also abound. It was an area untouched by tourism and its beauty was mesmerising. We crossed the Gran Sasso, a spectacular and eerie massif, beset by abandoned and semi deserted hill villages. This is the highest range in the Apennines and the feeling of wildness and bleakness is breathtaking.

L'Aquila was our destination for lunch that day. This town was founded by the Emperor Frederick II in 1240, as a stronghold against the Papal forces. L'Aquila boasts a lively centre with radiating crossroads, rather than a main piazza. The town is overlooked by the Gran Sasso and is very prone to earthquakes as are most towns in this beautiful region. There is a blend of old and new architecture, a daily market and a bustling street life.

After a satisfying lunch of pasta with a delicious lamb sauce - a speciality of the region - eaten *'al fresco'* under a pergola draped in sweet smelling jasmine, we pushed on through the Abruzzo National Park, a nature reserve and area of natural beauty. This lovely place is full of beech, maple and silver birch trees, as well as an abundant wild life.

This was followed by the more mundane A24 motorway into Rome. Fiona had to drive fast to keep up with the traffic and poor old Doris was stretched to her limits. The A24 cuts through the Sabine hills of Lazio and into the hinterland of Rome to the east. This led us to the Grande Raccordo Anulare, which encircles the city and is connected to all the major arteries running into the historic centre.

On this road, the traffic was fast and furious, and Fiona had to really concentrate to prevent poor Doris being hit by mad Roman drivers. We actually stopped talking for once, and hardly dared glance out of the window at the mayhem around us. Traffic was speeding bumper to bumper then stopping for no apparent reason. It was really quite scary.

We arrived in Rome at about five o'clock, tired, weary and hungry. Some wild exhilarating countryside had been traversed, and now we were entering one of the world's oldest civilizations. The juxtaposition of the two seemed surreal. Doris bore us into the industrial sprawl that surrounds Rome, with its factories and high rise developments. We entered the ancient centre and parked her somewhere along a street by the name of Via XX Septembre.

This long and usually bustling street was quiet, and many of its premises were closed for the long August holiday. Luckily we were able to book rooms in the first hotel that we chanced upon. It had an old world charm and a feeling of grandeur, with beautiful oak carved beds and twinkling chandeliers, spilling light from the ceilings.

After settling ourselves, we returned to the car and Fiona parked her right outside the hotel. However we were warned by the proprietor not to leave anything inside Doris, as thieves were known to frequently roam the area. Consequently, we had to lug all our baggage and camping gear up to our rooms.

We were disappointed at this turn of events, as we had saved enough money to treat ourselves to the luxury of a hotel room, just so we would not have to unpack everything. It was frustrating to learn that it would be foolhardy to leave our belongings on a Roman street.

"Better safe than sorry," groaned Suzi, pulling her suitcase up the marble travertine staircase.

"I feel absolutely drained now," I declared, flinging myself on my bed, in the room I was sharing with Suzi. The long journey and the hauling of our belongings up numerous flights, was beginning to take its toll.

Fiona and Michele were in an adjacent room. They also felt exhausted and were sprawled out on their beds, looking wan.

"Oh!" exclaimed Suzi, reviving a little and jumping off her bed. "Just look at this bathroom!"

It was indeed spectacular - marble with a black and cream chequered floor. An enormous walk-in shower was situated at the end of the room, and the basin, bath and toilet were of an Edwardian design or the equivalent of that era in Italy. Luxurious fluffy cream towels were hung at various intervals around the walls.

We refreshed ourselves, changed, and joined the others in their room to decide where to spend our first Roman evening. Food was definitely the first item on the agenda. After our long day, we were starving and could not wait to find something to eat.

"I wish I had some earrings!" Michele sighed. "I lost my only pair while we were camping."

She gazed at the chandelier above.

"Wouldn't those droplets make a fantastic pair!" she exclaimed, standing on a chest of drawers to examine them more closely. "They just hook on to each other. I'm sure no one will mind if I borrow two of them for the evening."

She stood on tiptoe, while we all held on to her to prevent her from toppling over, and she carefully unhooked the twinkling glass droplets. Jumping down off the drawers she attached the small glass objects to some fine twine she found amongst the camping gear, and managed somehow to thread these through her ears. She looked grand!

We were a noisy exuberant party, as we made our way out into the sultry night air. Dusk was falling and the heat of the day subsiding. Many restaurants were closed but we eventually found an out door *trattoria,* where we ate *spaghetti carbonara* and drank some good, red wine. After satisfying our hunger, we wandered further down the street and found an amazing *gelateria* or ice cream parlour, with the greatest choice of flavours we had ever seen.

We ordered a range of *gelati* and were incredulous when they arrived, as they were far more imaginatively and elaborately presented, than any we had ever laid eyes on before. Michele had requested a 'coconut ice,' and it arrived big and fluffy, wrapped up in a coconut shell, topped with slivers of mouth watering coconut and black and white chocolate. The rest of us were in for similar treats.

The ice cream man was called Gian-Franco.

"Why are you ladies visiting Roma now?" he demanded, as he laid our ice creams down with a flourish. "There's no one here - only turisti!"

"Well we're tourists," Suzi answered "We have to visit now, because this is when we have our holiday."

"You should come in spring time," Gian-Franco declared. "Roma, she is beautiful then - not too hot - just right."

That evening we turned in weary, after our long journey from east to west. We had just one day and another evening left in the Eternal city, before moving on to Tuscany where my parents had rented a house, and where we would be breaking our journey back to England, staying near Siena for a night.

The following day, it was difficult to decide which part of the monumental city to visit during our short stay. The Romans say that 'A lifetime isn't enough to do Rome justice,' and we had only one day! A unanimous decision was reached by all, to just wander around towards the centre and take in the sights that we happened to stumble upon, and try to feel the atmosphere of the great city.

"Let's go in the direction of the Trevi Fountain," suggested Suzi. "I can't come to Rome and not see it."

"I'd like to see the Forum," continued Michele, squinting at her guide book.

Fiona took out her map.

"We can't leave without seeing the Coliseum. It looks awesome."

"After that I'd like to sit on the Spanish Steps, and walk around the area where Keats lived." I added. Keats had been my favourite poet whilst studying the Romantics at school. We had been taught literature by a sort of Miss Jean Brodie type figure, and she had inspired some of us with embroidered stories about his short, tragic life.

After a simple breakfast of rolls and jam, and after donning our stoutest walking shoes which were not, in fact, very stout, we set off on our Roman adventure. The day was hot and cloudless. Deep shards of brilliant sunlight fell between the buildings. The streets were quiet and the interminable traffic much less frenetic than I remembered it years before, when visiting with my sister Joanna. It was relaxing to see Rome in August when the city was empty, even though it lacked its usual bustling, electric atmosphere.

La Fontana di Trevi or the Trevi Fountain was a complete shock to us. Tucked away behind narrow Roman alleyways, the vast ornate fountain is completely out of proportion with the tiny piazza where it has been built.

La Fontana di Trevi is an enormous, grandiose Baroque piece of sculpture, from which water gushes and spills over statues and rocks. Designed by Nicola (which, by the way, is a man's name in Italy) Salvi, in 1732, it features mythical creatures, archways and columns and the water that splashes over the sculpted rocks, is said to be the purest in Rome. In the celebrated film *'La Dolce Vita,'* Anita Ekberg became an icon of decadent hedonism when she threw herself into its glittering waters.

The little piazza had a cheerful ambience. People were sitting around the fountain's ledge, dipping their fingers or toes into the purifying waters. The trickles and splashes were soothing and cooling in the oppressive heat.

"If you throw a coin into the fountain it means that you'll return to Rome again." I told the others. We scrabbled around in our bags to find some loose lira to chuck into the watery depths.

We continued our *passeggiata* in a northerly direction towards Piazza di Spagna. Fronting the square is the house that Keats inhabited and where he died at an early age in 1821. Apparently he did not particularly enjoy living in the 'Eternal City.' He spent his last months there in great pain, and was also suffering from the unrequited love of a certain Fanny Brawne. He is reputed to have morbidly remarked to his room mate, the artist Joseph Severn that he could "already feel the flowers growing over him."

We reached the Spanish Steps and stopped for a well earned rest. In the spring time, gorgeous pink azaleas cascade down the sides of the travertine steps, but now in August they were flowerless. The twin belfries of the 16th century Baroque church, Trinita del Monte, loom over the three tiered staircase, which sweeps majestically upwards in a cascade of balustrades and balconies, whilst rustling palms stand like sentinels along the top.

We began to climb, and from the summit, the view of Rome spread before us was breathtaking and worth the effort involved in toiling up the many steps. We sat for a while chatting, and marvelled at the view, trying to identify various famous landmarks.

In the afternoon, we sauntered south down Via del Corso to Piazza Venezia, and stopped to gaze up at a huge edifice known as the Vittorio Emanuele Monument, which was started in 1885 and completed some forty years later, to celebrate the first king of a unified Italy. It seemed an incongruous building, dwarfing all its neighbours, its white Brescia marble glaring in the dazzling heat.

The Monument was completely out of place amongst the pink travertine and the other subdued colours of the city buildings. It has been nick-named the 'wedding cake,' 'Rome's false teeth' and even the 'typewriter,' and is generally considered to be a monstrosity and is loathed by most. It also obscures the Capitoline Hill which sits behind it and which played an important role in medieval and Renaissance times.

Next we strolled to the Forum area, a much more tranquil and idyllic spot, where the history of ages lay buried alongside graceful columns, arches, porticoes and other Roman remains. We did not have much time to explore this ancient market place, but were content to just drink in its unique atmosphere.

It was a peaceful spot in the heart of a great city. Butterflies swooped, insects droned and zizzed, and the hum of cicadas filled the grasses between the ruins. Sweet-scented oleander bushes were planted along one side of the Forum, and tall palms stood on the horizon jostling for space with ancient buildings and landmarks. I have been to this little oasis many times since and its beauty and serenity never fails to move me. It really is one of my favourite parts of Rome.

We tore ourselves away from this perfect place. The Coliseum beckoned and time was short. We walked around the awesome exterior and imagined the gladiators of long ago. This huge amphitheatre was commissioned by the Emperor Vespasian in AD 72. This massive building could hold up to 55,000 people, and they were seated according to their rank. The Roman Gladiators were the sportsmen and celebrities of their day, and slaves, prisoners of war or criminals, were made to fight them, or wild animals to the death. There was much bloodshed!

The next morning we arose early, as we had a long journey ahead. We traipsed down the stairs with our belongings, huffing and puffing with our heavy gear. That morning when I awoke and glanced in the mirror, I decided that I was definitely having a very 'bad hair day,' and just had to plug in my heated rollers, much to the annoyance of the others who were doing all the work and just wanted to get on. We loaded up Doris - me with my unpopular rollers jammed onto my head, in an effort to look presentable - and waved goodbye to *Bella Roma.*

Taking the A1 motorway northbound, we travelled through a gently undulating patchwork of green hills. In time, this became slightly monotonous and soporific with its velvet uniformity. As lunch time approached, we decided that the town of Orvieto would make a good stopping point.

Orvieto is an amazing place, built by the Etruscans and boasting one of the greatest Gothic cathedrals in Italy. Pope Leo X111 declared that on Judgement Day, 'it would float up to Heaven carried by its own beauty.' The façade of the *Duomo* is stunning with its lacy pattern of saints, apostles and prophets, grouped in a golden mosaic around the Virgin.

This jewel of a town is perched on a huge platform of tufa rock, six hundred feet high, and we spied it in the distance long before we arrived there. Its magnificent cathedral, zebra-striped in grey and white basalt and travertine, was poised on what seemed to be the edge of a precipice, all spires and pinnacles pointing heavenwards.

"What a dramatic place!" Michele said, as we viewed Orvieto, dominating the countryside for miles in every direction.

Its position on the tufa rock has meant that very few modern buildings have ever been constructed, giving the town an almost perfect medieval charm and character.

Parking Doris, we climbed upwards through serpentine, narrow streets towards the cathedral, which was built in medieval times to commemorate the 'Miracle of Bolsena. The building benefited from being decorated with the art work of some of the greatest artists and sculptors of the day. The massive interior contains frescoes started by Fra Angelico and completed by Luca Signorelli, depicting scenes of Resurection and Hell-fire.

The miracle of Bolsena is reputed to have happened, when a priest from a nearby town suddenly had doubts about 'transubstantiation,' i.e. when the bread and wine is supposed to change into the body and blood of Christ. Suddenly, the host he was blessing began dripping with blood, which in turn, seeped into the linen covering the altar. These relics are now contained in a beautiful gold and enamel reliquary, which is displayed on the feast of Corpus Christi and at Easter.

We sat for a while on the steps of the cathedral, looking at the radiant, glittering mosaics and the golden aura of it all. Ambling down Via Duomo and Corso Cavour, we did a spot of window shopping and were impressed by the ceramics with brightly painted medieval designs, and the wood sculptures, for which the town is noted. Taking a road to the left, we found ourselves in the old medieval quarter, with its narrow alleys and crumbling walls brightened by pots of tumbling, fuchsia coloured geraniums, and alive with the sweet sound of birdsong. These charming, confined streets led us back to the cathedral and as lunch beckoned, we found a small restaurant practically in its shadow.

The middle-aged owner of the eatery was called Rino. We engaged him in conversation and he told us, that besides owning a restaurant, he was also a wine maker. The volcanic slopes, on which Orvieto is built, are covered in vineyards that produce the famous fine white Orvieto wine. Some of the best Umbrian wines are produced here.

When the great artist Signorelli was painting the frescoes in the cathedral, he asked if he could be paid with the white stuff. The tufa rock, on which the town sits, is honeycombed with caves, used to ferment the Trebbiano grapes that go to make the great Orvieto vintages.

"Would you lovely ladies, like to taste my wine in my cellar?" Rino asked. "Venite, venite! Follow me," he gestured, leading the way down some rickety steps.

We trundled after him with much giggling and exclamation. We found ourselves in a cavern, where the soft rock had been hollowed out into wine caves. The walls were covered with a velvety mould and stalactites also made from mould, hung from the ceiling. Stacked around the walls were numerous stout wooden barrels. Rino produced a glass pipette and implored us to sample all his different wines. There were delicate and dry white wines and heavier sweeter red ones.

"Oh my God!" exclaimed Fiona. "Just look in this barrel - there's lots of flies floating on top of the wine!"

"Don't worry," Rino assured us. "They're harmless. They're dead and the acid has killed any germs. They add to the flavour!"

We giggled nervously, unsure whether to believe him or not.

"I can't drink anyway," declared Fiona. "I'm driving!" she explained; glad to be able to wriggle out of a difficult situation.

"Come, come!" Rino commanded. "Follow me!"

He led us up and down some stairs carved out of the rock. In one of the caverns, Rino showed us his potter's wheel, and picking up a lump of clay, threw it expertly onto the wheel and produced a beautiful turned vase in a matter of minutes. He proudly showed us other pots he had recently created, some glazed with Etruscan scenes. Rino told us that further down the hillside, there were Etruscan tombs dug into the side of the precipice.

We returned to the restaurant, blinking at the bright sunlight streaming through the windows. We discovered that our excursion through the caves had actually taken us under the cathedral, and we were thrilled at having had this experience.

The day was wearing on, and we still had to reach the foot hills of Siena and find the villa that my parents were renting. It would be late evening before we arrived. Feeling satiated with good food and Orvietan culture, we tumbled into Doris and rejoined the A1, also known as the *l'autostrada del sole,* or the sunshine motorway, and drove northbound.

Rolling hills, olive groves and the carefully terraced vineyards to the north were full of shadows and surrounded by a misty bluish haze. This was an area of Umbria as yet untouched by the mass tourism of somewhere like Tuscany. Its unassuming hilltop settlements do not boast the artistic accomplishments and wealth of its neighbours such as Florence, but they do harbour their own hidden treasures - beautiful churches and cathedrals, and an abundance of artistic works. They are well worth a visit and most of the towns exude a peaceful, old-world charm.

In times gone by, Umbria has been the scene of many a battle. Hannibal destroyed a Roman army on the shores of Lake Trasimeno. The never ending conflict between the Guelph-Ghibelline clans occurred on Umbrian soil. Dante declared long ago, that it was the most violent place in Italy. The memories of its bloody and turbulent past, still hum under the veneer of civilisation, and the proud peoples of this region, often re-enact scenes from times gone by, with cross bow tournaments and elaborate, colourful pageants.

The villa that my family had rented was somewhere just south of Siena. We were now in the heart of quintessential Italy, driving through glorious undulating countryside. Doris bore us through the dramatic Crete region, where bare rounded clay hills are punctuated with slender cypresses and the occasional terracotta coloured farmhouse. Ethereal mauve misty hills lay on the horizon and formed a background and contrast to the yellows and ochres of the Tuscan landscape.

All the windows of the car were open and a refreshing breeze blew about our faces. Suddenly a wasp flew into the car and Michele and Fiona started screaming, causing Doris to wobble dangerously. I had recently been on a transcendental meditation course in England and as I was deep on another level, did not notice the kefuffle around me. Apparently the wasp had landed on my knee where he stayed for a while. I just ignored it much to the amusement of the others. Eventually waspie flew off, everyone relaxed and I came out of my trance wondering what all the commotion was about.

Doris came to an abrupt stop several times while we consulted our map. Eventually, we found ourselves pushing up a narrow winding road that seemed interminable. Poor Doris lunged and rattled, and we all started to feel nauseous as we climbed the hair pin bends to our destination. Out came the chewing gum as we nervously contemplated the precipitous dip to the right of us. This particular drop was very difficult for Fiona as it was literally right under her window. She kept her eyes peeled on the bumpy road ahead. We could almost feel her terrified concentration.

"Are we nearly there yet?" she demanded, chewing furiously.

"We've got about 15 more kilometres to do yet," answered Suzi, consulting the large map spread out on the back seat of Doris. "Would you like me to drive for a while?" she offered, feeling that Fiona coud do with a rest.

"No, no it's OK." Fiona replied.

Fiona preferred to drive Doris. Neither Michele nor I could drive and Suzi often offered to help – but to no avail.

The house we were looking for was called '*Casa dei Fiori*' (House of Flowers) and it was solidly constructed from local stone, with an enormous, double front door. Over the portal entrance was a semicircular fresco of flowers, painted with red and blue pigments and the occasional touch of gold. Surrounded by cypress trees, the views over the Tuscan countryside were stupendous.

On arrival, we gratefully stumbled out of the car and rang the big jingly bell. My father opened the door He looked relaxed and was in holiday mode.

"Oh so you've found us then," he laughed. "You're just in time for dinner."

My mother and sisters were preparing food in the open-plan kitchen, and it smelt delicious and inviting. I introduced Suzi and Fiona whom they had never met before. Sitting around a huge table, we opened some bottles of Chianti and Orvieto, and later tucked into a hearty meal of lamb and roasted vegetables. There was apple pie and cream to follow, in true British style.

The following day, a trip to Siena had been planned on our way to Florence. As usual, the day presented as bright and hot. Apart from the storm south of Ancona, we had been lucky weather-wise with coast to coast sunshine.

We said our good-byes and piled back into Doris, who was looking decidedly dejected and dusty. Hoping she would have enough power and umph to see us back to Britain, we drove the short distance downhill to Siena, spying the wonderful medieval city in the distance. Silvery olive groves, oak and cypress forests were behind us - in front, the full splendour of Siena was unfolding before our very eyes.

Leaving Doris outside the ancient walls, we climbed the winding streets with their medieval and Renaissance buildings, to the main square, Piazza del Campo.

"Wow," enthused Fiona. "I have never seen a square this size. It's tremendous!"

We stood and gazed. I told the others about the Palio, and about my experience of almost being crushed to death in the crowd all those years ago.

"Trust you Doris," laughed Michele. "It could only happen to you!"

"Let's get a drink?" suggested Suzi. "I'm parched."

We moved to a small café in the shade and ordered four Martinis. It was a good spot for people – watching and the mellow medieval buildings provided music for the eyes. A small rotund waiter arrived at our table bearing four cups of tea and laid them on the table with a dramatic gesture.

"Erm, excuse me," said Michele. "We ordered Martinis not cups of tea."

"But you're Inglese – you always drink tea! Martinis aren't good for you – they're bad for your *fegato* (liver) and make you silly! Drink up your lovely English tea!"

With that comment, he disappeared, leaving us no option but to drink the murky substance which bore no resemblance to the drink as we know it!

We were happy for a while people watching and we received our own fair share of inquisitive looks from passing Italians. Fiona's hair always aroused curiosity and admiration. Michele was wearing a perky little hat over her short dark hair, which was obviously not Italian and rather bohemian in style. We stayed in the bar for ages. It was a great place to 'chill out,' and watch the world go by.

The atmosphere in Siena is very leisurely and has much to offer tourists. Apart from the Palio, Siena is famous for its cakes, the most delicious of these being *Panforte* which is a mouth watering mixture of nuts, honey, fruit and tiny pieces of biscuit. It is quite chewy in texture and has subtle flavours of aniseed and spices. This delicious confectionery can be bought whole or in pieces from one of the many bakeries, or it can be purchased as a gift in a colourful presentation box, made by a firm called Nannini.

The patron saint of Siena is Santa Caterina or St Catherine, and she was the first woman ever to be canonized. Her first vision occurred when she was six years old, but her father reacted against her holy destiny. However one day, so the story goes, he saw a dove hovering above her head whilst she was at prayer, and he relented realizing her holy vocation. This important Italian saint, performed many charitable as well as political works throughout her life and stars as co-patron of Italy, along with St. Francis. In 1999, Pope John Paul 11 declared her co-patron saint of Europe.

We lunched at 'La Lupa,' and I regaled the others with stories of previous visits to the trattoria. They particularly liked the tale about Paolo and the Alsation dog. After a hefty lunch, it was time to take our leave and soon we were racing through 'Chiantishire' with its picturesque villages. We took the N2, and passed through Monteriggioni, a hilltop town built in 1213 as a garrison, to guard the northern extremes of Sienese territory. This ancient place is surrounded by walls and has no less than fourteen towers.

We roared through rolling hills, dominated by rows of vines growing the Sangiovese grapes, which are pressed to become Chianti wines. Terraces of olives vied with tall willowy cypress trees and medieval castles adorned the landscape.

Suddely, we came upon Florence. The great city of the Renaissance was lying encapsulated in the emerald green hills of northern Tuscany. Bruelleschi's dome stood proud, rising massively but elegantly, above the terracotta roofs of the city.

This great artistic centre became an inspiration for travellers in the past doing the 'Grand Tour' and the poets Keats and Shelley loved to stay there. Our own 'Grand Tour' of the Renaissance city was to be relatively short, as we only had one night booked in a small pensione. The following day would be spent travelling northwards to Modena, where we had been invited to stay in the empty Contarini apartment, the entire family apart from Paolo, being up in the mountains at Casa della Fontana.

We headed for the area around the magnificent Duomo and wandered around the medieval streets, chancing upon a lively market where we browsed for a while, and purchased a few small items.

Later, we made our way to Piazza Signoria where we stopped to have a coffee and a *gelato*. This Piazza is the one, where in 1497, the fanatical monk Savonarola, bade his followers hurl all their worldly goods on to a bonfire. A year later, Savonarola was hanged as a heretic and then ironically, burnt. A bronze plaque set in one of the piazza pavement stones, marks the exact spot where the execution occurred.

The piazza was packed and we could not find an empty table for four, so we split up into two groups. Suzi and I eventually spied a couple of empty places with a great view of the copy of Michelangelo's 'David.' It took ages to be served, but finally our long awaited *gelati* arrived and we pounced upon them with dribbling anticipation.

After consuming our fill, we asked the waiter for '*il conto*' or the bill and after what seemed to be an interminable wait, he emerged with the tariff on a little saucer and then disappeared into the crowd. Suzi picked up the bill.

"Oh no!" she exclaimed. "It's 16.000 lira." (About £9)

"It can't possibly be?" I questioned incredulously "I don't think I've got that much money on me!"

"Neither have I," said Suzi looking despondent.

We pooled our money together and it amounted to 15.000 lira, minus the hotel money and some traveller's cheques that we could not cash until the following day.

"This price is ridiculous," I said. "It's day light robbery!"

Normally sitting down in an outside café and eating two ice creams, would total between 6.000 and 10.000 lira, at the very most.

"I suppose we are in the centre of Florence," declared Suzi. "What shall we do?"

"Well!" I pondered. "We can explain the situation and hope they don't hand us over to the police, wash dishes for the rest of the day or leave what we've got which is more than the stupid ice creams are actually worth!"

We decided on the latter plan. When the waiter was well out of sight we casually put our money onto the little saucer, as is the custom in Italy, and walked as nonchalantly as we could away from the café. Once we were around the corner, we ran like mad and finally, well away from the crime scene, collapsed in a heap of nervous giggles.

"Oh my Goodness!" Suzi exclaimed. "I never want to do that again!"

I had to agree with her!

That evening we took a leisurely stroll down to the river Arno. It had been a hot and sticky eventful day and the breeze from the river was welcome. The sun was just about to set - a round red orb, slowly sinking towards the horizon, slicing the sky with ribbons of gold, red, purple and magenta. The colours were less vibrantly reflected in the murky waters under the Ponte Vecchio, and signs of the 1966 Flood were just visible on some of the buildings. A faint tide mark encircled some of them indicating the level to where the fetid water had risen.

We stood by the banks of the great Arno and watched the sun sink. Gradually, the sky became an inky, starry void and a myriad of lights twinkled from the nearby buildings. Our 'Grand Tour' was coming to an end. The next morning would take us to Modena.

~

The following day we were loading up Doris once more, when we realized how efficient we were becoming, at packing in our belongings swiftly and tidily. I was not quite as organised as the other Dorises, and they used to moan at me - quite rightly so, because whenever I opened the car door, most of my possessions fell out. I am afraid that I have never quite got out of this bad habit, and now whenever we go on family holidays, my husband grumbles about exactly the same thing.

On that Florentine day, we took the A1 to Bologna, traversing a series of viaducts and tunnels through the hilly, densely forested landscape and then we joined the E45 to Modena. The countryside was changing subtly, and soon the flatness of the Po valley was upon us. The Pianura Padana stretched ahead - broken only by thrusting poplar trees whispering in the light summer breeze.

As we entered Modena, I could not believe how the *periferia* or outskirts had expanded. High rise modern dominiums had sprouted everywhere, blocking the landscape outside the city. What had once been rural farming hinterland, worked by old peasants picking radici and other edible leaves, was now a sprawling urban mass.

Driving into the centre of Modena, we parked Doris in one of the designated areas. I felt very emotional, as if I had come home. I was delighted that, after ten years of having first set foot in this beautiful city, nothing much had changed in its old historic heart, even if the outskirts were unrecognisable.

However, as I write this in 2004, I have reliable information that many alterations have occurred in the city centre since then. Standa and Upim, the two old-fashioned department stores I used to love pottering around in, are no longer there, and Bar Molinari where all the young set used to meet has vanished, having been replaced no doubt, by some other drinking establishment.

We traced our steps to Piazza Grande and walked around the beautiful Duomo and gorgeous Ghirlandina. We sat on the steps, as Jemp and I had done all those years ago and stroked the grinning lions. The city was quiet. Like Rome, most of the inhabitants were on holiday, having fled the oppressive sultry heat that pervades the towns of the Po in the summer months.

Sitting in a café called Bar Gino, we ordered *caffellatte,* and I found a coin phone and rang Paolo, to let him know of our arrival. He had returned from Casa della Fontana earlier in the day and was now staying at his parent's apartment, on the periphery of the city. He promised to be with us in about twenty minutes.

"Ciao Ragazze," he greeted us, brushing through Bar Gino's door. *"Come state?* Have you all had a good holiday?"

We recounted our adventures and stayed in the bar for a while. It was siesta time and everywhere else was closed up - shutters tightly locked against the world. For the second time that day I was reminded of my first afternoon in Modena, when Jemp and I had set foot in what seemed to be a deserted city.

Later, we drove up Via Giardini to the Contarini apartment and dumped our luggage. That evening we dined on pizza. Paolo had rung many of our old friends, including Claudio and we passed a jolly evening, reminiscing in the same pizzeria, where Lindsey from the City Language School had taken us newly appointed English teachers, during our direct method course, many years ago.

Clare Stimpson

Our 'Grand Tour' was practically over. Tomorrow we would begin the great trek north, leaving Italy and crossing France. We planned a stop-over in Paris, and for me this went a little way to assuage the loss of leaving Bella Italia. I wondered when I would return again to this wonderful land.

Teresa on the sun-drenched balcony in Sestri Levante

Teresa, wondering whether to go in for a dip

Walking down to the Campo in Siena

Three of the Dorises in Bella Roma

Three of the Dorises awaiting their coffee

Glimpses of Siena from just outside the walls

Clare Stimpson

A moment of respite, with the Virgin Mary looking on

The family relaxing

PART THREE

ENIGMATIC ITALY

CHAPTER 19 ALLA SICILIANA!

Sicilia - the very name conjures up images of scented orange and lemon groves and deep secret valleys - of beautiful lush landscapes, dotted with a profusion of wild flowers, contrasting with a barren inhospitable interior terrain. It sits like a jewel in the Mediterranean surrounded by the glittering sea and wrapped in the history of Greek, Roman and North African invaders. Often overlooked and ignored by the Italian mainland, Sicily is a land of proud warm-hearted people, of tension and Mafiosi, of bloodshed and violence and when my mother hitchhiked to this last outpost of Italy in around 1949, it was a land of brigands and bandits.

In the 1940s, it was a tourist's no-mans' land, and certainly a part of Italy that had rarely encountered young English women hiking through its countryside. My mother and her friend had their own Italian adventure in 1949, when they hitched through the peninsula and down to the *Mezzogiorno* - or south. Her stories inspired me during my teenage years, and I dreamed of living *'la dolce vita'* in a country I really knew nothing about.

271

On their trip to the *Mezzogiorno* where the summer sun is king and colours are intense, the two girls managed to hitch lifts into Italy as far as Venice, although cars must have been scarce in those days. By all accounts they had a lively time there, and my mother told me that they met some American chaps who bet them that they could not drink a litre of wine each, in one hour flat. This they did with dire consequences and there are rumours of them diving into the Grand Canal, inebriated and fully clothed. It is a wonder they lived to tell the tale!

Florence was their next stopping-off point and they stayed in a lovely youth hostel, which sadly has long since disappeared. In those days, the Renaissance city with its wealth of architectural features and artistic masterpieces was as much a tourist magnet as it is today. At the end of the 1940s, a new species of younger visitor was arriving to replace the elderly English ladies and the rich aristocratic Europeans. The two girls had a wonderful time sight seeing, and the highlight of their stay in Florence was a visit to the Uffizi Art Gallery, where they viewed celebrated paintings, that had only just returned from hiding after the Second World War.

Following World War II, Italy was in a state of complete upheaval. The country was more transformed by the war and its aftermath than any other place in Europe. The end of the conflict left much of Italy in chaos, and many buildings were reduced to rubble. Reconstruction began almost at once, providing jobs and opportunities for a new generation of craftsmen and construction workers. These were the halcyon years of expansion for Italy, and the North in particular, was poised on the edge of an industrial boom.

Of course, the style conscious Italians did not opt for the ugly post-war architecture that epitomises many British cities smashed by the Blitz, but expressed themselves artistically, with imaginative and tasteful buildings that blended seamlessly into the environment. The fact that they were generously aided by the Americans, of course, helped matters and new industries in the north promised a new prosperity. The ebullient Italians with their national characteristics of humour, imagination and a willingness to work soon had the country functioning again.

However, help was slow to arrive in the South, particularly in Sicily. At the end of the 1940s, the majority of people there existed in poverty. In this 'other' Italy, citizens lived in primitive surroundings. Villages existed in Sicily and the southern mainland, where the inhabitants lived with their donkeys in caves. In Calabria, there were many desolate villages which were unreachable because of the lack of roads, and could be approached only by streams.

In some parts of the *Mezzogiorno,* children were auctioned for farm labour and infant mortality was ten times higher than that in the north. The famous writer Danilo Dolci commented in his book 'To Feed the Hungry,' that at this time, almost half of Sicily's population was semi-destitute. He vividly describes the slums and squalid living conditions of many homes, some alive with flees and worse still, cockroaches. Epidemics of typhus and tuberculosis were endemic. Dolci tells us how the people subsisted on a starvation diet and he exposed the role of the Mafia in this lifestyle.

There was once an enormous rift between North and South. The economic post-war miracle had not been extended to the South, and the prosperous North wanted to wash its hands of the impoverished *Mezzagiorno*. This provided tension between two very different economies - and still does to a certain extent.

Sicily was once a land of plenty; a centre of culture and civilization, brought across the sea by the invading, ancient Greeks. It was the place where Plato dreamed of establishing his Republic. Ruled also by the Arabs, the Romans and the Normans, there is a mixture of bloods and it is not unusual to see blond, blue eyed people living in its cities and countryside.

When the Greeks first settled there, the island was carpeted with rich forests of oak, ilex, laurel and myrtle trees. Deforestation occurred, and now, away from the built-up cities there are few trees to hold moisture. The soil in Sicily is thick, cloggy clay, not conducive for growing crops and plants. The extremes of climate do not help. In winter there are rains and quagmires and the rivers turn to raging torrents, washing away the soil and loosening the mountain slopes, causing avalanches and devastation. In summer, the boiling sun and hot winds from Africa turn the soil to dust and dry up the rivers.

During this time, Sicily had an abundance of princes, marquises, counts and barons, many of whom drained wealth from the land. Through the 19th and early 20th century, many Sicilians emigrated to places like America, but the American immigration restriction laws of the early 1920s, caused the South to sink even deeper into poverty.

During the Fascist era, Mussolini banished his political opponents to the South. Many southern writers of the time described the conditions of their land, and reawakened the Italian conscience to the misery of the southern people.

After the allied soldiers had landed on the Sicilian beaches, they also made the world aware of the suffering. The Americans provided aid and this in turn caused the Italian government to take interest in the area. However over the years, much of the money ear-marked for the South did not always reach it. Most private capital has stayed out of the region, which has resulted in it lagging behind the rest of the country.

At the end of the 1940s, when my mother and her friend arrived in Sicily, the island was still sunk in desperate poverty - the sort that was rare in the Western world. The Sicilian people that they met were fascinated by the two English girls, who were unchaperoned, wearing northern European clothes, with rucksacks on their backs. Whole families came out to stare at them as they trudged along the stony paths, bordered with pungent aromatic wild celery and jasmine. They were a novelty and everyone, once they had recovered from the shock of seeing the two northern Europeans, wanted them to stay as their guests - even very poor Sicilians who had no room to spare, with the whole family sleeping together in one room.

En route to this wonderful isle, with its mule paths and Greek ruins, my mother and and her friend Jilly had stopped in Rome. Jilly had had all her money stolen, and eventually they were forced to visit the British Consul who charmingly sorted out the matter for them, before they continued on their way to Sicily.

However, on a subsequent visit the following year, a similar misfortune befell them further south, and this time the same consul was not quite so accommodating and refused them any help, thinking that they had engineered the whole thing. Instead, his more sympathetic secretary directed them to an English ship, which was docked in a nearby port where they were given a cabin, food and a working passage back to Britain.

On the rural road to Sicily in 1949, the girls met a family who lived very happily in a cave. The father worked as a policeman in a nearby town. The whole family insisted that the girls stay with them, but my mother and her friend found the cave claustrophobic and politely refused. Another hospitable family invited them into their tiny, barely furnished house for a meal and begged them to stay for a few days, inviting all their relatives around for 'a look.'

Very few foreigners ventured into these parts and it was a novelty to entertain the two English visitors. After a couple of days it was time to leave, but the warm kind-hearted Southerners would not hear of it and refused to let them go, keeping a close eye on their every move. Finally, they had no choice but to escape under cover of night and a giant luminous moon to guide their way in unfamiliar terrain.

A couple of days later, my mother was devastated to discover that she had left behind a much coveted swimming costume and against her friend's advice, almost went back for it.

Later that week, the remainder of what little funds they had were stolen and as they were hiking around the coast, they had no option but to sleep on the nearest beach. Early next morning, they were rudely awoken by an officious policeman who questioned them in a dialect they found impossible to understand, and eventually carted them off to the local police station, as he thought they were accomplices of the famous outlaw Salvatore Giuliano.

Giuliano the 'bandit' began criminal life as a popular folk hero. In 1943 he was captured by the carabinieri and was arrested for smuggling. In the scuffle that ensued, he killed one of the policemen and fled into the mountains. The news quickly spread and he was celebrated as an 'honorary murderer' by the people, who helped him and his gang find hide outs for which he repaid his helpers handsomely. He also had links with the Mafia and the Separatists who wanted independence for Sicily. Two important fighting troops were placed under his command and many crimes were perpetrated, under the respectable guise of Sicilian independence.

However, when the Separatist party was dissolved in 1947, Salvatore Giuliano and his brigands continued to terrorise the Sicilian people, with kidnappings, robberies and murders. His downfall from popular hero occurred on May Day in 1947, when he became a tool of the allied reactionary and Mafia force, and he opened fire with an automatic rifle on a group of peasant workers and their families who were holding a May Day picnic. Eleven died and fifty were seriously wounded, amongst them women and children, and this completely destroyed his status as a freedom fighter.

Two thousand carabinieri were sent from Rome to arrest the outlaw, and he was betrayed by one of his own rank. This infamous bandit has been the subject of two films - 'Salvatore Giuliano,' directed by Francesco Rose in 1961, and more recently, 'The Sicilian,' by Michael Cimino in 1988.

Feeling bewildered, my mother and her friend followed the stern-looking policeman to the police station. As they walked down the main path, they were amused (as well as being terrified) to see about a dozen or so carabinieri shaving '*al fresco*,' all peering into little mirrors hanging from courtyard trees.

The *Capo* or Chief of Police was charming, and laughed at the crumpled state of the two English girls, but nevertheless, locked them up in a cell for a few hours. Later he produced a huge key, releasing them and issuing an invitation to accompany him to the nearest village, to partake of coffee and cakes - a late breakfast!

On their release, the fact that the girls had no money presented few problems. Everybody they met wanted them as their guests. They were in danger of becoming minor celebrities, solely because of their penniless plight and because they were English!

Their journey continued around Sicily. The Sicilians that they stayed with gave them addresses of relatives living in different regions, and assured them that they would receive a warm welcome - although how the Sicilians managed to convey this in dialect, I have no idea!

Palermo and Castelamare in Calabria were visited, and the girls met up with some social workers who invited them to stay at an orphanage they were working in, somewhere in the mountains.

My mother told me that their stay in Palermo was particularly memorable. The Palermo of 1949 was a bombed heap - a melancholy place of contradictions, some of which continue even to this present day. Even now, the decaying elegance of the city's Baroque past, sits side by side with unrestored crumbling buildings and rubble from World War II. Baroque churches and palaces are everywhere, intermingled with slums, ruins and high-rise apartments. The rate of unemployment in this city is one of the highest in the whole of Italy. These differing historical and cultural forces, all come together to make Palermo a fascinating place with an edge of danger.

The two girls were given the address of a convent, where some nuns kindly put them up for a few days, on the condition that they go to mass every morning. It was a small price to pay!

Both girls were interested in art and history, and they visited many museums whilst staying in this fascinating city. They loved the stunning 12th century Arab-Norman mosaics in the Palatine Chapel, and the wonderful church of La Martovana, with its mystic Byzantine mosaics.Together, they wandered past bombed out zones, through bustling markets and down to the harbour, where fishing boats sailed on white capped turquoise waves, their sails swelling in a hot sultry breeze.

They wove their way through streets, brimming with fruit vendors and teeming with vespas, and they walked under canopies of billowing washing. Sicily had a different feel from the mainland and in fact the natives still call the rest of Italy *'Il continente.'*

The girls were given addresses of other convents, where they could be sure of a roof over their heads and some food. They managed to hitch a lift to Taomina, Sicily's most picturesque city, with its majestic views of Mount Etna, beautiful beaches and lush vegetation. They saw the Greek ruins of Selinunte, and wandered amongst the fallen marble capitols and uprooted columns that spoke to them of the history of long ago. They snacked on wild celery and plucked oranges and lemons, which grew in abundance in the wild countryside.

I too, once hitched from Modena to London, accompanied by Paolo and a bulging rucksack. Paolo's father drove us to the motorway, just north of the city, and then we were on our own. I remember the experience as being daunting, not knowing how or with whom we would be travelling, or even if we would ever arrive at our destination! We had taken enough money for the train, just in case there were no forthcoming lifts on our lonely journey north.

After obtaining a ride with a jolly truck driver as far as the border with France, our confidence grew immensely, and our next lift transported us to Paris, where we decided, tired and hungry, to catch the Metro to the Gard du Nord and finish our journey by rail.

I am still not sure to this day, how my mother and her friend managed the journey back to England. Perhaps they hitched a lift on a shipping vessel - who knows! Even my mother cannot remember after all this time. All I do know is that I am glad that she inspired me with stories of her epic journey which I nurtured. The seed turned into a flower and eventually I made my own Italian adventure a reality.

CHAPTER 20 BELLA ROMA

My mother and I continue our Italian saga, by trying to visit Italy at least once a year. Gone are the days of hitching and twenty-four hour gruelling train journeys. Now, we jump on an Easyjet or other low cost airline and land within two and a half hours. This relatively painless form of travel is worth our mutual fear of flying.

Our first ever destination together was '*La Bella Roma.*' The evening before we set off on our travels, we had attended a big family party and mama had drunk too much champagne. Consequently, she could not eat anything the following day and we arrived at the airport with her looking ashen faced and not well at all.

On the plane, the man sitting next to us had suggested that we share a taxi into Rome, but my mother dismissed the idea thinking that it would be too expensive. We decided to do the half an hour drive by bus. We would live to regret this decision.

We boarded the bus after a lot of messing about with ticket machines that were difficult to understand. Immediately, after turning very pale, mother collapsed. An ambulance arrived within minutes and we were both bundled into the back of it, as it sped off, sirens wailing. The paramedics began their job and my very rusty, but essential Italian, was quickly called into play.

After a short while, my mother recovered, sat up and declared rather smugly, that at least we would be heading nearer to the centre of Rome and it was a good job that we hadn't taken the taxi, after all. Little did we know that we were zooming in the opposite direction - miles from anywhere - to a *'Pronto Soccorso,'* a sort of accident and emergency unit, somewhere in the foot hills of Rome.

Our destination was be a hostel for *studentesse* or lady students, which closed at the midnight hour. On arrival at the *Pronto Soccorso* it was about 7.30 p.m. so we were slightly worried when we found that we were thirty kilometres from the centre of Rome. We had no idea how we would get back.

The doctors were excellent. I wish I could say the same about the hospital. The medics did their best in the shabby, unkempt building that housed the accident and emergency centre. There was graffiti everywhere, the bed linen was dirty, there was no loo paper in the toilets and even the picture-less walls were grubby. We moan about our National Health Service and our dirty hospitals, but by comparison, they are like palaces.

Of course this must vary considerably from region to region in Italy. During my 1970's stay, I had had my appendix taken out in a lovely, orderly, clean little clinic run by nuns.

After much examining and prodding, my mother was discharged.

Outside, the night was velvet black. No stars or moon or streetlights to indicate any form of civilisation. The medics were kind and phoned for a taxi. What sweet irony! However, no form of vehicle arrived.

"Where on earth will we stay, if the hostel is closed?" I pondered anxiously.

We were seriously worried, as by now it was eleven o'clock.

My mother was getting really cross, and I was anxious in case she had a relapse and we had to stay overnight in the hospital from hell.

As if by magic, a taxi arrived just before the midnight hour, complete with mad driver and mobile phone. By this stage, my Italian was improving by the second and I managed to relate a garbled message by phone to the hostel receptionist who promised to keep the doors open for us.

The next morning dawned bright and hopeful. To my amazement, my mother, who the evening before had almost been at death's door, was up early making tea for both of us, with her little portable and faithful tea maker that she always takes abroad with her.

We flung open the windows to greet the Roman day. To our horror, there were homeless people camped out in cardboard boxes below us. I immediately felt guilty as I had slept in a warm, albeit hard bed, whilst these poor wretches had had cardboard for blankets and a shop doorway as a bedroom.

From our hostel, the busy Via Nazionale was our gateway to the Eternal City. We battled to get on one of the No 64 buses, that constantly wound their way down this cosmopolitan and chaotic thoroughfare, risking our lives each time we crossed the road, literally praying that none of the totally mad Roman drivers would run us down. After all, we had already spent our first evening in hospital! Not many drivers stopped at the pedestrian crossings even when the lights were red. Instead, they would screech to a halt, in the middle of the black and white zebras, beeping and gesticulating and cursing everyone in general. It was quite stressful, noisy and exhilarating.

After a while we abandoned the No 64 and explored on foot. The buses were hot and sticky. People were packed in tighter than sardines and it was impossible to reach the ticket machines. It was much better to walk at leisure down the narrow historic streets, stopping to marvel at an unexpected wall painting here, or a beautiful statue or ornate door carving there. To smell the waft of garlic on the air, and listen to the odd snatch of Roman music or singing from an open window was heaven. However, our feet suffered as we trawled up and down the Via Nazionale, and we began to feel as if we almost belonged to the place.

I should explain that both Mother and I are mad art gallery freaks, which was one of the reasons why Rome, was at the top of our holiday hit list.

We found ourselves being enticed into every church we stumbled upon. We marvelled at the rich, sumptuous interiors and the amazingly intricate marble patterned floors, worn and uneven by centuries of passing feet. Richly decorated ceilings, adorned with celestial stars were above us, and beautiful works of art, by masters such as Titian, hung on many of the walls. We did indeed feel as if we had been transported to a calm serene heaven compared to the disorder of outside.

Virtually all the churches in Rome are Catholic. The warm glow of candlelight in these houses of God, adds to the serene atmosphere almost causing time to stop. Many people come into church for a few minutes to take time out and replenish themselves, both physically and spiritually.

The churches are always full, not just with tourists but also with working Italians.

On one of our journeys, we discovered a lovely Anglican church, with an outside garden, seats and colourful flowers. The interior was a little corner of England. Beautiful rich stained glass windows threw cascading pools of brilliant light upon the floor. I had forgotten, surrounded as I was, by Baroque Italian pomp and splendour, just how wondrous our more simple churches can be.

Back out on the Via Nazionale, the incessant traffic never ceased to wane. Whirring mopeds and scooters added to the confusion. The side streets with their ochre coloured *palazzi* offered some refuge. Every corner had some treasure which stopped us in our tracks: a pleasant green and leafy court yard with a bubbling fountain and the sweet twitter of birds; an exuberant Baroque façade; a thriving, colourful market or an imposing marble statue. The Italians kept a more leisurely pace of life here, in these little streets. Few tourists interrupted their everyday tasks, away from the main life veins of the city.

No wonder so many British painters and poets had wanted to live here, in Bella Roma. Byron, Shelley and Keats were all seduced by its crumbling charm. They were the Romantics - exiles, misunderstood by folk in their own country. My mother and I went to see where

Keats had lived in Piazza di Spagna - a beautiful, mellow artistic place. We sat at the top of the Spanish Steps, amongst the flowers and the gently swaying palm trees, and surveyed the city spread out before us.

We thought about poor Keats dying at the age of twenty five from consumption, and remembered his wonderful odes. He had been my favourite poet at school and his 'Ode to Autumn,' never fails to move me.

What a fantastic place Rome was! Ruins living happily with the more modern layers of history. Red pantile roofs with quaint chimney stacks punctuated the sky line, and famous monuments were dotted like thrown dice amongst this plethora of colour. The golden city was revealed in its decayed and gilded splendour!

Piazza di Spagna was sun drenched with vivid light. Crowds jostled with the bright azaleas on the Spanish Steps. To the left of us was Keats' house painted a mellow pink and now housing the Keats-Shelley Museum. Works, including prints, paintings, books and death-mask are all on display. Nearby is the Café Greco, where many famous intellectuals passed the time of day, including the Romantic Poets and Baudelaire, to name but a few!

We tried to avoid the Via Condotti. It is a street full of designer label shops and packed with milling people spending lots of money. Art was our aim - culture our gain - although I would not have minded frittering away some of my lira on some gorgeous clothes! However viewing art is a cheap pastime and very fulfilling and absorbing. We did look in some of the windows though, to see what we were missing, and we swooned over the fantastic Italian shoes and bags made from soft silky stylish leather - as only the Italians know how.

The Coliseum was a must! The day we decided to 'do' the Coliseum, it was raining! Of course, we had forgotten our umbrellas so we spent our time dodging the onslaught, under a smattering of scented umbrella shaped fir trees, in the vicinity of this great historic monument.

In Roman times, the bravest gladiators fought to the death there, spurred on by jeering or cheering crowds. Christian martyrs were thrown to the lions, dying heroically for their beliefs, amongst the screaming euphoric spectators.

It was with a sense of awe that we viewed this great amphitheatre. It had seen so much bloodshed. Tuscan, Ionic and Corinthian pillars had been placed one upon the other to create its round, massive, monumental presence. Underneath, the dungeons, cages and endless passageways, reminded us of its gruesome macabre past.

The Forum was a gentler place of interest. Quiet and subdued, its former glory lying in ruins around our feet. The Temple of Castor and Pollux seemed almost surreal, rising supremely out of the treasure-laden grounds, against a backdrop of Roman apartments and villas. This was a very tranquil scene after the circus and vendors of the Coliseum. Statues and artefacts lay littered on the scrubby ground. We sat and contemplated, basking in the sun.

Excavation began on the Forum in the eighteenth century and most of the area that we know today, was buried under mounds of rubble until then. Many temples, memorials, halls and basilicas were unearthed, all of which now stand in various states of ruin.

Clare Stimpson

Everywhere in Rome, one is constantly reminded of greatness and decline. We all remember the story of Romulus and Remus, the twins who were suckled by a wolf and became the founders of the great city.

Somewhere, there is a statue of this famous pair. In Rome statues abound everywhere. There are so many that one becomes quite blasé about them.

Of course, we could not travel to Rome without visiting the Vatican, that tiny independent state, housing the Basilica of St. Peter, the home of the Pope and the centre of the Catholic Church. Swiss guards dressed in colourful costumes, guard and protect this holy place which also houses one of the greatest art collections in the world. The Sistine Chapel and the Vatican library contain untold art treasures.

We visited the Vatican State on our first Sunday there. We filed into St Peter's with hundreds of others to hear mass. Droves of people were milling around. I was amazed at so many comings and goings during the service, which all seemed quite natural to the Italians. I think in England the parish priest would have something to say about that!

Outside, the sun was hot, and in the midday shimmer St. Peter's Square looked beautiful, surrounded by imposing colonnades and statues.

Our walkabouts in Rome, always left us hungry. On our first evening, we stumbled upon a little known *trattoria* run by just one elderly lady. She seemed to do everything - the waiting, ordering and cooking, all by herself. Her food was fantastic - simple homemade Italian cuisine at its best.

A *trattoria* is a type of local restaurant, frequented by Italians in the know and often overlooked by tourists, who prefer the more flashy and expensive variety of restaurant, mistaking a *trattoria* for a poor man's eating place. How wrong they are! Fresh homemade lasagne bursting with luscious tomato *sugo* or sauce; freshly picked flavoursome salad tossed in virgin olive oil and chunky freshly baked bread; these simple but delicious foods were all on the rustic menu.

Italians are very fussy about their food - always declaring that it is the best in the world. I actually agree with them, but I find their attitude amusing and sometimes it can be irritating. They have this notion that the food from other countries is just not up to scratch. Consequently, there are fewer foreign restaurants in Italy than practically anywhere else in Europe. Even the big cities are not very cosmopolitan when it comes to food.

I remember teaching a group of Italians at a summer school in the 1970s, when English cuisine was really disgusting. Most of the students arrived with big suitcases, which I imagined to be filled with the latest Italian clothes. Imagine my surprise when my students unpacked packets of spaghetti, *ragu* for sauces and Italian coffee. Some had even brought their own saucepans! Admittedly, English cuisine did have a bad reputation during that time, but I was stunned! I did not realise then, that food comes high up on an Italian's agenda and that that food, has to be Italian!

CHAPTER 21 VENEZIA - LA SERENISSIMA

Our next port of call was Venice. What a dazzling, magical and fantastic city. This time, compared to last year, our arrival was relatively painless and Mum and I spilt out of Marco Polo airport and into the Mestre or mainland, to catch a bus to the city of lagoons.

All was well. We found a vaporetto or water bus heading in our direction which was that of the Accademia, and had planned that we would have enough time for a quick change and meal, before our hostel closed for the night.

We had booked to stay in another hostel for young ladies, run by nuns. It was wonderfully clean and very cheap compared to most hotels in Venice and it was fairly central. The only drawbacks were, that it closed at 10.00p.m. each evening and the nuns awoke at 5.00a.m. and broke our sleep with their monotonous chanting and melodious hymn singing. Still, this was a tiny price to pay for a large room complete with lovely en suite bathroom, at a fraction of what it would have cost in a hotel.

It was mid evening and we were enjoying our ride in the vaporetto. The day had been hot. The cool air and the proximity to the water was refreshing. I looked around - to me Venice had always seemed surreal.

We felt that we were part of a film set. Initial exposure to the city is mind blowing. I had forgotten how incomparable it was to anywhere else I had ever travelled to. Venice is city of dreams - a work of art that we were actually moving around in. It was bizarre.

The clink of eight o'clock dinner plates resounded through open palazzo windows, which were hung with vivid red geraniums reflected in the foamy green-grey water. Snippets of conversation layered the bright evening air.

Everywhere was calm and serene, partly due to the fact that there are no cars in Venice. Instead, there is an eerie stillness that most of us are really unused to. Byron described the city as 'the greenest island of my imagination.' It has a life and culture uniquely its own. Now however, many of its young are leaving as there are no opportunities to be had, other than tourism.

The first time that I visited Venice was in the 1970s. It was January, and the place was bleak and cold - a grey and mysterious city. St. Mark's Campanile or bell tower rose dreamily out of the shrouded foggy mist, that often lies damply around the lagoon at this time of year. There were very few tourists and I was able to explore the city with ease, and marvel at its exceptional beauty and light without bumping into hoards of people.

At this time I had just seen the film 'Don't look Now,' the psychological thriller starring Julie Christie and Donald Sutherland, which was set in Venice. The film describes the city as a creepy, slightly sinister place especially at night. When visited in the winter months, it can take on a chilling and sad atmosphere - almost forlorn and forgotten by time and men.

So, we were sailing along the Grand Canal, my mother and I, wallowing in our breathtaking surroundings and looking forward to arriving at our destination. Suddenly, my mother looked very alarmed. She shouted to me that she had lost her bag. Now this was her only bag and practically all her luggage was packed inside. It contained her massive collection of vitamin pills, her passport and some other valuable documents.

She indicated that she was getting off the *vaporetto* at the next stop. I had no option but to follow. We ran down narrow back alleys or *Calle.* My mother raced like the wind, as she had no luggage, while I puffed and panted behind, trying to keep up, my huge rucksack banging painfully against my back with every step.

Venice is not a place where you can run freely from A to B. The *Calle* zigzag in all directions, often joined by bridges with steps. I was feeling more panic-stricken and breathless every minute, as we flew up and down the uneven stone steps.

"What on earth will we do Mum," I gasped, "if your bag isn't at the ticket station?"

"I really don't know!" Mother answered grimly.

Luckily, the wayward bag was produced with a flourish as we arrived, red faced, gasping for breath and gabbling in Italian. We had to spend about fifteen minutes recovering before we boarded the next *vaporetto* to the Accademia.

One of the first things that hits you about Venice is the lack of any serious noise. There are no cars, no honking horns or traffic jams. Just lapping water and other canal sounds, the clank of church bells ringing out the hour, the quick tap of footsteps upon stone, and the musical intonation of the Italian language, as gondolier and other street folk shout across the water to each other. Time feels suspended.

"This must be one reason why so many young Italians prefer the mainland and leave as soon as possible." I suggested to my mother.

"That, and the fact that you cannot have a car in Venice," she replied wisely. The Italians love fast cars and noise.

Venice has also been called *'La Serenissima.'* During the Middle Ages, it was a thriving maritime power. The Grand Canal snakes its way through the centre of the city, splitting it in two - the more middle class and tourist bank of San Marco, and the other more working class bank, where many Venetians live and work. This great waterway winds its way through the heart of Venice.

My mother and I used the Grand Canal a great deal, on our travels around the water-bound city. We marvelled at the intricate, Venetian Gothic traceries of the Ca'd'Oro, the Ca'Foscari and the Accademia, as we glided past them. The Ca'd'Oro is my favourite building - so called because of the gold ornamental detail, used by the Contarini family, (not the same ones that I knew in Modena), who owned it between 1422 and 1440. Now it is the Galleria Franchetti and houses many works of art, which of course we had to see. The view along the

Grand Canal from one of the huge upstairs windows was breathtaking - I could have stayed there all day watching the river traffic.

We tried to avoid the main tourist areas and often made for the quieter, smaller backwaters. One day we took a *vaporetto* to San Georgio Maggiore, a small island which could be clearly seen from the Zattera where we often took a stroll. How different it was from the smart piazzas and the great *palazzi* of *La Serenissima*. We were greeted by small dusty streets and crumbling grey buildings, hung with colourful washing drying in the heat. This was another world away from the hustle and bustle of St. Mark's Square. From this island, we crossed to the Giudecca and visited Il Redentore, a massive Palladian church.

~

Just as everything was going well, disaster struck! As I described earlier, the hostel we were staying in was run by nuns who were very charming, but who insisted on closing the main door at 10p.m. every evening. We had to be back by then or we were locked out. The hostel had recently been renovated and new fire doors fitted. Once closed, they were extremely difficult to unlock. Each evening, many frustrating minutes were spent turning our keys this way and that, in an attempt to gain entry to our room.

One evening we returned after a pleasant *passeggiata* at around 9.55p.m. just before locking up time. We could not open our door and asked the only nun who appeared to be awake to assist us. The poor woman who seemed very tired could not open it either. The three of us stood there helplessly, wondering what to do. The kind but exhausted nun suggested that we sleep in another room, as there were many empty ones. It was May and the peak tourist season had not really begun yet.

We were dismayed at this turn of events, as we had no night apparel or any of the lotions and potions which we heavily relied upon to make ourselves presentable to the world at large. We were particularly upset about not having our mosquito repellent, which was an absolute necessity for a good night's sleep in this lagoon infested area.

Mosquitoes or *zanzare* are an Italian nightmare. Never have I seen such huge and prolific zizzing creatures, as the ones that reign in Italy. When I lived in Modena, set in the swampy Po valley, they were the bane of my life and I spent many an evening chasing and executing them, before they could take great juicy bites out of my flesh.

Venice was no exception. Mother and I entered our new room in trepidation, resigned to our chilling fate. We knew what lay before us! We could already hear the ziz and whirr of several *zanzare*. We had been very careful to shut our windows in our own room, but in this one they had been left open.

The empty room contained only beds and fluffy white towels, so we were devoid of any weapons. Climbing wearily into bed, in make shift night gear, we tried not to leave any exposed areas of flesh and settled down uncomfortably. It was of course, impossible to sleep. Mosquitoes ducked and dived everywhere, but mostly around us!

We simultaneously jumped out of bed and grabbed the two available towels. A mad purge followed, as two wild women in a rage, flailed and swiped the evil foe, spurting their blood (probably our blood!) against the clean whitewashed walls. Having completed our holocaust, we climbed wearily back into our beds, only to hear yet more zizzing creatures trying to get their revenge!

All night long we battled against the enemy. The following morning we were exhausted, badly bitten and horrified by the state of our blood splattered surroundings. What on earth would the nuns think! We tried our best to clear up the evidence of the blood bath, washing the crimson splashes from the pristine white walls.

~

The quiet part of Venice is often mysterious and intriguing. A real stillness and sense of illusion pervades the air. It feels and probably looks the same as it did one hundred years ago. Sounds of domesticity float from open windows. Small boats create gently lapping waves, quaint bridges span canals, and picturesque squares are stumbled upon by accident. One feels that the very essence of Venice and her elusive ways are locked within the crumbling walls of the shabby, yet magnificent *palazzi.*

St Mark's Square, is of course, the jewel in the crown. Visitors flock here all year round, to view two of the city's most important sights - the magnificent Basilica di St. Marco and the Gothic Palazzo Ducale, also known as the Doge's palace which was home to the former rulers of Venice. It is the only square in the city that is entitled to be called a *piazza,* and is the focal point of the city's political, religious and administrative history. It has been the scene of many a festivity and state celebration.

My mother and I loved the *piazza,* but preferred to visit it at night when the atmosphere was magical. The great Basilica was illuminated, making the gilded façade mosaics and coloured marbles, gleam in vivid splendour against an inky, indigo sky. The string orchestras, playing outside the cafés Quadri and Florian, have always attracted groups of on-lookers, some of whom would begin to waltz dreamily across the uneven flagstones of the square, oblivious to the crowds, hearing only the music. The great square entertained all, on an extravagant scale.

Outside the many bars, were endless rows of tables and chairs, waited on by immaculately dressed *bariste,* bearing trays of sparkling drinks and tasty titbits. Austrian blinds hung from the huge archways shading the colonnades behind, and pigeons perilously swooped and dived.

During the day the *piazza* was packed with people from all corners of the earth but as night fell, they thined out and there was room to walk and breathe. We loved wandering around the *piazza* in the evening, bathed in the glow from the illuminated buildings. In the distance above the chatter and laughter of the crowd we could hear the slap of water, as the gondolas bobbed up and down on the Grande Canal.

A highlight of our stay was a visit to the Peggy Guggenheim collection, housed in a one storey *palazzo* which has the nickname *Il Palazzo Non-Finito,* meaning The Unfinished Palace. Apparently it was intended as a four storey building, but was never completed, and this gives it a modern feel which is very out of character in

Venice. Its airy look is completed by the fact that its exterior walls are whitewashed - a rarity in the watery city.

In 1949, the building was bought as a home by the American millionairess and socialite, Peggy Guggenheim, who was a prolific collector and patron of the arts. She was married to a painter, the great artist Max Ernst. More recently her home was turned into an art gallery, containing works of modern art, by artists such as Braque, Chagall, de Chirico, Duchamp, Kandinsky, Magritte and Mondrian to name but a few.

My mother and I were enthralled by this beautiful building and its wonderful works, and we were fascinated as we passed from room to room. The setting was magnificent. From the windows, river craft trawled the Grand Canal and the interior, housing the paintings, boasted light filled rooms and some of Peggy's furniture such as her marvellous red leather sofas and rich dark wooden tables. Outside, we stood on the terrace overlooking the Grand Canal and for a while watched the busy river traffic, amongst statues and modern art.

Sometimes during our stay, we hopped on a *vaporetto* or water bus to take us from one place to another, but often we found it quicker to explore Venice on foot. The *vaporetti* were crowded, but the welcome cooling breeze off the water in the humid clammy heat compensated for the jostling crowds.

Route No.1, along with several other routes, operates from one end of the Grand Canal to the other and affords a wonderful view of the ornate palaces lining the waterfront. The Grand Canal or the '*Canalazzo,*' as the Venetians call it, is a busy thoroughfare and as well as vaporetti there are *motoscafi* or water taxis, *traghetti* or gondola ferries, all manner of private water craft and of course the ubiquitous gondolas. Water ambulances, police speed-boats and funeral corteges decked with splendid flowers, all travel along the canals.

The deceased of Venice are buried on a small island called San Michele, which contains a huge cemetery consisting of a series of gardens planted with cypresses and studded with funereal monuments. The beautiful, small cemetery chapel was designed by Coduzzi, whose other lovely churches like Santa Maria dei Miracoli enrich the city.

We really preferred to see Venice on foot where we could breathe the spirit and atmosphere of the place. We loved the back waters, with the tiny bridges and tall narrow *palazzi* with crumbling faded pastel coloured façades. However shabby the *palazzi* exteriors were, they were almost always smartened up with colourful window awnings and cascading geraniums.

Here the water would be calm with just the faintest ripple touching the surface, and the feeling of quiet would be immense - as if time had halted. Sometimes, we would stumble upon ornate gondolas moored to the *palazzi*. I remember seeing one that was like a miniature living room with a carpet, velvet seats and tiny lacy table cloths, complete with fancy cushions and even a vase of lilies. Some have painted floors and most have a high, elaborate sofa area where couples can sit and romantically while away the evening. Most gondolas are reserved for foreigners and many are used for weddings. The Venetians do not often ride in them - they have their own forms of water transport, otherwise they take a *vaporetto*.

Near our hostel was a lovely waterfront café where we would sometimes have breakfast. It was decked with flowers and overlooked some pretty *palazzi* with lacy Gothic façades.

On the whole, we were rather disappointed with the food we were served in Venice. It did not seem up to the standard of other Italian cities. However, there was a tremendous choice of relatively cheap places to eat and a lot of fast food seemed to be available.

One day on our travels around the city, we came across what seemed to be an exquisite place to eat. It was open-air and situated alongside a canal. It looked interesting and although it was outside in a sort of passageway, it also had a beamed ceiling. We vowed to return that evening and dine there - but when night fell, we simply could not find it. It was as if it had vanished! A few days later, we chanced upon it and as it was lunch time, decided to eat, there and then, in case we lost its location again.

The restaurant was in a lovely position and we could watch the boats gliding up and down as we ate. Mother ordered spaghetti and I chose lasagne which looked delicious. I was halfway through eating it when I noticed a big, dead fly mixed up in the béchamel sauce.

"Ugh!" I exclaimed.

"What's up dear?" enquired Mother.

"There's a fly in my lasagne," I shrieked, laughing at the cliché.

"Are you sure?" asked my mother looking concerned.

"Of course I'm sure," I spluttered, pointing at the large black and green shaped object that was floating legs upwards on my plate. "I'm going to have to tell the waitress!"

I tried to catch her eye as she sailed up and down, bearing plates and dishes. It took ages. Eventually she came over to our table and was very upset and flustered when she discovered what had happened.

"I'm so sorry," she cried "I'll get you another lasagna. Just you wait moment! Please don't tell anybody!" she added conspiratorially, putting her fingers to her lips.

She returned some minutes later, with a plate of fresh lasagne and told us that we did not need to pay for our meal. She even plied us with some more wine which was also free.

Our hostel was near the Zattere, or the quayside region of the city. This was a workaday area with a little supermarket, local bars and a view of the Giudecca. The quayside was wide and provided a pleasant place to stroll along, away from the throngs of tourists. Sometimes Great Ocean liners rolled up to the docks - a little further on, and the proximity of the huge liner to the quayside was breathtaking and slightly surreal. Passengers lined the decks and waved to the people of Venice.

Most days we crossed the famous Rialto Bridge, which spans the Grand Canal in the commercial heart of the city. This was one of the first areas of Venice to be inhabited long ago, and the bridge afforded a wonderful view of the Grand Canal and all its traffic.

It was first constructed in 1264, as a wooden drawbridge. However it burnt down in 1310 in an insurrection, and was rebuilt, only to collapse under the weight of the crowds that gathered for the wedding of the Marchioness of Ferrara. Another wooden bridge was erected, but it fell into disrepair and in 1524, it was decided to construct the next bridge out of stone.

The streets around this crowded bustling area used to be lined with stalls, selling mysterious spices and fabrics from far away exotic places, but have since been replaced with tackier tourist merchandise. Further on, the *Pescheria* or fish market is a fascinating venue where it is possible to buy fresh fish and all manner of sea food. Around this part of the city are many market traders, selling a wide variety of goods, including tall plastic cups filled with delicious watermelon and grapes, which were a 'must' on a hot afternoon.

In the 17th century, a terrible plague hit Venice and wiped out a third of the population. By 1630 it was over, and the people of the city decided to build a church in thanksgiving for the end of the epidemic. The monumental church of Santa Maria della Salute was built, in an area known as Dorsodura meaning 'firm backbone.' This part of Venice, as its name suggest, is fairly stable ground built on a stratum of solid subsoil.Before the church could be constructed, more than a million wooden stakes were driven into the ground to reinforce and support the foundations of the vast edifice, which is one of the most imposing landmarks of Venice.

This huge octagonal shaped church is Baroque in style and was designed by Baldassare Longhena. As the outside was so imposing, we could not wait to see the interior. Compared to the outside, it was comparatively plain with a large octagonal space below the cupola. However, there were paintings by Tintoretto, namely 'The Wedding of Cana' and by Titian - 'The Sacrifice of Abraham, Cain and Abel and David and Goliath,' which my mother was glad not to have missed.

All too soon, our short stay was at an end. It has been said that one can spend one's whole life in Venice and still not see everything - there are so many secret hidden *palazzi* and squares, so many little nooks and crannies to be explored. We agreed to return as soon as time permitted.

~

Our next sojourn to Venice was a couple of years later. This time our trip was at the end of August. The weather had been unseasonably hot in England that year, but we were not prepared for the unremitting stifling heat of *La Serenissima*.

We had booked a hotel for one night on the mainland, as we were arriving rather late in the evening, and we boarded a bus for a small place called Tessera a few kilometres away, without any real idea of where we were actually going. Outside it was pitch black with no moon, stars or street lights to cast light on the scene.

"I had better ask the driver to tell us when we arrive at Hotel Gianni," I said to my mother.

"Yes," replied Mum. "Tell him it's about eight kilometres away."

I conveyed this information to the driver, striving to keep my balance as the bus tried its hardest to break the speed record. The terse looking fellow nodded, without taking his eyes off the black void that was the surrounding Italian countryside

We sped through open terrain. Peering out of the grimy windows, we could see nothing. Suddenly the bus rattled to an abrupt stop.

"Ecco ci siamo al Hotel Gianni!" shouted the driver.

"Grazie." We thanked him, as we jettisoned ourselves and our luggage into the balmy night air.

The night was inky black. We looked around for Hotel Gianni but it was nowhere to be seen and we appeared to be in the middle of a vast, very dark desert.

The driver, seeing our confusion disembarked and pointed us in the direction of the hotel.

"È ottanta metri giù in fondo," (80 metres down the road) he shouted above the roar of his bus. He then sped off into the night.

"Why on earth didn't we get a taxi?" I grumbled. "We're in the middle of nowhere!"

"Mmm," agreed my mother. "I thought he would drop us off outside the hotel."

"Oh well we're in Italy!" I said. "Weird and wonderful things always happen to us here!"

Would any arrival of ours in this country ever be normal? I thought. We always seemed to be jinxed - but that was half the fun - the unpredictable!

We travelled along the dark and very busy road. Cars with dazzling headlights, doing about eighty kilometres an hour, hurtled past. It was quite dangerous to be an English person, walking with a suitcase on wheels in this strange situation. There was no pavement and we were virtually forced to walk on the edge of the road.

On either side of us the land dipped away and appeared to be marshy. Cicadas chirped and frolicked in the bushes and the sound was almost deafening.

"This looks like mosquito land," I remarked to my mother.

This time we had packed plenty of insect repellent. We were taking no chances with the dreaded *zanzare*.

Hotel Gianni was reached with great relief. It was good to tumble into the bright reception area and be handed the key to a spacious and comfortable room. The hotel was decorated in art nouveau style, which surprised us, as the façade was very plain. There were lovely period fittings throughout the hotel, such as lamps, doors and coving and there were interesting paintings hanging on the walls. The atmosphere was humid, and as we sat on our beds to unpack a few things, sweat ran in rivulets down our backs.

The next morning dawned just as hot. We were greeted at breakfast with steaming bowls of frothy *cappuccini* which were delicious. We paid our bill, packed up our few belongings, and caught a bus to Venice. There was standing room only and we were fortunate to be positioned at the front, so that when we travelled over the causeway, en route to Piazzale Roma, we had a stunning view of *La Serenissima* rising triumphantly out of the lagoon.

We caught a *vaporetto* which transported us along the Grand Canal to Piazza San Marco. From there, it was a short walk to our hotel, which was situated along a small picturesque canal. The hotel was very pretty from the outside, but inside there were numerous flights of stairs to climb before reaching our room, which we found to be rather disappointing. We were at the rear of the hotel and had a view of an alleyway and another hotel window.

"At least we have a fan," said Mother. This was a godsend as the temperature was in the thirties.

"Well we won't be here most of the time and at least we won't have to be back for 10 o'clock," I chuckled.

We unpacked our few belongings and set out to explore the neighbourhood. We were in the *sestiero* or quarter of San Marco and although we were only a stone's throw away from the famous crowded *piazza,* our hotel was situated in a quiet but interesting back water.

Each *sestriero* hugs its own square called a *campo,* usually complete with church, pealing bells, bars, outdoor cafés and tiny local shops. Our nearest *campo* was that of Santa Maria Formosa, a lovely wide sunlit area with a fountain in the centre. The church of the same name is unusual, as it has two main façades one of which overlooks the *campo* and the other which overlooks the canal. We were drawn to the inside which contains a triptych by Vivarini painted in 1473, and which reminded us both of the artist Stanley Spencer's work.

Later that day we chanced upon the Querini Stampalia gallery which was also in the *campo,* and were fascinated by a collection of 18th century Venetian genre paintings, depicting life in Venice at that time. Entering the brilliant sun lit *campo* after being in the gallery for a few hours, we remarked on how much there was to see in this celebrated city and how we would never manage to see it all.

That evening we ate sea food and retired to bed at a reasonable hour. We congratulated ourselves on our choice of hotel, away from the main hubbub, with just a nice quiet alleyway beneath our window. However our complacence was to be short-lived. At around midnight, we were both awoken by the gruff sound of voices. They became louder, and someone somewhere very near us, was playing a guitar badly and singing gustily.

We both groaned and I padded over to the open window, to try to find out what was happening. Outside there was a bright light from a window directly opposite ours, illuminating an interior with about eight men playing cards, drinking and singing.

"There's nothing we can do Mum," I said exasperatedly. "There's a load of men in that building over there - we can't very well tell them to shut up. They'll just laugh at us!"

"Close the window then," murmured my mother sleepily.

I was reluctant to do this as the temperature in the room was stifling. We could still hear their voices, and the whirring of the fan made sleep fitful. We awoke next morning feeling irritable through lack of quality sleep. We asked the proprietor if we could have a change of room, but alas, there were no alternative ones available.

"If they keep us awake again," said my mother as we crossed the small bridged canal into Campo Santa Formosa, "we'll look for another hotel!"

We had a leisurely *cappuccino* in the *campo* and decided to head northwards to the Fondamente Nuovo.

Our route took us through some very pleasant untouristy areas, and we began to cheer up as the hot sun melted our frustrations. We came upon a beautiful Gothic church called Santi Giovanni e Paolo - known colloquially as San Zanipolo. This grand church is also known as the Pantheon of Venice and is next door to the city hospital. One of its cloisters actually forms part of the rambling medical building.

Alongside the canal were a series of water ambulances, bobbing gaily on the iridescent water.

People in Venice must be rather healthy, as we only saw one water ambulence in action during our stay in the city. Apparently, it is very difficult for paramedics to transport ill people from the top floor of their *palazzi* to the ambulances. Many old buildings do not contain lifts, and the ill and injured have to be carried down many flights of stairs, some of which are very narrow. It must be a nightmare job!

We pushed open the doors of the hospital and entered a vast reception hall, expecting someone to ask us what we were doing there and would we please go away. Nothing happened, so we continued on to the wards and passed through an incredible façade with a *tromp-l'oeil* painting from the fifteenth century.

Continuing up some wide worn marble steps to the next floor, we admired the beautiful patterns and tessellations that were created long ago, to give colour and interest underfoot. A great window overlooked a stunning courtyard garden, with palms and other tropical plants. We returned to the ground floor and still no one asked us what we were doing in the building. Perhaps we looked like visitors and not tourists.

Once outside, we continued along a canal path to the Fondamenta Nuove - the rather plain but busy quayside, overlooking the melancholy lagoon and the cemetery island of San Michele. There were many fish restaurants along the quayside and we decided to stop for lunch, treating ourselves to a platter of *fritto misto,* which included octopus and whelks, amongst other fishy delicacies.

"Why don't we visit the islands of Murano and Torcello one day?" suggested my mother, playing with a piece of octopus on her plate.

"I'd love to do that!" I exclaimed. I had never been to the islands, but I knew that each one had a character of its own. "I'd like to go to Burano as well," I added. "Let's go tomorrow!"

"We'll find the times of the boats on the way back. They all leave from this quayside and I seem to remember that they're fairly frequent. It will make a nice change to go somewhere else," said Mother. "The islands are so interesting."

I knew what she meant. Venice is a fantastic place but it can get claustrophobic. It is easy to lose touch with reality as one is folded into its cocoon.

~

That evening we strolled through the narrow *calle* or little lanes, to Piazza San Marco and listened to the open-air orchestras outside the cafés. The music was rousing and some people were dancing, waltzing and twirling across the famous flagstones. There were street vendors, selling mainly tat to the tourists, and the great *piazza* was overflowing with folk from all corners of the world.

We wove our way through the *piazzetta* and onto the Molo San Marco or waterfront, past the Palazzo Ducale with its wonderful Gothic traceries, over the Ponte della Paglia where we stopped briefly, amongst the throngs of people, to look down the canal at The Bridge of Sighs which was illuminated in fluorescent greens and pinks and looked glorious - its reflection shimmering in the water below. This famous bridge was built in 1600, as a passageway between the

Palazzo Ducale and the prison, and is said to have taken its name from the sighs of the prisoners being led away to trial.

Battling our way through the merry crowds, we continued along Riva degli Schiavoni, named after the slaves who were brought to Venice once upon a time. It was quieter here, and we admired the opulent waterfront hotels and their marvellous views across the great lagoon and the small island of San Giorgio. The Palladian church of San Giorgio Maggiore, on the tiny island was lit up against a starry sky, and the island seemed like a stage set floating on the glittering water. Venice is an adult's Disney World.

The weather seemed to change as we made our way back to the hotel. It was oppressive and ominous with a sultry leaden sky. Once back in our room, my mother took out her little travel kettle that she carries on her trips abroad and we had a nice cup of decaffeinated Red Bush tea before turning in for the night.

"Let's hope we get a better sleep tonight," I yawned.

I peered out of the window and all seemed quiet. At around 3a.m. a huge crash woke us up. The sky was alive with dramatic silver sheet lightening. Great peals of thunder boomed, and massive drops of rain fell from the heavens. It was impossible to sleep with this mighty storm in progress, so we turned on our light and wrote our post cards.

"I wonder if we'll ever get a decent night's kip in Venice." I mused. "You would expect it to be such a quiet place with no noisy traffic."

"I think because it's so quiet, all other noises are exaggerated and seem louder than they really are. There're lots of echoes around canal corners," answered Mum.

The storm raged for about two hours. Eventually, we fell into an uneasy sleep and awoke late. The sun was streaming through the window, casting sharp edged shadows on the floor, and it seemed as if a storm had never taken place. However, the air smelt fresher and the buildings looked perkier - as if they had had a good wash.

We only just caught breakfast, which had to be eaten quickly as we had a boat to catch.

Retracing our steps to the Fondamenta Nuove, we caught a *motonave* which is a large boat to the island of Murano - famous world wide, for its superb glass making. As we glided over the lagoon, Venice receded into the distance; a fabulous silhouette against a perfect blue sky. Murano drew nearer and from the boat appeared to be quite a workaday place. We skirted a rather decrepit glass factory which looked as if it had seen better days, and we pulled up at a small quayside where we disembarked.

Murano, like Venice, is a cluster of small islands joined together by bridges. It is tiny by comparison, and we soon found ourselves in the picturesque centre, dominated by a long canal and little shops selling fabulous glassware of all shapes, sizes and colours. The canal sides were bustling and colourful. Stripy boats were moored at the water's edge, adding to the liveliness of the scene.

We looked at the many boutiques full of tantalising Murano glass. There were huge jugs, dishes, lampshades, goblets, vases and delicate jewellery made from millefiore beads. Crossing a bridge, we entered

311

a large emporium, exhibiting and selling the most wonderful glass objects imaginable, and we spent a while viewing them.

On our return to the quayside to catch the *motonave* to Burano, we stumbled upon a minuscule Greek Church which was only big enough for about four people to fit inside. The atmosphere had a slightly musty tinge mingled with incense and there were votive candles, elaborate plastic flowers and old sepia pictures of saints hanging on the crumbling walls. It spoke of a bygone age.

The *motonave* was late, but soon we were sailing towards the small island of Burano where we planned to have lunch. We pushed through the reedy lagoon, passing tiny islands and isolated houses. In the distance the tilting tower of Burano's church could be seen, punctuating the horizon. Landing amongst crowds of other tourists, we made our way to the small centre, where we found an outside trattoria beside a very picturesque canal. We ordered *spaghetti carbonara* and a carafe of local wine, and were pleased to note that the prices were extremely reasonable.

This island is famous for its kaleidoscope of colourful houses and intricate lace making. After lunch, we wandered along the waterways looking at the brightly painted houses - every one a different joyful colour, from midnight blue and crimson red, to sorbet yellow and pretty pink. Brilliant white washing was strung between some of the dwellings, creating a vivid contrast.

One house 'Casa Bepi,' is even multicoloured, with geometric shapes of every hue decorating its facade. The main thoroughfare was busy, containing market stalls selling lace and other linen goods.

Inviting cafés and open-air trattorias selling fresh fish were dotted along the way.

The last island on our list was Torcello - a sad, mysterious, seemingly deserted place. On this island there are marshy reclaimed fields, which is unusual in the lagoon area. Long ago, it was a flourishing city with 20.000 inhabitants, but its people were decimated by malaria and other diseases, and it was later eclipsed by Venice.

Also over the centuries, the canals of Torcello clogged up with silt from the lagoon and the great decline began. There is only one remaining canal, which runs from the *motonave* stop to the celebrated cathedral of Santa Maria dell'Assunta. Now, only about a hundred people live on this melancholy island. There are green fields planted with artichokes and fruit trees, and a few small farmhouses are dotted around the place.

Our aim on disembarking was to stroll along the rather straight canal path bordered with long grasses and trees, as far as the splendid cathedral with its adjoining Byzantine church of Santa Fosca. The interior of this building is vast, part Byzantine part Gothic - it is where east meets west. At the end of the nave is an enormous mosaic covering the entire west wall, illustrating the Cruxifiction, the Resurection of the Dead and the Day of Judgement.

At the opposite end of the cathedral is the apse mosaic, depicting a 13th century Madonna set against a glittering gold, *tessere* background. This is said to be one of the most beautiful mosaics in the whole of Venice. We stood transfixed. The Madonna loomed above us, tall and slender, and there were tears on her cheeks as if she were grieving for the world.

Outside, the sun was low in the sky and we decided that it was time to return to *La Serenissima*. Before we left, we took our turn at sitting on Attila's Throne - a big seat hewn out of a chunk of marble, placed on the square of grass outside the cathedral. We took photographs - as everyone does. Rumour has it that the 5th century king of the Huns used this seat as his throne.

The sun was setting as we sailed back to Venice, across the weedy lagoon. A red orb floated in a pink hemisphere, streaked with splashes of crimson and gold, and I thought of the great English painter Turner, who often visited the city to gain inspiration for his sunset masterpieces. Apparently, some evenings he would jump on a gondola and float out across the labyrinth of canals. From this watery vantage point, he sketched his marvellous ideas and drawings, which he later translated into paint, with vivid, expressive, almost abstract splashes of colour.

~

That night we slept like babies, exhausted by our explorations of the islands and our two nights of broken sleep. On our travels around the city the following morning, we came across a lovely little hotel with Gothic windows. It was situated right on a small canal not far from the Bridge of Sighs. We peered through the door. The interior looked very posh, with either real or reproduction antique furniture, and huge lamps casting great pools of light on beautiful Persian rugs. There were fabulous Venetian mirrors hanging on the walls of the long open plan area, and big vases filled to overflowing with flowers.

The little hotel presented a very cosy atmosphere and we were tempted inside, to ask a rather formidable looking woman the price of a double room. The answer was surprisingly cheap, so we decided that later we would check out of our present place, providing the room that we were just about to be shown was up to standard.

We followed the impeccably dressed woman up numerous flights of marble steps. At the top of a small landing, she opened an oak door with a flourish, revealing a tastefully, but simply furnished room, with three large windows overlooking a canal. We could hardly believe our luck!

We returned to the first hotel to pack up our few belongings and to check out. Just before we reached our room, a small maid with a big trolley of cleaning equipment, beckoned us over. She led us down a narrow corridor and up a short flight of steps. We stepped out on to a roof terrace covered with billowing white washing, drying in the midday heat. To the right of us was a shaded area, with an old table and a couple of chairs, and over the terrace walls - in between the washing, were enticing views of Venice's rooftops. Ahead of us, we could see the Campanile and the ornate roof of the Basilica.

"This is lovely!" I exclaimed. "I wish we had known about it earlier. We could have written our postcards here or read for a while."

"Let's do our packing and then come up here before we leave," suggested my mother.

We spent a very pleasant hour or two, up on the roof top amidst the washing, soaking up the sun before winding our way to our next hotel, which was in the vicinity of the first one. I had my old faithful

315

rucksack but my mother was pushing a small case on wheels. Cases are very difficult to manoeuvre in Venice because of all the steps and bridges, and we were quite out of breath with all the pushing and pulling, by the time we arrived at our new location.

Once in the haven of our room, we flung open the windows. I lent out and surveyed the scene before me. Three bells clanged the hour. Opposite was a beautiful *palazzo,* painted a deep burnt terracotta colour with a small balcony, containing chairs and table and cascading pots of white geraniums. The windows were shuttered with green wooden slats against the glare of the sun. Below, the canal water slapped against the *palazzi* and a gondola glided around the corner. We had views down two canals. It was the epitome of Venice.

Our room was on the end of the building and so had windows on two sides, which let a delicious breeze flood through. This time we had no fan, but our room felt reasonably cool because of the proximity of the water. The ornate twin beds were made from walnut and the room contained big lamps, comfortable chairs, a good sized wardrobe, a small en suite bathroom and a beautiful Venetian mirror, aged with the patina of time. It seemed that everything had been chosen with attention and care to the last detail.

We rested for a while, listening from the open windows to the calls and shouts of the gondoliers as they rounded a tricky corner. When pealing bells announced that the hour was six o'clock, we decided that it was time to go out and look for our supper. Dusk was falling, and I lent out of the window mesmerized by the view and the glinting lights reflecting on the canal.

The gondoliers were doing a roaring trade. There were so many of them they could hardly move and it was a miracle that there were no crashes. They glided gracefully and effortlessly and when a traffic jam occurred, they just waited patiently, chatting to each other, punts in hand, until they could move.

Most of the gondoliers were dressed in black. Some had black and white striped tee-shirts and others donned jaunty little boaters, tied with a red or black ribbon. Many sang *'O Sole Mio,'* or played jolly Italian tunes on an accordion. They all shouted *"Oi"* as they deftly rounded the corner to warn other gondoliers that they were approaching. It was a delightful and entertaining view, and I had to tear myself away once my mother was ready to go out.

Later that night, we found it difficult to sleep (again!) being so close to the river traffic. We had not bargained on the gondoliers plying their trade well into the night. The *'O Sole Mio'* and the shout of *'Oi,'* which had seemed so enchanting earlier on in the evening, was now merely a great inconvenience. The heat was intense and we could not shut the windows, so we had to lie there and hope that everybody would soon go to bed. To make matters worse there was an occasional zizz, which told us the mosquitoes were in town. At least this time we had protection against them!

We drifted off to sleep, but at around two o'clock we were rudely awoken by a ranting banshee of a woman, screaming and swearing in dialect at three men, somewhere on a canal bridge or path below. I wearily stumbled over to the window wondering if I were dreaming, to see if I could find out what was going on.

Clare Stimpson

The banshee was obviously drunk and in a real rage, and looked as if she was going to push one of the men into the canal. Venetians from other surrounding *palazzi* were flinging open their shutters and adding to the argument, ordering the four peace-busters to go away or else…. An old woman threw a bucket of water over one of them, and eventually they moved off to another quarter of the city, their quarrels receding into the distance.

The next morning we woke bleary-eyed and wondered if we were jinxed where sleep was concerned.

"We're going to need another holiday to get over this one!" I commented to Mum as we sat down at a beautifully laid breakfast table. We drank strong coffee and enjoyed rolls and jam - a typical continental breakfast. The Italians do not put much emphasis on the first meal of the day, but they certainly make up for it at lunch and dinner.

This was to be our last day in Venice and we agreed to visit the Cannereggio area, taking in the Jewish quarter. Cannereggio is the most northerly *sestiere* in the city, and closest to the railway station and the mainland. It is a bustling, working class area and one of the most densely populated parts, giving the visitor a glimpse of the real Venice, far from the madding crowds and theatricality of San Marco.

Here in Cannereggio, women peg their washing precariously from iron-work balconies whilst chatting through the open window to their neighbour opposite. Children play in the street below, old men sitting on benches chat about football, and there are small neighbourhood shops such as *il fruttivendolo* (the greengrocer) and *l' alimentari* (the grocer).

We took the *vaporetto* from San Zaccaria near San Marco. Once away from the main hub of Cannereggio, we found ourselves in a quiet melancholy place, where few tourists ever venture. Here the back water *palazzi* had an air of wistful crumbling decay about them. We strolled along the network of wide canals and open windswept austere quaysides. Our mission was to find the Gothic church of Madonna dell'Orto where there are paintings by Tintoretto, who lived nearby and was a parishioner.

This church was originally dedicated to St. Christopher, patron saint of travellers, but in the early 15th century the dedication was changed, when a statue of the Virgin Mary, reputed to possess miraculous powers, was found in an adjoining vegetable garden (*orto*). This beautiful church is situated in a pleasant square, and we admired the exterior with its onion shaped cupola before entering the cool airy interior.

My mother is a great fan of Tintoretto and we spent some time gazing at his dramatic masterpieces, which adorn the chancel. The right wall is magnificent and contains the 'Last Judgement'- a violent and fiery depiction, which apparently caused the art critic John Ruskin's wife Effie, to run out of the church in fright after seeing its content.

Later, we headed for the atmospheric and unassuming Jewish quarter, which apparently is the oldest in the world. The name *'ghetto'* comes from the Italian word 'foundry' - this Jewish area surrounded by canals was within sight of the local foundry and so took its name from it. We came across citizens dressed in typical Jewish garments, and we looked in the windows of workshops selling liturgical goods. There were synagogues and even a kosher bakery.

I had been here before on one of my trips to Venice and loved the solitude and serenity it exuded. It was quiet, this area, as if Venice had forgotten about it. The tall, almost tenement like houses were in a state of disrepair, but there was a calm atmosphere as if the ghetto had come to terms with its turbulent past, when its inhabitants had been segregated and discriminated against, although sometimes protected and often tolerated by Venetian society.

After our thought provoking walk through the ghetto, we hurried back to the hotel to pack our suitcases, as we were catching an early evening plane. For the second time that day we boarded the vaporetto at San Zaccaria and bid a fond farewell to Venice as she slid silently away. The sky above grew the colour of slate, and great raindrops cascaded from the heavens, splashing on the Grand Canal like silver bullets.

Our plane was delayed for a couple of hours, and through the airport windows, we could see flashes of sheet lightening and hear clashes of thunder. Mother and I looked at each other nervously. Neither of us particularly liked flying, and I for one had never flown in a storm.

"I'm sure they won't let us take off if it's dangerous," I assured my mother, although I was not feeling very confident about the situation.

We boarded the plane with the horrible dread feeling that we would shortly be flying to our doom. The rain was so heavy we could hear it drumming on the roof and outside the thunder and lightning continued its battle overhead.

As we took off over Venice, I tried to take my mind off the present situation by looking out of the window hoping to identify certain landmarks, but it was too dark and all I could see was the lightning hovering over the wing of the plane. Certain films came to mind, and I had to shut them out. The storm subsided as we flew over Austria and we both started to feel a lot better.

We had left Bristol airport a couple of days earlier in an English heat wave, but arrived back to howling gales and what seemed to be subzero temperatures. Such is the British summer! Although we had moaned about the searing heat in Venice, we longed to be back there amongst the evocative canals, the marvellous architecture, the colour, light and enchanting vistas that define this unique city.

CHAPTER 22 BOLOGNA AND MODENA AGAIN!

It was May 2001, when my mother and I touched down in the sublime city of Bologna, some twenty-five years after I had first set eyes on the city. I loved visiting and exploring regions in Italy that I had previously never set foot in, but it was an equal joy to be back in Emilia-Romagna.

We had booked a family orientated hotel, right in the heart of bustling Via dell'Independenza. It was situated on the top floor of a nondescript building, and we had the choice of either walking up a few hundred steps to our destination, or gliding up to the summit in a rickety but beautiful art nouveau lift.

The compact hotel was light and airy, with a tremendous variety of potted plants crammed into its tiny vestibule. Magnificent patterned tiles covered the floors and comfy little sofas were placed here and there, for people to rest upon and maybe read a magazine, or chat about their forthcoming plans.

Our room was enormous with a cheerful, sunny aspect. There were three beds, a couple of chairs and ample wardrobe space for our few belongings. We had learnt to travel light, carrying only a couple of changes of clothes and the bare necessities - including the portable kettle and tea-bags - of course! A pair of large windows opened out on to the street several floors below, letting light and muffled noise flood in.

Later that evening, we strolled along Via dell' Independenza and marvelled at the wonderful Renaissance buildings, with their rosy brick facades. We turned into Via Rizzoli, and there in front of us were the two famous towers or '*i due torre*' of Bologna, old medieval structures, leaning precariously towards each other like two leaning towers of Pisa. These are the '*Torre Pendente*' - Torre Asinelli and Torre Garisenda, which were constructed in the 12th century and were mentioned in Dante's '*Inferno.*'

Torre Garisenda leans ten feet or three metres from its vertical baseline, and had to be shortened soon after its construction for safety purposes. The other tower, Torre Asinelli, is said to be the fourth highest tower in Italy, and it is possible to climb the five hundred steps to its summit, where a wonderful view of the terracotta pantiled roofs of Bologna are spread in a kaleidoscope of different hues beneath. My mother and I declined this intriguing prospect, as neither of us was fond of heights. We were both feeling peckish and decided it was time for supper instead.

An elderly Italian man, who saw us looking up in wonder at the towers, approached us and after the usual preliminaries of 'who were we and why had we come to Bologna?' told us that originally, there had been two hundred towers on Bologna's skyline. In the early Middle Ages, it must have looked like a medieval Manhatten.

After an interesting conversation with the old Bolognese man, we turned and made our way through the evening *passeggiata* to Piazza Maggiore, an enormous magnificent stately square surrounded by Renaissance architecture.

Bologna has one of the best preserved historic centres in Europe, with churches, towers, squares and buildings linked together by thirty seven kilometres of connecting porticoes. These give the city an attractive picturesque appearance, as well as providing shelter from the scorching summer sun and the squally blasts of winter gales and rain.

We found a table in one of the numerous outside cafés, where we could sip an aperitif and watch the Italian world go by. Dusk was falling, and the sky glowed with the last remnants of the pink and gold sun. As it was May, the evening was pleasant. The humid suffocating nights of midsummer had yet to arrive.

We drank Campari in the *piazza* and once again the seductive magic of Italy folded around us. We felt the intense theatricality - the surreal that always pervades this country - almost as if we were onlookers in some grand, dramatic production.

Later, strolling around the *piazza,* we found a very cheerful and reasonably priced restaurant where we enjoyed mouth watering mammoth pizzas. It was difficult to choose our meal that evening, as all the dishes on the menu sounded tempting. Bologna is the gastronomic centre of Italy and boasts some astounding culinary dishes.

As evening was turning to night, we sauntered back to our hotel, appetites satiated - ready for a good night's sleep. However, that was not to be! Unbeknown to us that day, Bologna had won some sort of sporting trophy and at about one o'clock a.m. strange noises from afar, drifted through our open window.

The sounds grew nearer and nearer. What seemed like a massive procession of people, blowing whistles, cheering, throwing bangers and fireworks on to the street, greeted our ears.The noise below our window was explosive.

"Oh Heavens, what on earth is that?" murmured my mother sleepily.

"I'll go and have a look." I volunteered, padding over to the window and leaning out.

Under us, and stretching far into the distance, was a motley assortment of folk, most of whom were wearing strange hats, waving flags and chanting what appeared to be something like, 'Long live Bologna. We are the champions!'

It was impossible to sleep, so we stood at the window and watched the procession below us. The crowd was really excited, shouting and gesticulating and making an almighty din. This part of the city centre is not very residential; just a few apartment blocks and hotels were dotted amongst the shops, restaurants and bars. Eventually the police arrived amidst the wail of sirens, and managed to move the jubilant supporters into the next street and the noise abated somewhat. It was about three a.m. when we made our way back to bed, to sleep a deep and restless slumber, punctuated by dreams of football supporters.

The next morning we felt fragile, but soon revived after a cup of strong creamy cappuccino. We wolfed down a few cakes or *paste* as well; after all, we needed our strength to walk the city streets. Our itinerary for that day included a visit to the Pinacoteca Nazionale.

This wonderful place is Bologna's principal art gallery and it houses one of Italy's most important collections, including some magnificent works by the Bolognese painters Vitale da Bologna, Guido Reni, Guercino and the Carraci family. Two marvellous paintings 'Madonna in Glory' by Perugino and 'The Ecstasy of St. Cecilia' are present in the gallery - both these artists worked in Bologna some time during their artistic careers.

Stepping out into the strong brilliant sunshine after our gallery visit, we voted to explore the university district as we were virtually on the edge of it. We picked our way through the historic centre and down wonderfully shady, arcaded medieval streets. Bologna brought back so many memories. Wandering through the porticoed and flag stoned alleyways was deja vu.

Via Zamponi, the heart of the student area had not changed much. Red left wing graffiti still adorned the faded walls and it retained a scruffy air of intellectual untidiness. Music blared from dark cavernous bars set under the arcades, and the pavements were lined with cheap bistro tables and chairs.

This place felt a million miles away from the smart elegant shops of Piazza Cavour but in fact, this up-market area was just down the road. Distant memories of the Frank Zappa concert when Jemp and I were chased by the police came to mind, and the reminiscences were bittersweet.

We sat down on some rickety chairs feeling a mite conspicuous, as most of the other tables were occupied by young gesticulating and debating student types.

"It really hasn't changed much," I said to Mum. "It even smells the same."

We ordered *caffellatte*, sprinkled with a liberal layer of sieved chocolate. The frothy, delicious looking drink arrived on our table in long tall glasses.

"Mmm, very nice," commented Mother "But I suppose this isn't the thing to be drinking in this heat. A nice cool white wine would perhaps have been better."

I had to agree - but the *caffellatte* was superb.

It was very pleasant sitting in the university surroundings, under the cool of the arcade whiling away the rest of the morning. The pace of life in Bologna is leisurely. Working sounds like the chink of china cups, glasses being washed, the chatter and banter of the *bariste* calling to each other, and the animated discourse of the students filled the air, punctuated by distant traffic noises.

After lunch, we strolled back to Piazza Maggiore and looked at the Fontana del Nettuno - one of the symbols of Bologna dedicated to the sea god Neptune. This beautiful fountain is the work of Giambologna and was constructed between 1564 and 1566.

We were surrounded by beauty. To the right of us stood the Palazzo del Commune or Town hall, built in medieval times, with its glorious Gothic windows and unusual bell-tower, complete with carillon clock and green verdigris cupolas. The façade of the palace is impressive, boasting three important works of art, including the 'Madonna di

Piazza' by Nicolo dell'Arca, the statue of Pope Gregory XIII, and the 'Eagle' reputed to be sculpted by the great Michelangelo.

The interior of the building houses many great works of art and it is also home to the Museo Morandi, one of the most interesting little museums I have ever had the pleasure to visit. Giorgio Morandi is Bologna's and in fact Italy's most famous contemporary artist, and both my mother and I are great fans of his exquisite work.

Morandi painted landscapes and still life subjects in a restricted palette of pale greys, duck egg blues, beige browns and muted pinks. He painted tall bottles, jars and vases said to be inspired by the tall towers of Bologna itself. We were able to see a reconstruction of his studio, with his paint splattered easel, rags, turpentine, jars full of paintbrushes and row upon row of assorted, jumbled, dusty bottles. The studio was quite Spartan, although there was a day bed of sorts. It was a glimpse into his fantastic world.

Many happy hours were spent walking the arcades of Bologna. Those near the centre were beautifully appointed - pale terracotta in colour and lined with elegant shops. Some even possessed Austrian blinds, reminiscent of the great *piazza* of San Marco in Venice. Others, like those in the university district presented a crumbling and forlorn dusty air and were adorned with political grafitti of the left wing variety.

There were many interesting bars and cafés to be explored under these porticoes and most extended outside, with a smattering of tables and chairs. Often we would stop on our travels around the city, to sit under a shady vaulted portico, protected from the heat and bustle of the street, to drink a coffee or a glass of chilled white wine.

~

Before setting off on our short holiday to Bologna, I had rung my friend Antonella, to let her know that we would be in the area. She cordially invited us to join her in Modena for a day. I was excited at the thought of seeing both my friend and this city again, as it had been well over twelve years since my last visit.

We arrived at Bologna station early one morning, near the end of our Bolognese sojourn and bought two return tickets for Modena, which is situated about thirty kilometres further north. We had forgotten how cheap it is to travel by rail in Italy. Our return fares totalled about £3.50p each.

The station in Bologna is massive, and like most in Italy was built during Mussolini's Fascist regime and is decorated with lots of opulent and creamy polished marble and high cavernous ceilings. Various small outlets selling newspapers or *panini* (sandwiches), line the perimeter of the station and as we walked out onto platform 1, we could not help but be reminded of the awful tragedy that occurred there in 1981, when a terrorist bomb ripped apart the restaurant and adjacent waiting-room. The glass memorial inscribed with the names of all who lost their lives on that summer's day is a very poignant reminder.

During my stay in Modena, most of the trains that I ever caught had been *in ritardo* (late), so we were very surprised when an exceptionally clean looking train slid smoothly alongside the platform, exactly on time. Inside it was spotless, comfortable and well designed - a far cry from the old grey locomotives I knew and loved!

In the 1970s, I used to smugly comment on how superior English trains were in comparison to their Italian counterparts, but now I have to admit that it is the other way round!

The journey took us through familiar landscape. The hilly and forested terrain around Bologna soon gave way to the flat lands of the Po basin. We caught fleeting glimpses of the northern plain, bordered by tall gently swaying poplar trees and home to isolated square built terracotta farmhouses. It had its own lonely type of beauty.

We had arrived in Modena earlier than expected. It was only ten o'clock and we had arranged to meet Antonella in Piazza Grande at around 12.45p.m.

"I'd love to go and have a look at Via Paolo Ferrari, as we've got some spare time," I said to Mum. "It's only just around the corner and if we walk to the centre it's actually on our way."

"Can you remember where it is?" asked Mother.

"Yeh, I think so." I answered confidently.

We took the main street from the station and arrived in a small piazza with a large domed church, a cinema and some local shops and bars. If I remembered rightly, Via Ferrari was somewhere vaguely to the left. We sauntered down what I was sure was the right street but nowhere seemed familiar. Feeling puzzled, I wandered around looking out for landmarks, but nothing quite seemed to fit. I was mystified.

"Look Clare, isn't that house over there the old post office depot?" urged my mother.

"Of course it is!" I answered in surprise. "It's been done up. I really don't recognise the old place! Doesn't it look different?"

It had indeed been spruced up. In fact the whole street had been given a make over. Gone were the dusty, grey, dilapidated buildings and rusty ironwork that I remembered so well. The houses and flats in Via Paolo Ferrari now presented smart façades in tones and hues of yellow ochre and burnt terracotta.

We stood in front of the building I had once lived in, admiring its change of fortune. A middle-aged and care worn looking woman stepped out from behind the big wooden main door, and approached us.

"Cercate qualquno?" (Are you looking for someone) she asked.

"I used to live here a long time ago - up on the top floor." I responded.

She stared at me quizzically. "When did you live here?"

"In 1974. There were two of us to begin with. My friend Jemp and I taught English at the City Language School in Modena."

The woman remained perplexed for some seconds and then broke out into a huge smile.

"È la regazza Inglese!" She grabbed my arm and shook it enthusiastically. "Don't you remember me? We lived in the adjacent flat to yours!"

I did remember her. We had not exactly been on speaking terms, as she spoke with a broad southern accent and Jemp and I struggled to understand the Modenese intonation in our first year there, without having to grapple with Sicilian. Then, she had been a young mother who always seemed to be scrubbing her hall floor with her front door left open to dry it quickly. We always bade each other *'buon giorno,'* but that was about all.

"Via Paolo Ferrari has really changed," I said.

"*Ah, si.*" She answered proudly. "*È bella, non è vero?*"

We agreed with her that it looked good.

Continuing our journey to the centre, we followed the signs for '*Il centro città.*' By now the sun was high in the deep turquoise sky, so we decided to cut through the shady park that led to the Piazza containing the Military Accademy. Sunlight filtered through the trees, creating dappled patterns on the winding paths and greenery.

"It's lovely here," I said. "I remember I sometimes used to come and sit here to read a book if it was really hot. There used to be a zoo with monkeys and flamingos but it must've closed down."

There was no sign or sound of animals - just peace, shade and quiet.

By the time we arrived in the centre, the shops were beginning to close for lunch and siesta time, and the narrow arcaded streets were emptying of people. We bought some cakes, beautifully wrapped with trailing ribbons, as a small gift for Antonella and preceded to Piazza Grande, where we had arranged to meet our friend.

The great Piazza was bathed in sunlight. It was practically empty save for a few souls hurrying home for lunch, and a row of bicycles and various mopeds and vespas chained to some railings. The cathedral looked magnificent in all its Gothic tracery. It radiated a pinkish white colour, with the Ghirlandina spiking the brilliant noon day sky.

There were the grinning lions, guarding the main entrance. I went and sat next to one of them - he seemed like an old friend, his tactile marble coat smoothed by centuries of people stroking him. There was no time to enter the cathedral as Antonella arrived, rushing over to greet us.

"Come state?" she cried, hugging us both. "It's such a long time since we've seen each other!"

Antonella spoke very good English with a charming Italian accent. For many years now she had been a teacher in a middle school a little way out of Modena. She still lived in the same beautiful apartment that she shared with her husband, and every day after work she visited her mother - La signora Contarini, who now lived alone and was practically house-bound. Sadly, we learnt that Antonella's father had passed away some years previously.

Antonella's car, a small modern Fiat, was parked in a little side road and as she drove us through the city, she chatted about her family and told us she had prepared lunch for us at her home.

I hardly recognised the road to Antonella's apartment. It had changed vastly over the years. Many trees had sprung up and the periphery of the city had grown to enormous proportions. Previously, Antonella's home had been on the outskirts of Modena, but recent development and expansion had put it back in the centre.

Gone also, were the ubiquitous little Fiat 500s that used to characterise the streets of all Italian cities. Now they are a cult car, and most Italians drive modern Fiats and Alfa Romeos.

Antonella's apartment is unique. It is situated over two floors, so that inside it appears to look and feel just like a house. Long floor to ceiling windows are shaded with white linen Roman blinds that are lowered and raised with an intricate pulley system.

Both Antonella and her husband Alessandro are inveterate travellers, and their apartment is filled with artefacts from exotic places like Afganistan and Thailand. Pictures adorn every wall and carefully chosen antique furniture is scattered around the place. Wonderful Afghan rugs litter the floors, and the bathroom towels which are stored in battered but chic leather suitcases, are edged with antique lace. There is an aura of calm and faded elegance about the place.

The table was laid with a spotless white lacy cloth and silver cutlery. Slender Venetian wine glasses contained linen serviettes. Numerous bottles of Lambrusco were dotted amongst crystal bowls containing fruit. It looked very welcoming.

"I'm sorry Alessandro could not be here today. He has some clients to attend to at work," apologised Antonella. "He sends his regards!"

We sat down to *pollo in brodo*, a special Italian soup made with the carcass of a chicken and tiny pasta shapes.

"I have to confess," laughed Antonella, as we complimented her on the broth, "that I did not actually make it! La zia Vita prepared it yesterday and I picked it up on my way to meet you. All I did was heat it up!"

Creamy lasagna arrived on the table next, accompanied by a salad of radici, spinach leaves and other greenery. Antonella tossed the salad with virgin olive oil and some balsamic vinegar.

"I'm afraid I did not make the lasagna either. I cheated and ordered it from Fini."

Fini is a well-known and rather expensive restaurant and retailer situated in the centre of Modena.

"Life's too short to be cooking," said our friend, saluting us with a glass of lambrusco.

We chatted about the old days and our families, and reminisced about summers spent at Casa della Fontana. It all seemed so far away.

I glanced around the room and remembered a time about twelve years before, when my husband and three small boys, who were then aged between one and four, had called in on Antonella and Alessandro on our way home from a camping holiday in Florence. We were tired and needed somewhere to stay for the night, and our Italian friends kindly offered to accommodate us.

The apartment was arranged in much the same manner on that particular day, with small occasional tables dotted between wonderful Victorian settees. On the tables, exquisite tiny silver photo frames were arranged with great precision amongst delicate pieces of china. To the embarrassment of my husband and me, one of our sons rampaged around the place - having been used to the freedom of the camp site - and knocked over one of the tables, shattering some of the precious items.

I reminded Antonella of that day. She laughed.

"But don't you remember when Gabriella and I visited you in Southampton before you were married, and Claudia (Gabriella's daughter who was in a pushchair at the time) got hold of one of your trailing ivy plants on top of your wardrobe and pulled it down, smashing the pot and ruining the poor plant!"

We laughed as we remembered these past episodes.

With lunch ended, Antonella asked us if we would like to visit her mother, and following that, auntie Vita. We said that we would love to see these two ladies again.

It was a short drive to Signora Contarini's flat. The landscape, like that all around Modena had indeed changed, although mainly for the better. Trees had matured, and shrubs gave the area a more decorative, well-established look.

I could remember when the apartment that the Contarini family lived in had just been a building site, and the land around the new development had consisted of parched sun-baked earth in summer and a muddy quagmire in winter. Now the apartments basked in the afternoon sun, amidst pleasant flowering bushes and fragrant roses.

Signora Contarini greeted us enthusiastically. She had obviously aged much since I had last visited and was now unable to walk around without a stick. Antonella told us that her mother rarely ventured out, preferring her own domain where she lived alone, with the help of a housekeeper. Apparently, she loved watching television and whiled away the day immersed in old T.V. films.

We sat at the table and talked whilst Antonella prepared some coffee. Although neither of them could speak the other's language well, my mother and the signora exchanged animated conversation about the Second World War, with translation imput from Antonella and myself.

I enquired about Uncle Fred, Signora Contarini's brother, whom I had met on several occasions at Casa della Fontana. He had been a prisoner of war somewhere in England in the mid 1940s, and he had told me that they had been some of the happiest days of his life. His love of England and his happy memories of wartime camaraderie, had earned him the nickname of 'Uncle Fred' (instead of Lo zio Frederico), amongst his family.

After a couple of happy hours, we agreed it was time for our next visit to see zia Vita and her daughter Portia, who lived near-by. Sadly zio Berto had also passed away some years ago, and now Portia, her husband and daughter resided with zia Vita, along with another sister of Vita's - zia Benedetta. Since I had lived in Modena they had moved apartments, and I was surprised to discover that their new flat was in Corso Emanuelle II, opposite the park with the shady winding paths that I loved so much.

We parked outside, and Antonella led us through a potted palm filled courtyard and up to the first floor apartment. Auntie Vita greeted us with outstretched arms and insisted that we sit at her table and eat the cake that she had just baked. She looked as I had always imagined her - rotund, cheerful, dressed in a flowery pinny with a ready smile on her lips.

The apartment was smaller than her previous one, and the huge dining room table that is the focus of so many Italian families, practically filled the small cosy room. There was just enough space for the numerous chairs surrounding it. Some knitting that Vita had been working on lay in a fluffy mass in a small wicker basket. Portia and her young daughter Martina were seated at the table, but zia Benedetta who was the youngest of the older Contarini generation was absent, being at work in the centre of Modena.

We gossiped about the old days and our present lives for hours. It was strange to see Portia with a daughter of her own. When I had first met her she had only been fourteen years old. Now she was an elegant young mother.

"How is La Carolina?" she asked of my sister who had lived with the family for some months in the mid 1970s.

I assured her that Caroline was fine and filled the family in with all the details they requested. It was good to catch up on news of all the Contarini family and hear about Casa della Fontana. It appeared from their conversation that the conglomeration of houses nestled beneath the Apennines had not changed at all, and that various members of the family still frequented the area most summers, in order to escape the heat of the city. I learnt that Paolo had married some years previously and now had two young sons of his own. He no longer lived in Modena, but resided further north - somewhere near Verona.

After a wonderful afternoon, Antonella escorted Mother and me back to Modena station to catch the train for Bologna. As we drew away from the platform, I mentally waved good-bye to the city and wondered when, or if, I would ever visit again. Dusk was falling and as the train gathered speed and we slid further away from the city lights, I could see the Ghirlandina proudly etched against a darkening evening sky.

It was a long walk from Bologna station to our hotel, and after a momentous day we were both exhausted. We agreed that visiting Modena and seeing some of the Contarini family, had been one of the best days of our short holiday. That night, worn out by the excitement of the day we slept like logs.

~

We decided to spend our last day in Bologna very leisurely, with a visit to some of the department stores in the centre of the city, a mooch around the market stalls - where we were amazed at the size and colour of the luscious looking fruit and vegetables, a gourmet lunch and a lot of sitting around in open-air cafés in Piazza Maggiore, watching the world go by, campari in hand.

The slower pace of life and the absolute enjoyment of it that most Italians cultivate, were beginning to affect us and we felt our cares and worries ebbing away as we joined in the celebration of just being alive. Italians certainly know how to enjoy themselves and seem to derive pleasure from the simplest of things.

All too soon it was time to return to England. It was sad to leave this joyous, often ambivalent country. The spark that was lit for me long ago will never be extinguished.

I often yearn for Italy and always will do. Having dipped my toes in her glittering waters, crossed her hilly pastures punctuated with silent cypresses and giant sun flowers, having known the kindness of her people and spoken her mellifluous language, it is difficult to be content with anywhere else.

THE END

Sunday morning at St. Peter's in Rome

Mum looking down The Grande Canal — Venice

Piazza San Marco in Venice

Looking down the Grand Canal again!

The town hall in Piazza Maggiore

The University Area of Bologna

ABOUT THE AUTHOR

'Spaghetti in my Hair' is Clare Stimpson's first travelogue which is set in three parts. 'The Early days' tells the story of her life in Modena between the years 1974 –1978. Part II 'Italy Revisited' describes living in San Remo, holidaying in various resorts with a character from part one, and travelling through Italy in a V.W. called Doris with three girls to the Gargano in Puglia. The final part 'Enigmatic Italy', describes how Clare was influenced by her mother who hitchhiked to Sicily in 1949

As a young girl, Clare was brought-up on stories of her mother's adventures in Italy and determined that one day, she too, would live in that land of dreams

In 1970, before setting foot on Italian soil, Clare trained to be an art teacher at Shoreditch Teacher's Training College in Surrey. She taught pottery for a year in a west London comprehensive, before fleeing in relief to Italy to teach E.F.L. or English as a Foreign Language to a more receptive audience. On return to England she retrained to teach design and technology in Winchester and has been employed in many teaching posts. Her present job involves teaching art and English GCSE.

Clare has always enjoyed writing and used to entertain her sisters with bedtime stories that she invented spontaneously. She has always been fascinated by travel and at teacher training college, studied geography alongside art. As a teenager she kept various holiday journals and at the tender age of thirteen had a poem about autumn published in the 'Liverpool Echo'.

Clare now lives in Southampton with her husband Gordon and three sons Joe, Alex and Jamie. She describes herself as being obsessed with Italy and feels that her Italian experience has played an enormous part in shaping her life.

Printed in the United Kingdom
by Lightning Source UK Ltd.
117147UKS00001B/219